Viva

A jour ~~~gh Mexico
and the
Southwestern United States

MoWuKnuffels?

This is the lovingly combined crew of a camper. It consists of two affectionate dogs and one aged lady. These three ladies wanted to experience it again as they had already crossed the North American Continent on their own some years ago.

A woman alone? In a camping car? With two dogs? It is possible! Why, certainly! And, it is fun! In her richly illustrated diary, the author continuously describes her daily experiences and shares her thoughts about the host country. RV travelers are addressed in this humorous work as well as dog lovers or solo traveling women.

Monika von Borthwick already belongs to the older generation of travelers and lives in the culturally rich Upper Bavaria on the border with Austria. In addition to her professional activities, for decades she coached bus travelers as tour guides in European countries. Even then she wrote down her experiences extensively about land and people, but without publishing them.

After the death of her husband, she explored numerous areas in Europe on her own with her newly acquired RV and her two dog ladies. Equipped with these experiences, they ventured the leap over the big pond with an organized group a few years ago. During this five-month journey from Washington to and through Mexico she decided to do it again on her own. She discovered the love of storytelling and detailed travel reports were sent home by email.

These blogs are now for the first time published for an audience interested in traveling.

Monika von Borthwick

Viva Los Topes!

With the MoWuKnuffels
and their motorhome through
Central Mexico and
Southwestern USA

An entertaining diary

© 2020 Monika von Borthwick
Translation into English (2018): Patricia Troncho
Production and publishing:
BoD - Books on Demand, Norderstedt
ISBN: 9783751994880

The work, including all its parts, is copyright protected. Any use beyond the copyright is inadmissible and punishable without the consent of the author and the publisher. This applies in particular to reproductions, translations, microfilming and storage and processing in electronic systems.

Introduction

The desire to travel had touched us again. This year I wanted to spend the winter in Mexico accompanied by my two four-legged friends. The following spring, I intended to visit extensively the National Parks of the US from Utah in the Southwest of the continent.

I am a female chauffeur and diary author with my two dogs Wuschel and Knuffi. Both ladies are used to traveling in the camper and enjoy the many hours spent together. Wuschel is nine years old, Knuffi is five years old and I am close to sixty.
They do not like the flight across the pond that much, but once a year they make this sacrifice for me. What else is left for them when traveling? Wuschel acts (because of her size) as my bodyguard and Knuffi (due to her attentiveness) as a reliable alarm system. We make a good team for adventure in other continents.

My own "American Wuschelmobil" (made in 1994) was already waiting for us at a friends' parking lot in the State of New York. There were still some minor repairs and maintenance work to do before we could head south, along the American East Coast, to Florida and around the Gulf of Mexico. This time I wanted to cross the Mexican border from Texas. This was just an approximate schedule for me, because I hoped to escape from the cold in Florida. We would take our time on the journey, visit our friends in North Carolina and celebrate Christmas together with a longtime friend and her family in Florida. In mid-January we should – after about five thousand kilometers – reach the Mexican border.

Of course, there would have been a lot to report over the first three months on bigger and smaller experiences, but the focus of this travel book was on Mexico and Utah. The approach of the tour is to be found in "Highways and Gravel Roads" (II volume). Therefore, I won't include a detailed description and start our story with the new calendar year.

All photos were taken exclusively with my camera and are thus under copyright. Additional picture material in the form of a PowerPoint presentation on CD (Windows suitable) is in preparation and can be ordered. More information can be checked on my homepage
www.mvborthwick.de
Upper Bavaria in autumn 2010/2019
Monika of Borthwick

The used rolling home for our adventure:
Born in 1991
125 000 km, gasoline,
8 m in length
…. and very thirsty

Month of January
1ˢᵗ half
2400 km

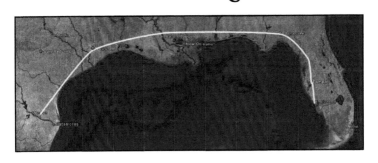

*Florida to the
Mexican border*

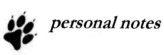 *personal notes*

New Year
Alafia River State Park

As announced, the sky opened all the locks at half past three in the morning and the rain pattered on our roof according to all rules of business. Delighted, I turned around once again. Last night I let the New Year enter through the side door – despite all the intentions of an early night's sleep. I was on a stupid game on the PC and could not stop playing. Regardless of all prohibitions the fireworks with its bangs were heard from time to time in the area. Probably all the pyrotechnic enthusiasts had gathered themselves in front of the park line. Here nobody could harm them. Nevertheless, it was peaceful in my area relatively early and the noise died soon.

Breakfast was served according to today's event: Ham, egg and toast, not the usual healthy muesli! After it continued to pour, I did the same as my dogs and crawled into bed again for my "Beauty sleep". The result is still pending! A short tour without rain and then several hours with my thriller novel in the chair until hunger tormented me.

Today I wanted to test whether my oven was working, and I baked a crispy garlic bread Texan style. In addition, I roasted a fine salmon steak. For dessert there were strawberries with cookies: attractive, sweet, soft, flat little round bakery in different flavors. Later, I was back behind my thriller! Before I took root in my chair, I took a longer afternoon walk with my dogs to the picnic area and to the off-road trails for mountain bikers. The park had a trail system that ran for miles, with many different training levels of difficulty. There were multiple usable hiking and riding trails, so we had a wide selection for the next days.

January 2nd
Compensation

Six degrees Celsius at eight o'clock in the morning! Not that hot! No wonder the heater did not stop working. In the camper it was at least 17°C. The sky was clear, no clouds visible and we had a wonderful morning sun. I could, however, resist taking my breakfast outside. Tonight, at around midnight I had serious fears when I rolled back the awning because of strong storm gusts. I was tired of the rattling and the rocking, which were transmitted to the car.

We were ready to go before ten o'clock. After the lazy day yesterday, I wanted to be outside and to breathe fresh air, armed with a thick anorak and headband. Meanwhile the temperature had gone down to 12°C, but the icy wind whistled around the ears. We were on the road for two and a half hours and met almost no one. Only when we arrived at the official parking lot did some mountain bikers past us. We had just started in time, before the crowd got bigger. We could confidently retire to our cabin and leave the track to the athletes.

First, I tried to make myself comfortable in the slipstream of the camper and in the sun, but it was too inconveniently cold for reading. So, I hid myself in the camper, regretting not being able to take advantage of the beautiful sunshine outside. Who sits and reads outdoor with 12°C? Our daily routine went on as usual until the doggies asked again for a walk at around half past three. The wind had eased, and we were one and a half hours on tour. I think we had compensated for yesterday's laziness.

Happiness must be human! The neighbors had left a lot of firewood behind. "If I don't get it, then the next person will," I thought to myself and quickly grabbed the stuff. Now I had some more firewood for the next two nights. I lit the campfire and sat straight down in front of it. At about six o'clock it was so uncomfortable that I retreated into my shelter. How can normal tent campers survive at these temperatures? The only possible option for me would be to hide in the sleeping bag or to play cards with gloves and a bobble hat, drinking a lot of hot wine!

It is still starry outside (8°C/9 pm), but my barometer continues to drop. Fine, let's wait for the surprise tomorrow. Soon we will be more restricted in our movements, so if possible, I want to hike a longer trail with my ladies.

January 3rd
Ice Cellar Florida

It will be hard to believe, but for the morning walk I was looking in the closet for long underpants (my leggings) and my musk ox headband (from Alaska). Two sweaters and an anorak! Six degrees Celsius! This was just unreal! By way of comparison I had "summer" in Portugal at the same time last winter. The heater had trouble warming up the inside to a temperature of at least twenty degrees in the RV. Nature made it through the day at not even ten degrees! And it was overcast!

Yesterday, as it was clear it made more sense, but today? Nevertheless, I went bravely on with my two ladies on a two-hour tour of the rider trails. The only oncoming traffic was in the form of six horses with their riders. Otherwise we were alone in the area and both my friends could sniff as much as they wanted and romp at the leash. They were doing well, and my nose was running! Since it was certainly too cold for   fire and being outside today, I packed most of my equipment – that would save time tomorrow.

Now we three are sitting again in a heap and hoping that the stove will provide the necessary heat. That night I will have several cups of hot tea instead of a cold beer. Three guesses why…

11

January 4th
Winter in Floooorriiiida!

The **Oscar Scherer Park** will be our last State Park here in Florida for a longer stay (4 nights). We will visit friends nearby – if they are not frozen yet! It will stay icy according to the weather forecast for the next few days.

This morning we had reached freezing point. It can only go up! The sun laughed at us again from a cloudless sky. Today I could do everything that needed to be done. At around nine o'clock in the morning we started and had our first stop at **Sun City Center**, near Tampa Bay. Walmart was quickly checked, cheap refueling too, but I had some trouble finding the library at the beginning. Understandable, if you stay on Pebble Beach Boulevard in the south and the address is in the northern part. There they had no Wi-Fi, so I was sent to another building. An elderly gentleman with an urgent need for discussion took me to a community center with a swimming pool and various leisure facilities. First, I was alone in the room, but then a lot of babbling ladies (above the "maiden age") joined us and sat at the tables for a parlor game. Entertainment was announced. The whole time I felt a bit out of place, as in a "Columbo" film: the noblest little houses, the lawn trimmed with millimeter precision in such a way that one neighbor competed with the next. The means of transport was not a bicycle, but a golf cart, clubhouse atmosphere... As far as the eye could see, no pensioner under seventy; very well-kept ladies and gentlemen, bowling in matching outfits: it smelled of money. The American pensioners' paradise par excellence – artificially pounded out of the ground!

I had that feeling, and after completing the mail I hurried away! (Yes, I know, I'm approaching sixty too!) That was probably why I forgot to attach my reports for my German friends and family. Sorry! Now they'll have to wait for the next opportunity.

The State Park was spacious and easy to find, in the middle of a residential area. It was not far from the coast, although you needed a car. But I could not go to the beach because... yes, because I was with dogs in Florida! In return, there were a lot of hiking trails, which we could diligently check.

I will save my firewood over the next days too, because who can still be sitting outdoors at seven o'clock in the evening at 8°C? Really only the stalwarts and the Canadians! No spoiled Northern Europeans like us.

January 5th
Frosty

At night we would get light rain, but no temperature recovery. As usual, dressed in Alaskan anorak, with headband and long underpants I put my nose into the fresh morning air. During our mandatory morning walk I discovered that the visitor center here in this State Park had Wi-Fi signal, but only outdoors! That's why I cycled there quickly to get rid of my overdue emails. I would have needed gloves and a warm pad for the session, but as it was, I froze silently with no complaints.

Back in the camper there was a hot foot bath and lemon tea to prevent any cold. It took almost an hour until I was warm again. I vowed: "No one is going to get me out of my home that fast again!" But when at half past three the sun could be seen and at least it looked like it would have warmed up a little, I chased my two ladies out into the cool air. We managed a walk of ninety minutes. However, I hid in the palm forest, so that we would not feel the icy wind. Meanwhile the temperature in the WoMo dropped from 25°C to 14°C! So much for the thermal insulation in my castle. That's why the electrical heater was running all night. At least I got something out of the expensive campsite fee: the electricity was included.

13

January 6th/Holy Three Wise Men celebration in Germany
Short and terse – meanwhile in Florida

* Sunshine and cold wind
* Temperatures of 13°C at around noon
* two-hour hike with red nose
* washed two loads of laundry
* Copying CDs in the evening

January 7th
Southbound to the "Angels" (Engel)

We could take our time, because we were meeting our friends at around 1:00 pm in Englewood, FL. I grabbed everything together to leave immediately after I tried a short walk with the pooches. But I soon gave up, because this time I managed (despite my plan) to get lost. So, we marched back the same way and left the State Park at around noon. To get to Englewood it was only about thirty kilometers to the south.

I was greeted by the new acquaintances as if we had always known each other. Pure coincidence that we had a such nice relationship? I don't believe it! "Coincidences" in life always indicate a new direction. During our conversation it turned out that Monika's father had the same job as my husband. Maybe had they met on "cloud nine" and brought our paths together? I hadn't had such a harmonious visit for a long time. That's why I decided to dock on their power and stay overnight in the driveway. How can you say goodbye and get away from good food, interesting entertainment and a German Christmas tree so fast?

In the evening Laszlo had the idea of taking me for a small sightseeing tour through Englewood and the surrounding area. I did not mind, and we had an extensive and interesting tour.

He showed me the former motel of his parents, told me about the town's old time and pointed out the serious changes, for instance an RV park, which could be considered a city in itself. Terrible for me, to see so many "Snowbirds" of older semesters in a pile! But maybe in twenty years' time will I think differently? In summer, the city was like a ghost town made from wooden buildings. We saw many beautiful and magnificent villas from the past. They were to the right and left of Manasota Key Road, an offshore island. On one side, the bay; on the other side, the Gulf of Mexico. There were more than a few dollars of fortune invested there. At the oldest house of Englewood (still on the island) we experienced a colorful sunset. The sun itself was invisible due to the clouds, but the color of the sky was impressive. The horizon glowed red and the light was mirrored in the dark water.

There was an interesting connection with the old building. After being "abused" for all sorts of purposes for years, it had been moved further and further away from the coast due to dune movement. You could now spend two weeks of unpaid nostalgic vacation in it. The only condition: You should be a recognized artist and be able to prove it. Would diary authors travelling alone with an attachment of four paws fall into this category?

Back home we were surprised by a visit from Monika's girlfriend, a vital and in many ways interesting personality. She has studied my language in Germany intensively and spoke very well. We only had to explain the word "Korinthenkacker" in more detail: literal translation: raisin shit/someone who is more than painfully meticulous. We talked in English, since Laszlo would have been otherwise excluded from the conversation. With Jean, I was immediately able to establish a trustworthy relationship. It is strange how fast and casually people often find each other. As a precaution, I said goodbye to my two hosts in the evening. I wanted to leave early tomorrow. Maybe they weren't "early birds" like us.

January 8th
Going northbound!

About four hundred kilometers were on the program today, ninety percent on Interstate I-75. At half past eight we left, sadly refusing an invitation for Jean's afternoon gossip, as I finally wanted to make kilometers again. Wandering around in Florida had come to its end.

Contrary to my previous intention to make the circumnavigation of the Gulf of Mexico and Walmart camping, I chose State Parks on the way. Right! The icy cold had ruined my desire to save money. I needed electricity so as not to freeze. Well, my gas heater would help, but it makes a terrible lot of noise and I wanted to reserve my existing propane (if possible) for Mexico.

As the first base I found a place at the intersection of I-75 with the I-10. The latter was on my way tomorrow. This park was only listed in the AAA camp book. Yay! Mistrust had been unnecessary. In **White Springs** we found the **Stephen Foster Cultural Center** with its attached campground. It was a lovingly managed State Park with an informative museum of the composer, arts and crafts, a pretty little church that still had a nice, tasteful but a bit kitschy Christmas decoration. The place had forty-five large pitches for $23, and it was not overcrowded! Strongly recommended! However, it was a bit colder here in the North than at today's starting point. The hiking trails would be suitable for a longer stay.

January 9th
A new time dawns

At home, if we had just 4°C or less in front of the door at eight in the morning, I would open it and let my dogs into the garden. Now I threw myself into several thick sweaters, thick underwear, warm pants and lined winter boots before my ladies could fulfill their morning needs. I had already fished out the

16

lined anorak of Wales (GB) from its hiding place. It just could not be any other way. I had not really imagined it to be so wintry! Ready for cold times! And in between always a hot foot bath, so that the cold had no chance.

We made good progress today and were able to skip a State Park. From **Tallahassee** (capital of Florida) onwards, the sun came out and we got a bright blue sky. Unfortunately, the temperatures did not keep up. After the **Apalachicola River** we switched into Central Time. So, it was now seven hours time difference to Germany, one hour to my friends in Florida, coinciding with my friend in Chicago and only two hours difference to Elfi in California.

We spent the night in the **Blackwater River State Park**, almost at the western end of the "Panhandle" of Florida, at the border with Alabama. The camping could only be found on tortuous paths but paid off for a visit. For twenty-two dollars, I got full disposal of the place. There were thirty spacious pitches in the middle of a tall pine forest. The sanitary building was well maintained and... heated! In the outdoor area, the water was switched off at five o'clock in the evening to prevent the pipes from freezing. There was even snow last week! The park was located on a small white sandy beach on the river and non-campers could stay in the parking lot for a small fee. I had never seen that before. Unfortunately, the time change brought the evening earlier (at about five o'clock), but I got out of bed earlier when the daylight came. My two Wuffis, however, were always hungry at the same time...

January 10ᵗʰ
Halfway

From our 2400 km to the Texas-Mexican border, we had made half of it since Englewood. We were close to **New Orleans.** Thank God I was able to drive Interstate I-18 all this time, because on my last tour I visited the whole surrounding area in detail (travel report "Highways... II"!). So, we could cycle the miles around the gulf with no hurries in six days. The weather was good today, temperatures below freezing. In the morning I had to remove the ice from the doors with the hair dryer, behind which I had stowed the utensils for disposal. The electric heating needed energy support from the gas heater, otherwise it would not have been able to fulfill its task. Showering was at the camper, since I did not really trust the general premises despite the heating.

Up and away earlier, my ass! What are you referring to hear? We kept up our usual rhythm and said goodbye to Blackwater at half past nine. It was amazing to see the cypresses frozen in the dark water. Wuschel wondered why she couldn't get into the water. It was so strangely hard!

Maybe I've been complaining a little too much about the weather lately! I'm sorry! I will just take it as it is and let no more disappointment arise. The sun is shining now, the heating is working, we have it warm, the right clothing is available. The car is running well, it only has a few start problems with the cold in the morning. So far, I have not needed a chemical remedy, just a little patience while warming up with the glow plugs. I do not want to complain anymore. Years ago, at that time, I was having a stressful period (writing student reports) that cost me the remainder of my nerves. So, I'm staying with this!

Today's State Park is not necessarily the "yolk of the egg" – as we say in my language. Maybe that's because they are rebuilding, and everything looks a bit grubby. On my last tour I was at the **Fairview Riverside SP**, very close to here. It was more appealing. But for nineteen dollars you can swallow the bitter pill for one night. **Fontainebleau State Park** is large and has access to Lake Pontchartrain. Judging by the parking lots, there should be a lot going on here in summer.

Since I had previously done the grocery shopping, I was busy in the evening with cleaning and cooking in advance. Wonderful Bavarian roulades are still steaming in my stove. (Can you smell them?)

January 11th
Going westwards

Four States in two days! It ain't bad! We left Florida the day before yesterday, drove through Alabama for an hour, left Mississippi after another hour and landed in Louisiana yesterday. We covered a good three hundred and forty miles. The departure was delayed, since an impeccable internet reception was available in the previous State Park. I had to call a few people, even got phone calls, forwarded mails and did important research. You never knew when the next opportunity would come. In addition, the engine needed some solar energy to start. That's why we did not leave until late in the morning.

Since there was nothing to do, we drove for four hours, except for one pee-break. I recognized place names everywhere from my last tour. The ride over the eighteen-mile bridge through the swamp area of the **Atchafalaya River** and the **Henderson Swamp** was impressive: as far as the eye could see, shallow brown water, with moss-hung cypresses, sometimes alone, sometimes in small groups, sometimes in a forest. Many were picturesquely reflected in the calm waters. Unfortunately, I was driving and could not behold this unique impression in the sunshine. At **Baton Rouge** we crossed the much-praised "old man river" (Mississippi) with its sweeping barges. Sometimes you saw several of them side by side and joined. At **Lake Charles**, I drove on familiar roads. I even remembered the somewhat expensive propane dealer.

I think that tomorrow I will seize the opportunity right away and fill my tank again for Mexico. Thus, I will get out of the annoying search near the border.

We almost got the same pitch as we did two years ago. The prices had increased a bit, but nineteen dollars could still be accepted. Oh, joy! On this little spot in Louisiana we also got a free internet reception! Apparently, many State Parks have endeavored to meet this communication need.

Although as usual I was hungry and tired on arrival, my two ladies could take a little walk with me first. After dinner, the bedclothes called me for half an hour, but remembering the growing darkness and the oncoming cold, I carried the three of us outside to the fresh air for another hour and we went round the lake. Once again, the many cypresses impressed me with their weird forms.

That's enough for today! When I close my laptop, the early birds will soon return to work back in Germany! For them: good morning!

January 12th
Paid twenty dollars apprenticeship

Sh... communication technology! I urgently had to increase my balance on the mobile phone. In order to skip the expiry date for Mexico, I got two prepaid cards of ten dollars each. I followed the instructions, but no accumulated sum appeared on my display. What had I done wrong? Once again, I did not understand which button to press.

Calling the customer service, I dreaded that the assistant on the other end often speak too fast and use too many technical terms. How should foreign speakers find their way?

I dared and got what sounded like "Chinese". Supposedly the added balance is already on my account. Why then no confirmation message? Later, I figured it out: they distinguish between SMS prepaid card and phone card. I had bought the first one at Walmart. Now I could send unlimited text messages by the end of February. To whom please? I only had the landline number of most of my friends! Verizon made a deal once again! That's what really annoyed me. Otherwise I was not stingy with my money, if I could choose what I spent it on. But I had no idea I was paying for this and that made me angry. Tonight, I was exhausted, and I was sure it wasn't because of the age factor.

We got away in time; my propane gas could also be filled up. So far, so good! Even the trip to the Texas border was a "walk". But then, suddenly out of nowhere, I encountered the heavy goods traffic with oil transporters in **Houston**. The road conditions, although we were on I-10, were miserable and interrupted with many construction sites. All that went along for three hundred kilometers at least. As I stuck to the speed limit, the heavy trucks passed rustling and thundering on my left and sometimes right side. For these vehicles, the speed limit did not seem to apply! Houston itself demanded full concentration from me, even though my navigation system steered me well through the freeway jungle of this city.

I finally reached the US-59 and was on my way to the present State Park. Only a hundred and fifty kilometers from Houston! Thankfully, the road was four-lanes and I could drive stress-free. At some point, the traffic got more fluid and I took a half-hour lunch break. At about three o'clock we reached **Lake Texana State Park** and were allocated a very nice spot right on the lake for eighteen dollars. Since I had already eaten on the way, I was able to go with my two ladies on a tour. It was surprisingly mild outside and the anorak could stay in the RV again. This time the squirrels were less of a problem on our walk. Rather, countless armadillos drove the adrenaline into the bloodstream of my hunters. I tied Knuffi securely around the belly and Wuschel behaved properly after a few good words. I had to turn on the boss in me again for the two of them. Secretly, after the long drive, I understood their hunting need, but I could not let that show. Otherwise they would have gone for a walk <u>without </u>me! Later, I managed to get such a remnant from the dinosaur past in front of the lens.

Tomorrow we are driving our last four hundred and thirty kilometers. Then we will have gone round the Gulf of Mexico on the US side. A direct flight would have been significantly shorter from Englewood!

We will stay in a State Park near Mission, because that's where I could find "Camping World" with their repair service. Before I entered an almost "third world country", I wanted to have checked all the technical details of my rolling home. I was also thinking that new front tires will be due. Since Alaska two years ago, they have not been replaced. Thus, they have run for several miles and not in the best condition.

<u>Side note:</u> Knuffi is whistling excitedly in her sleep and her paws tremble. Probably in the dream she is hunting a rat-tailed monster with chain armor....

January 13th
The thirteenth is doing the honors!

Is number 13 in the States an unlucky number as it is in Germany? Bad luck on the thirteenth? After a beautiful sunrise at Lake Texana we drove towards the rain. It was no fun getting our windshield sprayed by passing lorries. For safety reasons I did not want to drive my box faster than 80 km/h. So, the wipers worked at full speed, which was not particularly helpful for attention. But the four hundred kilometers had to be driven today. There was no way out, because there were no other State Parks on the way.

Once the rain had stopped, I could reflect on the boring, gray-brown and flat landscape. Here, there was a brown Texas steak grazing on the pasture, there a source for oil, but nothing else! A sign said, "Check your fuel! No tank options in the next hundred kilometers". The rough country was fenced, so it had to be farmed. Probably some ranches did it, off the thoroughfare #59 and #77. They were miserable rural roads full of bumps. After all, the #59 was four lanes and thus one or the other car was no obstacle, except for the fast trucks! It was called "Texan Tropic Highway" or something like that.

We made the trip to **Mission** in the estimated time and arrived at half past four at "Camping World". Excellent! The lift had been broken since last week, so the mechanic could not do the oil change. Tires for my size were not in stock. It would take a week to order. At least I wanted to have a look at my back light and my dripping water drain. But wait! I was assigned a mechanic who could perfectly solve the problem with my back light. A Mexican who was used to improvisation! Now I was able to use my blinkers again! Thank God!

I also had a problem with my greywater. The whole procedure lasted until five o'clock and I was a bit worried that I wouldn't reach the **Bentsen Valley River State Park** until the evening. Finally, I arrived but the next disappointment came unexpectedly: there was no camping possibility in this State Park anymore. There I was and it was getting dark! A ghastly RV Park nearby was overcrowded. However, an employee assured that there would be no problems with free accommodation in the parking lot of the State Park. Well, let's try it. If someone scares me off, the Walmart will still be there.

Now I'm sitting here, benefitting from the resort's Wi-Fi and typing in my lines. I have enough water and electricity. If it gets too cold tonight, I will inevitably have to run my noisy heater. Tomorrow I'll go looking for a Ford dealer for oil change and a tire dealer to get me some new "shoes". If I can find an insurance broker for Mexico, I can cross the border on Friday or Saturday.

January 14th
Is waiting really fun?

We were not chased away tonight, so we'll try it again tomorrow evening. Everything was quiet and peaceful. Only Knuffi had to warn twice in the night because there were black pigs in the area. Every time I was sound asleep, she barked!

The day was boring. Apart from waiting and turning thumbs, I had nothing to do. After all, some important matters have been settled:

- New tires were fitted.
- The oil change has been carried out.
- My car ran straight.
- All lubricants have been checked.
- A front lamp has been replaced.
- The drainpipe had to be fixed.
- Side mirrors were ordered so we have spare ones.

The only thing left was to reward my two ladies with a long walk. You really needed to look after such patient and good dogs. Either they slept under a table, or a chair, or next to me or they waited in the living room. I had two special treasures in the family!

January 15th
Some preparations left

This day can be told very quickly. In the morning I was able to complete my required Mexican insurance. Since the car had more than fifteen years under its belt, the agency only gave me a value of five thousand dollars in the event of damage. Thus, the insurance rate was low for half a year. If they had known that I bought the car for only seven thousand dollars two years ago and have traveled around the whole globe, they probably would not have insured me! I discovered a Walmart near the main road to the International Bridge (border crossing) for RVs. I will stay there tomorrow night. That way, I can save up to twenty kilometers the next morning. In addition, I'm also saving a few dollars "cash" for an emergency case or some change. I had barely saved any pesos from the last trip. And my hair is practically short again – I found a hairdresser! Now I look like

Knuffi after her four-month radical makeover. I spared my dog this procedure because of the cold!

At Ford, I picked up my expensive mirrors and found out that I cannot take them back if I don't really need them. That's why at the end of the trip I will have to look for an "eBay" or a flea market.

The afternoon time was spent again with a long walk along the canal at the Bentsen SP, before returning to McAllen before dark. I was so broken in the evening that at eight o'clock I was already knocked out. In addition, my notebook had low battery, so I postponed writing until later.

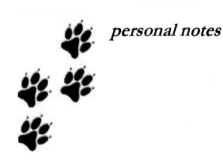 *personal notes*

Month of January
2nd half
1800 km

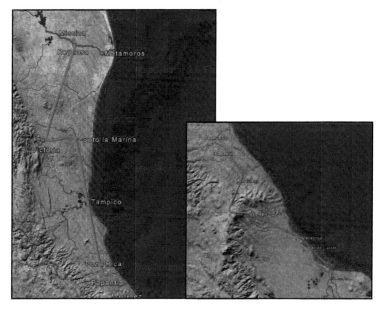

East Coast Mexico
to Tlacotalban
(State of Veracruz)

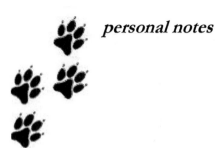 *personal notes*

First impressions of a foreign country

 *personal notes*

January 16th
Bavaria greets Mexico!

The night was restless and noisy as several trucks had their generators running and on Highway #83 there was heavy truck traffic. You get used to the background noise. At six o'clock I had rested and was a bit overwrought on my way to the border. How I hate these official procedures!

First, I went the wrong way and had to make a complicated turn with the help of a friendly guard. Then I found the right "house". There were only a few contenders to import cars. Nevertheless, all the formalities took more than one and a half hours. Obviously, I had caught an apprentice who had only mastered the two-finger system at the keyboard. It also took some time to explain to him what "maiden name" meant in my passport, as well as explaining the two different addresses. It was written in his face that he did not know what information he had to type into his PC. But that was not my problem. No one forced us and finally we were in Mexico. There was a different way of dealing with time here. It was unfortunate that I did not pass any American border controls to hand over the white document and thereby confirm my departure. Now, when I arrive in April, I will probably have to deal with the same disaster as California's "Corinthian Chaser" two years ago. Besides, my stay was temporary this time! Sh ...! However, since I will not travel to Acapulco, I won a few weeks.

Now we had entered this historical neighbor of the States. Like the last few times, the difference in quality of life was a recurrent culture shock for me. The first thing that came to my mind in **Reynosa** was a donkey cart, whose emaciated train animal carried cardboard-flap blinders and people through the hectic traffic. Only the main roads are paved, sidewalks were unknown, dirt and dust piled up in front of every front door and the cars looked accordingly grimy. Border towns were rarely the most well-maintained and attractive settlements. I had trouble finding the arterial road and drove around the city for half an hour. Consequently, I got used to the Mexican traffic right away.

Finally, I was out of the center and consciously looked for a chance so my dogs could pee. But we couldn't find an appealing stop. Once there was a spot, but it was littered with garbage. Only at an official road control could we rest and take advantage of the stop.

As the weather was nice today, the women in the villages seemed to have laundry day. But not with a washing machine! No! With a wash tub and a washboard on their doorsteps! The living conditions in these pseudo villages along the Mex #97 were not marked by luxury. Not even as a dog would I have wanted to be buried there. Small wooden barracks sparsely set and sealed, on dusty dirt roads, with lots of lumber around.

What future does the growing youth have here? What do people live from? Odd jobs? Support from distant family members in rich America? They cannot make much money selling oranges and honey in the wayside small stalls. And the lonely tailed cow beside the road? If she's unlucky, the rope breaks and then she's involved in a road accident, then she lies on the roadside for the next few days and maybe weeks with her stomach bloated, until the carrion vultures take pity on her. Such giant cow is noticeable, the many small dogs and rabbits, not so much.

We went south for a hundred kilometers until we came to Mex #101. As the main road, it was relatively well developed, with plenty of overtaking opportunities, but the undulating bumps in the pavement caused an eternal up and down of my carriage. Knuffi got the better part because her driver's seat absorbed some shocks. Wuschel, on the other hand, couldn't escape any because she was laying on the ground. Maybe that was the reason why both had no appetite this evening from all the bumps in the road.

At the fork in the road to Mex #101 we had lunch. We would reach **CD Victoria** at a good time. However, I had no more desire to drive into the city and find the RV Park. I was too tired from today's stress. Thus, I swung in front of the city limits to a motel, which I had found in my smart book.

We were alone for two hundred pesos with all supply options, on a large meadow, quieter than in the city and I made plans for our onward journey. I did not want to rush. It was better to take a look along the route to the Emerald Coast. That's why we will drive the hundred and fifty kilometers out to sea tomorrow and spend a night or two right at the Gulf.

January 17ᵗʰ
Finally!

Pure sunshine when we left the motel at around ten o'clock. I had a restful and quiet night with at least ten hours of sleep behind me and a nice warm private shower. Last night I was so exhausted that I closed my eyes at nine without reading. That means something.

There were two roads for the drive to **La Pesca**. I followed the signs and came to Highway #75, a minor road. It was surprisingly well-developed and had only a few potholes every now and then, but we also ran over a few of them the size of saucepan. Fast braking was advisable, and as soon as a shadow appeared on the road, all my senses were tense. I got away with most of the risings, though.

As soon as I wanted to praise the efficiency of the province of **Tampaulipas** in road construction, the road bent and I landed for about three kilometers on a better dirt road. To my right you could see the dug-up earth of the future road. A glimmer of hope for the next generation! I sank into mud, dirt and water. It was not bad enough to get stuck, a firmer surface was still there. But now I had the color of the Mexican cars because the dirt splashed up to the windshield as I drove fast through the unpredictable pools of water.

In **Soto la Marina** I met the alternative (return route!) and swung to the #70 and #52. These were excellently developed, and I could keep my hundred km/h well. The entire route and the landscape were interesting. I went through a plateau that was absolutely deserted and untouched. It almost felt like the Yukon: a wide view over a hilly scenic and intact nature, nothing else. The feeling lasted a hundred kilometers. Since CD Victoria was more than three hundred meters high and bordered on a mountain to the west, the road had to lower again at sea level. From Marina, it was lively as we were going down, with a latter view of the sea and the marshy estuarine delta of the river with the same name.

I arrived at a village of about five hundred inhabitants, the kind Mexico can only convey in a picture book. Every twenty meters we found a *tope* (speed bump) in the street, which forced you to drive slowly. I overlooked the first one and then my toilet paper unrolled itself off the roll: Next time I would be slower. I wanted to take pictures, but inhibition and respect for the privacy of the residents prevented me. Here, an elderly man was sitting on a rocking chair, dozing with his sombrero on his stomach; there a father was working with his son, cleaning the fish from the morning. In another corner, a family gathered for lunch, opposite a young woman breastfeeding her baby. All this on the open road. However, I knew about the fear of some Mexicans in front of the camera and the associated "evil eye", so I prefer to describe it. The cottages were low and small. Many were painted with bright and cheerful colors. Lots of junk (sorry, I meant offers!) were stored outside the door. The road led away from the paved road into the mud. The branching side streets were also unpaved. Woe, what would happen when it rained?

I searched for today's accommodation offer. I had overlooked the exclusive one in favor of the simpler one. I did not need knickknacks, just water and electricity and maybe disposal. Nobody was there so I hardly feared competition. We drove to the beach. I have promised it to my girls. You could freely spend the night directly on the shore and I didn't care that there wasn't

anybody else. However, I thought that it was now safer in off-season than during high season. I also thought that this beautiful beach was a Mexican insider tip as all North American tourists rushed south. If you have time, I'd recommend it. If you have the chance, this is by far your best option. Hundreds of shady *palapas* (thatched roofs) adorned the beach. My ladies enjoyed the water and the leash-free situation to the full: Into the waves! Rolling in the sand! Digging holes! Catching the game! What happy dogs! End of the American straitjacket!

We had lunch there and later we took another long walk. The saltwater had already affected Wuschel! I just couldn't stop her! I had hardly set up on my stand, when a hawker came with his pearl necklaces. Unfortunately, I had to reject him, and he left.

We were completely satisfied with our overnight stay. We did not pay more than in CD Victoria and got a beautiful sunset on the river. Again, we were the only guests and could feel safe. It was a nice place to camp, had a jetty and a *palapa* on the riverbank. In addition, attractive little holiday homes were to rent on the property. For my simple needs it was enough, and I had a lot of space for my pooches!

Now a little side story: I had just parked behind a *tope* to take a picture of the area. There was an old vehicle next to me with a

35

couple. The *caballero* looked at my camera and asked if I could take a picture of them with his camera. Of course! He took his *reina* in his arms, squeezed her and I hit the button. When I showed him the photo, he wanted to reward me with a beer. I waved and with a "buenas tardes" they went off! I can only emphasize again and again: Mexicans are friendly and lovely people! Although of course there are exceptions everywhere.

When the sun goes down at this season, the night breaks in very quickly. Now, the wind whistles quite nicely around our vehicle and the temperature has fallen to around 17°C. Tomorrow I will decide what to do depending on weather conditions. But more than likely it won't be an urgent program.

January 18th
Gut decision

This morning we were happy to spend another night in this nice place. We got up at ten o'clock and went to the beach. I wanted to stroll with the doggies and then make the inside of my vehicle shine. But then, during our walk, heavy clouds came up and that did not look good! We got our feet out of the water, jumped into our shoes, and went back to the camper. We did not need rain here! Since we were better off in CD Victoria, adios to the nice pitch and back on #52 to Soto la Marina.

We needed to refuel. A liter of diesel for 8,24 pesos! (I have not calculated the conversion in cents yet – but it sure is a ridiculous price!) Then I stood at the junction between the roads to Victoria and to Tampico. If I went straight ahead, I would be in Tampico in the late afternoon. I couldn't make up my mind! Finally, I dropped point 5-7 (see later!) out of the program and drove straight to the South. Why drive through the city and then through the mountains? I would win at least four days for me and my girls at the Gulf.

When I looked at the sky, our departure was perhaps a bit premature, because now the sun was shining again in its entire splendour! Whatever, the decision had been made! We drove the Mex #180 South. For Mexican conditions, it was drivable if you overlooked some generous potholes and patchwork on the pavement. It took us five hours for the two hundred kilometers to our overnight stop, north of Tampico. The average speed was not impressive. But you cannot expect more in Mexico, even if the road is marked on the map with two lanes.

We got to see a lot of the daily life of normal Mexicans. Here in the countryside, the tire specialist was probably the most sought-after profession, even if he practiced his skill in unsightly and catastrophic workshops. The second most important means of transportation was the horse or a donkey. Very often beautiful animals were tied somewhere for grazing at the roadside. The huts of the locals were very modest, if not primitive. All too often they were still covered with straw. I was sure there was more comfort in my RV than in these simple dwellings. Life took place in the dust or (after rain) in the dirt in front of the house. Cooking was usually outdoors, firstly to escape the heat and secondly to reduce the risk of fire.

The landscape was varied. The road ran between two mountain ridges: one down to the sea to the east, the other to the west. When I saw the ridge, I was glad I did not have to take that way and thanked my decision instincts. A lot of millet was grown here, with wide agave fields in between. This plant is the basis for the infamous Tequila!

We reached our destination **North of Tampico** at around three o'clock. You couldn't have everything for a hundred pesos. This time there were showers and a toilet nearby, as well as Wi-Fi from the hotel for free. For this reason, we had no electricity and no disposal. Never mind, I had done everything earlier. Tomorrow will be different. We will have bad road conditions ahead of us and a lot of truck traffic. That's why I anticipated at least five hours driving time for the two hundred kilometers.

January 19th
Phew! Done!

The overnight stay turned out to be a surprise! By midnight, I realized why there was this huge unpaved area behind the house. Little by little, one semi-trailer joined the other. They had all sorts of battered cars in tow, transports to Guatemala. The drivers stopped here to sleep, and they were noisy. Thankfully, they did not let their generators run overnight, so at least it was quiet until six o'clock in the morning.

I got into nice conversation with an American couple from Missouri, who was already on their way back home. They urgently warned me of the Tampico police: greedy and outrageous. They gave me so many useful tips. Alarm bells were ringing! How to face the danger? Was a Mexican an early riser? Certainly not! Rush Hour? The money-hungry law enforcement officers were likely to be concerned with other problems than with passing tourists. So – get out early!

We started at eight o'clock at daybreak. It was twenty kilometers to Tampico to access the bypass There was heavy fog and heavy traffic. The police seemed busy. I followed the description in the book, but nevertheless, I almost missed the entrance to the **Libramento** because of the haze and smog. Not even the oversized ship (that served as a landmark and signpost) was visible in the fog. Half a meter further and I would have landed in the middle of Tampico. If that had happened, I would have paid a fine, because the city transit is closed for heavy cars. With side indicators and inch by inch preparatory work, I forced myself on the right road. I was relieved that I had escaped the tricky order keepers.

At the entrance to the #70 I was stopped. Now they'd got me! An unfriendly face appeared at the window. I hadn't stopped at the entrance of the bypass and ignored the stop sign. With three words of Spanish and the sign language, I explained to him that there was only a "give way" sign but no "stop". Then he wanted to inspect my driver's license. The man was boring. When he saw Knuffi, he inquired about her name, whether she had a passport, whether she bit and whether she was vaccinated. He pulled a biscuit out of his pocket for her. When I asked Knuffi to look at the *hombre gentil*, he was quite taken by her brown eyes. Then he saw the big one. That made him more respectful. Nevertheless, he let me get up and gather my documents. I tried to stay friendly.

So far, he had not asked for payment. When I returned to the driver's seat with all my paperwork, his superior had apparently appeared. The whole banter had taken too long and with an *adios* I was released graciously. They could not find anything that they could accuse me of! After this successful low-cost interlude, we found the bypass to #180 **south of Tampico**.

When we finally got back on course, two hours had passed. Now we had to cover three more hours of miserable road conditions: potholes like I've only seen on the Alaska Highway, road ups and downs that were the perfect example of a rollercoaster, *topes* that could only be crossed at walking speed, (one after the other) and then heavy traffic in both directions. There was not much time for me to look at the area. Revenge would have been swift if I had taken my eyes off the road. At some point, I wondered why I was doing it all. I did not have time to find an answer.

About a hundred kilometers before *Tajin / Poza Rica* there was a place to stay for the night. I headed there, even though it was only early afternoon. Five hours of driving time had used up all my energy in these road conditions. Although the pitches were pretty behind the motel, I mistrusted tremendously the type of ground they were in. Everything soaked and spongy. Thanks, but I've already sunk twice with my box! I asked for another option. The lady offered to take a room. I could park the car on solid ground in front of the motel. The price difference was ridiculous: 150 pesos for the pitch and 230 pesos for the room with supposedly warm shower (I have checked: 100 pesos were currently about 5,50 Euros). The dogs could sleep in the car. All cats are gray at night, I thought!

So far, I have not decided where to lay my head to rest yet, in my own place or in the cool room on a hard bed. I can perhaps turn on my heater. If the fuse breaks, I still have my RV. Unfortunately, the disposal won't happen under this arrangement, but we can solve that problem tomorrow.

Now I must dedicate a kind word to my two companions. They hold out under this rocking and shaking with the patience of saints. There's no hesitancy in getting back in the car as a sign that they've had enough. I really must admire the long-suffering of both. No one has had a spat or behaved negatively to take revenge for the impositions, which is great! And that's why we're going to take a long break on the *Costa Esmeralda* to relax.

January 20th
Redeemed promise

In the RV it smelled of wet, happy dogs. Today we arrived at Zorro on the **Costa Esmeralda**, with direct access to the beach and we felt happy. The reason for the decision was the terrible

parking space in Poza Rica and the ugly city. The hotel there was great, but you feel like you are behind prison walls without green around and on deep gravel, even if you only paid two hundred pesos for neat showers and toilets. But let me tell things in order! All three of us had a good stay in the hotel room, even though it smelt musty. The trucks drove past our window all night and woke us up several times. Sometimes they sounded like jet fighters were flying overhead. Never mind, we had a warm shower! As someone already said: You could not have everything in Mexico!

At about nine o'clock we set out on the bumpy road to **Poza Rica,** about a hundred kilometers away. In two and a half hours we were there. It was foggy and I had the real impression of a tropical humid climate. After all, we were several miles south of the **Tropic of Cancer**, the gateway to the tropics. The northern tropic is the northernmost latitude where the midday sun is just at its zenith, namely on 21st of June, the day of the summer solstice of the northern hemisphere. The latitude is 23°26'22" north latitude and runs through the southern tip of Lower California near La Paz (Mexico), north of Cuba across the Atlantic to the Sahara through Western Sahara, Mauritania, Mali, Algeria, Libya and Egypt. The year-round trade winds often bring rain to this part of Mexico. Nature grows green and varied. Banana trees thrive as successfully along the route as all sorts of citrus fruits.

Again and again, we saw the small poor huts of the Mexicans, hidden under a crowd of banana trees, as in a jungle of natives. Somehow, I got off the Mex # 180 and landed on a crossing. There was a village with potholes and topes. Caballeros crossed my path on handsome steeds, many women carried their burdens on their heads, children scurried in the dirt and neat young ladies with their school uniforms stood out from the general confusion. I kept wondering how the population manages to be so clean and well-groomed in all the primitive living conditions. It's simply admirable!

My unscheduled detour brought me to **Alamo**, a rich fruit growing area. We constantly came across the loaded pick-ups of farmers, bringing their bananas and citrus fruit to the local fruit plant. I had to stop on a road with tons of fruit stalls, painted in orange, despite the many trucks behind me. For some pesos, I bought a bunch of these small bananas (plátanos), of which you can eat ten at a time, without getting full. I wanted to get a picture of all the colorfulness, but all batteries were on strike! Typical! Yesterday I forgot to reload. But there will surely be another opportunity soon.

We reached **Poza Rica** at lunchtime, a hectic industrial city with few attractions and tons of traffic. I needed eyes in the back of my head. There, an old beetle flitted past me on a road without a dividing line. On the other side I had the public bus, a truck was on my tail and the traffic light switched to red relatively quickly! I felt myself sweating. Somewhere a scooter popped up and flew past all the existing jam! No, it did not pay to stay here! When I saw the pitch, I decided to use the next two hours to drive to the coast. The road was for the most part very well developed, and we were moving forward. In addition, it was sunny. As the road was so good, we could easily master El Tajin with the excavations and Papantla from the coast in a day trip.

Therefore, we landed here on the **Gulf of Mexico**. I have not spotted a single motorhome on the whole trip. When I arrived at **Zorro** with its unusual architecture at around three o'clock, I was the only guest on the premises with 30 palapas. I hoped I wouldn't get bored! However, relaxing was good, and I should start to work. I hadn't started writing up the last journey yet and it was still sitting in the drawer. So, for the time I'll be here I paid a hundred and fifty pesos for five days, with full "Hook up", clean toilets, warm showers, palapa with table and chairs as well as two swimming pools. The pooches could run without leash in the "garden" and the beach with its black-brown sand was only a few steps away. After the dogs had swum in the water all they wanted, they rolled enjoyably in the sand. I could not let them stay too long because I saw myself later cleaning our little apartment (Knuffi loves to shake herself on my bed). I had therefore sealed my sleeping accommodation with several blankets, but some sand always crumbled through. Then good night! Hopefully the fog, which has messed up our view over the Gulf to Florida today, will clear tomorrow.

Costa Esmeralda / Veracruz
/Camping „El Zorro"

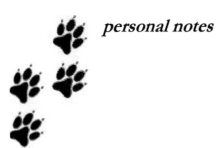 *personal notes*

 *personal notes*

January 21*st*
How is the weather at home?

Here the sun rose over a fog bank, while I made my first round on the Gulf with my dogs. At night, the humidity was so high that water accumulated on the car without rain. We got nice neighbours from Montreal yesterday. They will leave before us, but a little chat from palapa to palapa was quite nice. Then the fog came in again. A pity, I thought! But I did not give up hope so easily. I took advantage of the gloomy time and used it for the tiresome housework. The fridge and the RV were crying out for a clean, so I put the ladies outside and devoted myself to the inevitable chores. In between, the sun gained the upper hand and the day got wonderfully bright.

I celebrated the event with my feet in the gulf waters and a short walk with the girls. For a long time, I did not need to walk with them for too long, because they could run around within a radius of half a mile until they got tired. This did not help my laziness. Due to the water-wading in the gulf, I had the brilliant idea of testing the swimming pool next to my pitch. Daring, but I was almost out of breath! I thought I was a lot fitter! But I had finally cooled down – as much as an hour later my feet were still cold. We enjoyed the sunshine for the rest of the day.

Tomorrow I'll look for an opportunity to fix my hammock under the palapa. On the beach bars are installed for this purpose, but unfortunately there is no shade.

47

January 22nd
Casual...

...or how to spend a day without getting a bad conscience. Casually my dogs without leash, casually their mistress in dealing with the time – according to Mexican example: Mañana (tomorrow, maybe the day after tomorrow) or si dios nos presta el tiempo (if God lends us the time). Can one explain more clearly unclear dates? Although the sun was struggling to get through the dense fog today (trade winds!), we had our second walk at half past four. Later, I sat in my extensive park under coconut palms until sunset and studied all kinds of Mexican info for the trip.

Yesterday, a coconut fell a few inches from the camper and the milk disappeared and so did my scared dog Knuffi. I hope we don't get another one of these bombs hitting my roof!

We had the second walk behind us and the two dogs were dozing off and dripping wet in a corner. The hike this morning was a bit shorter due to fog. We were alone again in our area; the Canadians having moved to the South.

While planning the route, I discovered interesting details that offered a whole new timetable and excursions. Good thing I checked first, I thought to myself. After the stay here I will take a chance on unprepared paths and hopefully take interesting pictures and attend cool events. The accommodation question, however, is open. If I cannot find a parking space, I can stay at a motel or at a Pemex gas station in the parking lot as a last resort. These expenses will not be my financial ruin!

Thus, I spent the morning planning, and the time until lunch ran between my fingers. I don't know why I bothered cleaning yesterday because although I brushed both ladies every time, they entered the apartment, the sand was crunching everywhere again. But if they were happy, then I was too!

We will still stay here this weekend hoping for more sun. If not, we will not spoil the mood with trade winds! The night is as clear as yesterday; the crescent moon is lying on its back in these latitudes. Let's see, what is waiting for us tomorrow morning!

January 23rd
Attention! Sunburn danger!

Our jaws dropped in the morning! Again, this beautiful (!)... fog! Well, then at least I get to work! First, pee walk in an anorak and then breakfast. Was it getting sunnier outside?

That was right, the sun continued to fight, leaving a Mexican sky for us at ten o'clock. Jaws up! I grabbed my friends and started walking, barefoot, feet in the refreshing Gulf Water, short-sleeved and jeans up. Gorgeous! Were we doing well? I guess so!

How could I make better use of the location of the RV Park along the water? Without any shade, the sun became (in the truest sense of the word) too scorching for me. I remembered my oversized family umbrella. That could be the solution! I grabbed it and tied it with elastic to the rail. The shadow we got with the umbrella was enough for all three if we sat together. I did not hang the hammock because I could not deal with that much sun.

At noon we received a visit from a walker from the State of Washington. He wanted to see who the owner of such a lonely RV from Illinois was. The dogs adopted the friendly newcomer right away and we had a lot of fun talking about Mexico and, what do you know... It turned out that he later stayed under my palapa for lunch and invited me to eat in the evening in his rented cabin. He was bored sometimes and on the lookout for people to talk to. This time I was his "victim". He was stuck here for several weeks because his VW-bus had to be overhauled and this would take a while. He had sent his wife back to

America to work and was now spending his time here on the coast. As a Mexican connoisseur, he gave me some tips and there were more over the next few days. Again and again, there were opportunities to make new friends.

After he had left, it was three o'clock and we headed for the beach again. As it got too windy and the beach was starting to get more and more crowded with Mexican teens, so I moved into my quiet palm garden. What else did I have to read? A lot of things came back to me from our first trip. I wanted to refresh or assimilate many things. The travel program had been overloaded at that time. That's why I would not join a motorhome group anymore.

I now realized how much I had relied on the – sometimes miserable – local guides and had not provided myself with information. However, I must emphasize that with the organizational and driving duties as a single traveller, there was hardly any time to spare. But I had time to catch up now!

Tomorrow is our last relaxing day here; then we'll go for some sightseeing days. My sunburn will accompany me to bed and hopefully tomorrow I can add some more colour.

The flying men –
Voladores – of Papantla

 *personal notes*

El Tajin with "Pirámide de los Nichos" and women from the Maya ethnic group

 *personal notes*

January 24th
El Tajin

Children and teenagers are always being told that they shouldn't trust strangers; that they should not get into a foreigner's car or go with an unknown person. In fact, I was about to do all this in Mexico, and without the protection of my dogs. No, I did not like the whole situation if I considered it properly. The invitation could be quite riskless and nicely, nevertheless ...! In an emergency, nobody would know where I was. You have watched too many movies right, Monika?

Therefore, this morning I decided to cancel on my "chevalier" and drove to *El Tajín* one day earlier than planned. The sky was overcast so the hike through the ruins would not be so hot. I left him a nice letter with a plausible excuse not to offend him. He had wanted to pick me up at four o'clock that evening by taxi. I did not even know his name or where he lived, and I was dependent on him bringing me back. I did not like the latter idea at all, so cancelling was not too.

At about nine o'clock I started towards *Papantla*, the place of origin of the *Voladores* (see below) and the center of the largest vanilla plantation in North America. The village itself would have been nice (!) to stroll around if there had been a parking possibility. But not for my carriage! Thus, I drove among buses, trucks, taxis, red, yellow, and green lights on a crossroads and waved them away happily. What else was left for me? I could not fly! *Mañana*, I prayed softly...

The road to *El Tajín* from there was terrible. They should consider that these archaeological sites are World Heritage Sites. One might think that such historic highlights would lead to a somewhat passable path. Not in Mexico! The worst spots on the Alaska Highway were motorways over these potholes and road messes. Everyone who got through here safely (including the passenger) should receive the first-class Federal Cross of Merit!

55

No exaggeration – my box rocked not only up and down but also back and forth at the same time. I was afraid that I would get stuck somewhere. Sometimes I had to invade the enemy side, for which of course I got a honk concert and hazard lights. Dear reader, these were the facts! Because of this experience I vowed to drive back via *Poza Rica*. This road seemed to be more frequented, even if the route was longer.

First, we arrived, somewhat exhausted, in *El Tajín*. I was extremely fortunate: just before noon, I reached in time for one of the *Voladores* shows, and on the other hand, I did not have to spend fifty *pesos*. The museum pleasure was free today and many Mexicans were visiting the ruins. I could park in front of one of the many small stalls. To stay on the safe side, the *señor* got a good tip from me, so that he would occasionally keep an eye on my "sanctuary". Also, the Wuffis had to guard our car...

Five years ago, I did not have any power left in my camera to even get one picture of the show. Who would have thought at that moment that I would visit this place again? This time I had enough power for video clips and pictures.

The ceremony of the *Voladores* is originally part of a cult drama, which revolves around the myth of the young corn and is portrayed in pre-Hispanic depictions using pictorial writing. After extensive preparatory ceremonies, five men climb onto a thirty-meter-high platform. The leader starts to play the flute and send prayers for the fertility of the land in all directions. As a result, four flying people (*Voladores*) descend from above in large spirals, with a rope connecting their feet to a rotating frame at the top of the pole. They start to fly around the pole with their heads down until the rope has unwound and they come back to the ground. Each person performs thirteen turns, all together 52 circles, corresponding to the 52-year cycle of the pre-Columbian calendar.

El Tajín is one of the most important excavation sites in Mexico. Surrounded by vanilla plantations, the ruins of the *Totonaken* lie in a tropical-green hilly landscape with a warm and humid climate. The vast archaeological area, which was inhabited in its heyday by 50 000 people, has been explored in recent years to about 40% and declared in 1992 by UNESCO as a World Heritage Site of Humanity. The most famous building is the niche pyramid (*Pirámide de los Nichos*). It is 25 meters high and 1225 square meters long. The pyramid has 365 niches, which most likely symbolize a solar year. In addition, several reliefs are preserved at a ball court. They show scenes from everyday life and the cult of the *Totonaken*. *El Tajín* was also known for its cultural ball game, which eventually ended up with human sacrifices. In this game, the teams had to put the ball through a high-mounted ring on a wall, using their hips. This ball was made of hard rubber, which is why the players also wore a large belt, of which stone figures exist. It is believed that either the losers or the victors were subsequently beheaded, and ritual sacrifice was considered a great honor at the time. The entire city is dedicated to the god of thunder.

I went through the grounds again and admired not only the old stones and walls, but also the visitors around me. Here, a school class dressed in uniforms followed their teacher's remarks; there, older Mayan women in traditional dress were resting from the strains of sightseeing.

In search of a quiet little place (toilet), I went to the back of the facility. I saw a solid building there. It was not a restroom. The cottage was full of older women and their daughters, who offered peeled oranges with chili and vanilla pods. They were separated by a wire fence from the museum area. Every time a few people came near, a chatter and advertisement for their goods started. Of course, I bought something. After all, I had never tried oranges with chili. What bothered me most about the whole situation was the almost desperate call for people to buy. In what poverty did a human being or a family must live to offer themselves this way? It is frightening to see how high a percentage of Mexicans live below the poverty line as we understand it in Europe. I remember one of the traveling participants of the first caravan group, bargaining with these poor people for every *peso*, displaying a well-nourished belly and driving a camper with a star (Mercedes Benz)! Disgusting!

At about three o'clock I made my way home. I wanted to return to the *Costa Esmeralda* to camp in another trailer park with Wi-Fi. I anticipated about two hours, as I intended to detour via *Poza Rica* for a better road. It turned out to be an absolute fallacy! The direct connection to the city was just as catastrophic as the other way from *Papantla*. For sixteen kilometers I needed almost an hour! Yikes! This slalom race was always exhausting – I had to keep my wits keen for new pitfalls or holes. I landed for the second time in *Poza Rica* in city traffic. Three-lane carriageways without a dividing line are five lanes for Mexicans! But I managed the drive well this time and was happy to have landed again on the better-developed road to the coast.

Now we are sitting at the exceptionally beautiful *Hotel Torre Molino*. We paid a hundred and fifty pesos. Although we don't have a *palapa*, there's Wi-Fi. I'll test it out tomorrow, because today I've had enough. I am glad that I have sent the daily report. Tomorrow we will enjoy pure relaxation before we approach the next two hundred kilometers. By the way: Fresh oranges with a little chili powder on it really taste spicy! Give it a try! Also, do not ask about the state of my cabinets and closets after such a bumpy day …!

January 25th
Bold mistrust!

I'm sitting in the camper with the door open and it is more than warm. Why? Although the current outside temperature is 22°C, the hot-air fan is on to somehow get Knuffi dry. The whole dog is dripping, despite rubbing off sand and seawater. Inside my house it is 28°C. I see no other way, because otherwise she will still have a wet stomach until tomorrow.

Why "bold mistrust"? My "caballero" has visited me again. At five-thirty in the afternoon there was a knock. There he stood outside, not at all annoyed about my refusal yesterday. He had received my message and invited other friends instead. Now I quickly had to come up with an incomprehensible disease for Wuschel. After all, a sick dog and an urgent visit to the vet had been the reason for my excuse. Her allergy was exactly right and so was the saltwater and he willingly bought the story from me. Now my suspicions had ruined a good dinner and probably a nice conversation. I just could not talk about *El Tajín* now.

The day before, he had realized that I wanted to visit this current place again because of the Wi-Fi and looked out for me, and we had hiked a bit with the dogs along the troubled sea. I got some good advice and we said goodbye in friendship, promising to keep in touch by email. After all, his brother will celebrate his sixtieth birthday in Berlin, when I'm back home, and he wants to be there. A good opportunity to see him again and a new foothold in the States – I should have become a diplomat!

We were ready to depart, so we would start early tomorrow morning for new adventure. First, however, there was a height difference of 1400 m to overcome.

January 26th
A day of extremes

We started early, at around nine o'clock. The sky was gray and rainy, not exactly unpleasant for driving. I expected about five hours of driving time for two hundred kilometers, according to my experience. As already mentioned, today we had to cope with a height difference of 1400 m above sea level on this route. The road was generally passable, at least a lot better than *El Tajín*'s. Why did we still need so much time? From *Martínez* it went uphill with many curves. Until then, most of it was still plain with many banana plantations. But then it went into the mountains! Good that my friends and I did not mind the curves too much. I drove slowly because of a lot of heavy traffic on the way.

Unfortunately, we drove more and more into the clouds and there was nothing to see. It was like that for three hours. Then, from one meter to the next, we left the wall of fog behind us and dived into bright sunshine. This was a few kilometers before *Altotonga*. In *Tlapacoyan* I got lost in the main square and once again I had to make a skillful turning maneuver. The police was kind enough to help me, as my destination *Perote* had no sign on the road.

A turnout in the sunshine was simply good for a break and to get something to eat. It was already half past twelve and we had only done half of the journey. I was looking forward to a more pleasant ride, and my joy lasted exactly twenty kilometers. In this section, one brick factory lined up after the other. Using the most primitive means, the brick was shaped and piled up to dry. It looked like there were half-finished Aztec pyramids everywhere.

Snow in Mexico! You wouldn't believe it! In front of me appeared the *Cofre de Perote* with 4282 m, covered in snow. It did not seem that high to me, but I think we were around two thousand meters above sea level.

I came through a village I had to stop and be amazed. Picture book Mexico! The meat hung from wooden stalls, the butcher brought his goods in the wheelbarrow, in front of the hut a woman stirred some unappetizing broth, there was the *Zócalo* (main square) in front of the church with plenty of seating, a lovingly decorated church (still Christmas for them) and road construction as soon as we were ten meters from the center, a simple *tortillería* with still warm *tortillas* (twenty-five for five pesos!), and behind all of it the snow-capped mountain in the sunshine! Guys, it was an experience!

Shortly thereafter, the stress continued. The road from *Perote* was well developed, but had several slopes, which made me turn on my engine brake, and it was foggy again! We dived back into the previous cloud soup. You couldn't see five meters ahead of you. I got behind a security-minded truck and the vehicle signaled me every *tope* by braking. Everyone could overtake me if they wanted, I had no problem with that. I can't imagine how trucks drive in this fog without headlights!

In the direction of *Xalapa* or *Jalapa* (capital of the state of *Veracruz*) the traffic flow increased, and I prayed that I'd find the correct main road to the anthropological museum, according to the plan in the book. No chance! There was nothing indicated. I (almost) landed in the *Centro Histórico*, but before the narrow lanes could scare me, I used trick 17 "New York": I grabbed a taxi, to take me to the museum. A large, newly built building must also have parking lots, I thought! I wanted to stay there until tomorrow, as it was too late for a visit today. The taxi driver delivered me reliably. I recognized the street through which I had just come. How come the town administration did not have information boards for such a place? No signs – but look, there it is at the front – very puny in a corner! I had discovered it, but practically needed a magnifying glass!

Now we stood in the rain in front of the museum <u>without</u> parking! What to do? I needed a place to sleep. I did not want to search around for a long time and so I asked my guide to take me to the next best hotel with a big parking space. It was within walking distance of the museum and the best place on the square. (Crown Plaza): wickedly expensive by Mexican standards, but affordable by European ones. I paid for a luxury room with breakfast the equivalent of seventy euros for the night! Downer: The dogs had to sleep in the car. No chance to smuggle them into the house. (But they would survive!) On the other hand, it was important to me that my car was safe, and I could find all the stuff when I came back.

It was an over-the-top luxury for my circumstances, though. The immaculate white sand in the cigarette racks wore the emblem of the hotel and the toilet rolls had napkin folds. But I had no sand in bed tonight, internet connection for tomorrow and a generous shower with all American comforts! Did they have a small coffee cup, they did not need? Mine broke at one of the last potholes …

A day with topes and potholes

Xalapa – Hauptstadt des mexikanischen Bundesstaates Veracruz – Anthropologisches Museum

 *personal notes*

Xalapa
Anthropological
Museum

 *personal notes*

January 27th
Picture book of the past

Today, as planned, the Anthropological Museum is on my program. It houses a comprehensive collection of the major Gulf Coast cultures, the *Olmecs*, *Totonaks* and *Huasteks*. Each culture is different from the other. The *Olmec* colossal heads are particularly famous, as found in *La Venta*. The museum is attractively bright and has green patios with beautiful exhibits.

Of course, after three hours I couldn't feel my legs anymore, but now I had to take a longer walk with my patient companions. After a little lunch and a siesta, and since it was not cloudy anymore, I decided to take a taxi to the center for twenty-five *pesos* to take a look. The most colorful was the *Zócalo* with its many bootblacks. The cathedral was closed at lunch time, so I could only visit the outside. In the Government Palace, a friendly security guard let me photograph the typical Mexican monumental frescoes. You could still see the variety of people everywhere on the street today. You could also see the bustle of the many taxis on the road who clearly dominated the streetscape. I had to walk very slowly at the beginning, because the fourteen hundred meters' altitude affected my breathing! But I got used to it quickly. *Xalapa* had a very hilly structure with quite steep slopes.

 *personal notes*

 *personal notes*

January 28th
The length of a nose and the width of a hair

After receiving no news last night from an old *hacienda* for accommodation, this morning I crossed out the location from the program and got up at six o'clock. We were ready to start at eight o'clock. There was a lot on the "menu" for today! As there was a big supermarket around the corner, I got all the heavy food, drinks, drinking water, dog food and canned food for my spoiled livestock, as I did not know if I would have another opportunity in the coming days.

In the rush hour of *Xalapa* I tried to find the road to *Coatepec*. It was Highway #7 with a collection of potholes and *topes*. Since it was close and tight in this colorful village (one-way system) I decided to go straight to *Xico*, another recommendation from one of my helpful books. In *Coatepec* every house smelled like coffee through my window. Since the small town with a beautiful church was surrounded by extensive coffee plantations, it was also called the "city of coffee", but I had no chance to stop anywhere. *Xico* was within reach and sight of the highest mountain of Mexico, the *Pico de Orizaba* (5610 m). In sunshine and clear visibility, it dominated the wide horizon, covered with snow at this time of year. It was sunny and, on the ride, I could see the summit well, although it was hazy.

In *Xico*, now, there seemed to be some community money for refurbishment. The streets were torn up, the *zócalo* was newly paved and the children's playground had got a new coat of colored paint. This was counterproductive to the size of my car. Anything bigger than my RV should not do this trip.

We were asked to stop behind the church. The policeman told me not to worry, that I could stay the whole day. A pee-round for my mice and then I went out alone with my camera. Around this time (or maybe all the time) Xico was a sleepy village with a lot of Mexican ambiance. Apparently, several local artists were based here, but I did not see one of them. There was an over-supply of lovely churches in the four thousand soul village, which was still decorated for Christmas.

Faith is still deeply rooted inside the population. Who among us (except in places of pilgrimage) still kneels in our parish church before the suffering Christ on the bare ground and audibly brings him our concerns, regardless of our surroundings? Who still respectfully touches all the saints and then kisses the cardboard lid, which serves as an extended arm? Who crucifies himself in reverence, even if he's not practicing? The pope will hardly find a humbler Catholic, young or old, than the Mexican. He could give these people more financial help and not let his travel to this country be paid by poor people. But this is my own humble opinion.

For me, there were a variety of picture taking motives. The inhabitants of the village welcomed me friendly and interested. Mostly I identified myself as German, not as American. I deeply regretted my lack of language skills to be able to talk to these warm people. I strolled uphill and downhill for a while because the village was located on a mountainside. Finally, I was able to shoot a nice picture of the *Orizaba*. An old woman wanted to send me more uphill, but it was too difficult for me.

When driving back, due to the roadworks, we followed a detour and we had to turn into a difficult small lane and then took a narrow turn into the next street. All this with a pavement of beautiful uneven cobblestones. As well as I could, I tried to look ahead to see if I could fit between the careless parked cars. I was lucky in *Xico,* but back in *Coatepec* I got caught. Not a piece of paper would have slid between me and the vehicles parked right and left. I did not want to lose the first side mirror so soon. I could not fold it with my old RV model. So, others had to be pushed away. Centimeter-by-centimeter-maneuvering was the order of the day before the critical and curious eyes of many *Coatepec* spectators. First, they enjoyed the spectacle per se and

72

second – a woman at the steering wheel of such a big box. That's why I was the sensation par excellence in the village. A truck got some scratches, but the owner wouldn't notice, as it already had more than a few! Where was the applause after my successful performance? I didn't care. I just wanted to get out of these curves and corners.

Done! The better road to *Xalapa* lay ahead of us. I did not want to go there but rather towards *Veracruz!* But don't even think about it – no signage! I ended up in the drive of the Mex #140 to the southeast. Behind *Xalapa* I saw the signposting to the hacienda *El Lencero*. It was set up as a museum. Then I saw the road and changed my mind from one second to the next. No, thanks! I had had enough changes today. I wanted to find the RV Park south of *Veracruz* for me and my two and if possible, without a detour. I guessed that we had been there with the group several years ago. This suspicion was confirmed when I recognized the locations again. The approach was a disaster with all its bypasses, as the road to *Anton Lizardo,* at the end of the bay, was being rebuilt into four lanes for the future. I supposed that there were several hidden holiday park projects in the community drawer. Why else, all this effort?

According to my calendar, we were able to stay here for two nights and enjoy the golf. The RV also needed a general servicing. From here you could reach the center of *Veracruz* within an hour by bus and for the ridiculous price of twenty pesos. As I had once strolled through this city, I will consider whether I do this tomorrow or not. I'll let the weather decide.

The full moon is shining on us and the dogs can move without a leash, *Veracruz* glows with its lights across the coastline, the beach is within reach, the showers and toilets are clean and working. We are together again. Why would I need the luxury of a five-star hotel? I am exhausted after today, but it's reassuring to hear someone breathe next to you again. I missed my two devoted traveling companions in *Xalapa.*

January 29th
Camping at the king's

I forgot about *Veracruz*! First, I had to struggle with my weak condition. It probably was the fast change of temperatures and the huge difference in altitude. It all happened within a few hours yesterday. (Here at the gulf, short trousers were announced again.)

Anyway, after the morning walk and the usual breakfast I crawled back into my bed. One and a half hours later I felt better, and I started cleaning my camper. A general cleaning was urgently needed. When else in the future would I be able to do it? There were also a few things to cook, to give the dogs their bones and not let my bread get moldy. Since there are virtually no useful treats in this country, I have relied on soup bones. They had the additional positive effect of protection against Wuschel's salt-water diarrhea. Accordingly, we spent the day relaxing at Camping *El Rey*. Now everything was prepared for tomorrow's departure when we would plunge into a new adventure. Hopefully, everything will work!

January 30th
Tlacotalpan – Fiesta Mexicana (Part 1)

Incredible! In front of my RV there's a mariachi group playing, the police parade just passed with blaring siren and the entire procession romps along next to us. Nearby, Mexicans dance to music on the street! Mexico, *olé*! My planning had worked...

Now to the day's events: Tonight, we had to bed in at "King's" behind a barn and another trailer because of a strong storm, otherwise we would have had a restless night. Would we be able to leave tomorrow?

Since the morning walk was not too stormy, we left for *Tlacotalpan*, about a hundred kilometers south of *Veracruz*. We

74

were not sure: Hotel? Free camping? Pemex gas station? There was no RV park or campsite in this little sleepy village.

This place was not described in any travel-guidebook, even though the town was declared a World Heritage Site in 1998, however, its celebration days for *la Virgen de la Candelaria*, (31.1. until 02.02 / and 09.02) were famous. The whole town was a *fiesta* on its own. I had read this by accident and planned the trip here around these dates. I wanted to arrive on time the day before to find a parking place. Good that I was so early. The police sent me behind the oldest church in the village. I could stay there. A tent city with young people had built up all around me. Every green spot, even some places between the house pillars, was covered with a small cloth hut. I was relatively close to the action, so I would see what each day brought. I would have to economize the use of water and electricity because it had to last four nights. If necessary, the generator could run for a short time.

Now I was here, among the locals for the time being. I felt safe at my stand. My watchdogs would (hopefully) fulfill their task. The nights could be a bit loud since the Mexicans like it noisy and hearty. For such an extraordinary event, I accepted the noise. With the dogs, I took a long walk around the camper and in the center, so everyone could see that I had protectors on board. With the camera and my appearance, I was clearly recognizable as a *guiri* (expression from my Spanish friend Felix for "tourist"). Everywhere was diligently prepared for the holidays – even the main church got a new coat of white paint. It would be dry tomorrow!

Unfortunately, I could not get hold of a program on my second walk so I had to leave it to chance. Today I was lucky. In the House of Culture, young dancers and musicians gathered with their local costumes. The participants later wanted to parade through the village and then prove their reverence in the Church of Our Lady. It was still being rehearsed diligently, make-up on and dressed in matching outfits. Nice boys and girls! How I envied them! Then they went through the village with a lot of music – of course!

After the service, people danced, played and sang in front of the statue of Mary. It was a first-class show. The pastor was enthusiastic, and the old dance teacher presented herself proudly with her pupils.

As a precaution, I had hidden all valuables and important documents somewhere in the camper. If someone was really looking for something, they had to be quick. Who would suspect one of my wallets in the dog food? Or the laptop in the dirty laundry? I even took off my car radio and the important papers were behind the stove. To avoid the short-term memory loss of old age, I wrote all the hiding places again in my notepad. No one understood German here, and in the tourist office not even English!

Now I will feed my guards and then march again for a short time to the center – maybe something is happening. There are so many riders along my street, probably residents of the surrounding area. Finding a parking space for a horse is easier in this bustle than for a car.

I was back from my stroll! Many people were on the way. *Tlacotalpan* resembled a huge bazaar and smells came from every corner. My dinner today consisted of sweet biscuit sticks (*churros*, deep fried biscuit, so nothing could go wrong). I almost ate all of them. In the main square in front of the church there was a dance performance. Since it was not to my taste, I strolled on to the illuminated *zocalo*, genuinely nice with the bright shining palm trees. Anyone who could get a bench had made themselves comfortable. As everywhere, the "artists" were present with their handmade jewelry. I suspected that a lot of them were tent guests in my neighborhood. If families with children and older couples were walking around and I avoided dark alleys, my solo walk wouldn't be dangerous. You couldn't hear a lot of noise in the center. To compensate this, someone turned his car radio on my doorstep at full blast. The noisier, the better!

I just hope the weather will be good for the festivities. According to the weather report, some rain clouds will sweep over us for the umpteenth time. Tomorrow I will have a look into two small local museums and when it gets nice, I can enjoy myself by the river or watch the people on the *zócalo*. Simply enjoy! Even though, now it is raining a bit, one advantage – the car radio was switched off for safety's sake!

January 31ˢᵗ
Fiesta Mexicana – Part 2

Well, the night passed a bit loudly as expected, with musical accompaniment and a lot of chattering around. At some point it became silent – until half past four in the morning. Were these people still out? Or early birds? At any rate, they were provided with blankets and mattresses by someone. At seven o'clock, the holidays started with a few firework salutes which annoyed my two ladies.

At about ten o'clock I set out for my first hike. I needed some batteries since I could not use my rechargeable ones without a generator. Many stalls were still closed, but the merchants already cavorted at the *zócalo* and the fishermen offered their morning catch along the river. Had this *señor* fished his fat pig out of the water using one of the boats?

It inevitably pulled me once again into the House of Culture. There, the old lady from yesterday was there with her students and she was dancing too. Two feet in high-heeled shoes! Excellent!

I got my batteries and I also found the bizarre museum several streets away thanks to my guide. What creatures the old gentleman had gathered there! He kept his crocodiles behind bars, while his turtles in plastic tubs did not live in a way that suited their species. In between, pelicans romped about.

You would not even believe how quickly it turned noon. Now I had to invite my two ladies for a walk. We could go to a less busy street with some green space in our neighborhood. Wuschel was so special!

For better or worse, I had to turn on my generator, because the notebook was vital. And you won't believe it: While I was writing, a young boy tried to force the side door! In a surprise counterattack I slammed the door open and against his head. His face had to be seen! I saw his face! If I run into him again, I "have" a passport photo of him! He obviously wasn't paying much attention. After all, my generator was running, and he was standing right in front of the sign "Beware of Dogs"!

A family offering warm food has settled down opposite me. Afterwards I will hand over some *pesos* to them so that they can keep an eye on my car. Since I was in the car myself during the attempted break-in, Wuschel and Knuffi naturally did not react to the thief.

Finally, I got a program for the next two days. Now I can plan a little better – as far as my energy will permit. Until four o'clock today I have free time, then the official opening of the Fiesta takes place. It was a matter of fate: at the next dumping walk I passed a school, which provided their guarded (!) parking for a fee. The place was big enough to accommodate my carriage. So, let's get off the road! Here we were at least under the watchful eye of a *señor*. At least during the day and at night I could lock everything well. This was a residential area and we were away from the turmoil and the concentration of tents. The *jefe* got a higher fee from me. Surveillance guaranteed!

Now, I was able to go to the official opening of the festival. Supposedly, it took place in the square in front of the sanctuary. But where did all the people go? Why were they sitting along the street? Was there a parade in the program? I saw so many pretty boys and girls on tall horses.

Along the way, I also managed a few snapshots. It was a long parade of musical groups, beautiful horses, pretty *caballeros* and incomparably graceful women, girls and even kids. An official government member on horseback have must been there, because there was a constant handshake greeting of children and adults. The riders, whose job it was to perform a few tricks with their horses, got a lot of applause. I could fill a whole book with my pictures, but since I wanted to see a *fandango* performance in the evening, I had to conserve my energy. I even skipped the fireworks today – there would be more of them the day after tomorrow, anyway. Plus, my anxious ladies were more comfortable when I was near them during the "storm". Next time, they would probably have to endure it alone! For dinner I got a peeled pineapple with chili (for disinfection, of course!), defrosted my ham and warmed up a few tortillas quickly! Gorgeous! I did not need to feed my two ladies because experience tells me that in this state of stress, they will refuse to eat any food, even if it were cooked chicken

 *personal notes*

 *personal notes*

Month of February
1700 km

Tlacotalpan
(State of Veracruz)
Isthmus
(State of Oaxaca)
West Coast
(State of Guerrero)
Morelia
(Michoacán de Ocampo)

 *personal notes*

Mexican youth
sincerity and enjoyment of life

 *personal notes*

 *personal notes*

February 1st
Tlacotalpan – day of the toro

My god, I must have looked starved! The parking attendant was urging me to take homemade tortillas with homemade chilies, made by his wife. The neighbor from the parking lot invited me for a sandwich with a drink. In the evening, I got another big meal from the *señor* and his wife, because I had praised their cooking skills so much. As quid pro quo, I collected sweets in my supplies and arranged them nicely. They did not take money, but they will get a good tip on my departure for sure! His family took turns guarding the parking lot, sleeping on the hard and cold stone as long as a car was still parked in the yard.

If you look at the other side of the city, where I can walk with the dogs, it looks as bleak as in any other village. Simple wooden booths, clay floor (because of parquet!), open spaces covered with corrugated iron; if made of bricks, then only the raw bricks. Paint and pavement are only affordable for better-off citizens. Everywhere I go along with my anxious companions I get a friendly *buenos días*, a nice *hola*.

The car neighbors engaged me for almost half an hour and listened to me with the patience of a saint, as I squeezed the limited Spanish vocabulary out of my brain. Even though they seemed to be better off and well educated, no one spoke any foreign languages.

But headline now: *Tlacotalpan* was known throughout Mexico, if not across the continent, for its tradition of letting bulls swim through the river and then driving them through the streets like in the city of Pamplona (Spain). The whole hunt was scheduled for noon. At ten o'clock I wanted to watch the *Voladores* once more along the river promenade. There were preparations for the event in full swing everywhere.

The streets were shielded with sturdy barriers to direct the bulls along the route. Behind them, the people would later stand to watch the show. Sand was piled up on the riverbank to make it easier for the actors to get out, and gauchos prepared with lassos to skillfully catch the coming bulls. Music groups were installed on the right and left of the street.

Where should I post myself? I wanted to see as much as possible. I saw people standing on a porch above me. Mind you: I was two hours early! I remembered my experience in Siena (Italy) at the Palio and bit into the sour apple (as we say in German). Two hours before, I also looked for a stand directly on the parapet for fifty pesos "entrance fee"! For that I got an exclusive place. God, I was thankful that it was overcast! I could not say that time was flying by. However, it was tolerable because of the many impressions in the meantime from my bird's eye view.

The otherwise empty river filled up more and more with larger and smaller boats, people climbed on roofs and trees, various dealers tried to get rid of their goods. The crowd bubbled and the music groups helped to get the mood going. Finally, the first night black bull arrived swimming. However, I only saw him when the hero got out of the water. The many boats that accompanied him had blocked the view, but I had a chance to see it twelve times. The *toros,* of course, completely stole the show of the *Voladores.* But the folk group undoubtedly had the best view from their tall pole. On the shore, the lasso-swinging riders stood ready to capture the totally unsettled animals and, if possible, to drive them into the enclosure in the village center. I write "if possible", as a desperate bull kept tearing away and tried to flee, either back into the water or among the crowd. Then of course the running and the screaming began because there were enough "courageous" passers-by on the way who wanted to be more than spectators of the event. The bull was completely irritated by all the different forms of attack and more than a few *matadors* fell, though luckily, enough ambulances were available. However, the bull had no chance to escape his fate.

I could not say that the event got me off the stool, although I shot one picture after the other. I was a guest in this country and had to refrain from criticism. My soul is European and not Mexican. Animals have a different status in this Central American culture than at home and I kept thinking about the terrified animal and the stress it was subjected to.

After two hours of spectacle I had enough and tried to escape the excitement. That was not so easy, because the sidewalks were crowded with onlookers and to dodge was not possible because of the barriers. But somewhere I found a hole through the fence, so I went home to my ladies. They had been alone for four hours now and had to endure the noise of the shots. I urgently needed a break, because I was not used to so much "humankind" around me any more.

Some events with the animals were advertised at about three o'clock. It was enough for me. In addition, a *corrida* was announced for the evening and this took place in our area. The music for the evening event with its deep bass was heard during my "homework" reaching all the way to the RV and making it vibrate again and again. The bangs wouldn't stop, and my two mice were totally scared. They even refused to eat normally– but treats and chicken meat were still accepted! So it couldn't have been that bad.

Only tomorrow left, and then they have survived. We will go back to calmer waters. Of course, in the evening everything is offered in different places. It's not only the official organizers who participate in the program, but the whole city, which is a spectacle. Music groups are playing everywhere, and you can listen to jazz as well as traditional *fandango*. This is a dance variation that is more or less the same as a tap dance, but much more intense, earthbound and with a pounding rhythm. Comparable maybe to *flamenco*, but also different! Just special! I do not have to attend the rodeo tonight. I had had enough of bulls for today. In addition, I would surely have to arrive two hours before to get a good place, and it's enough for me if I hear the crowd roar from far. In contrast, tomorrow will be more Christian-oriented.

 *personal notes*

Tlacotalban – day of the toro

 *personal notes*

 *personal notes*

February 2nd
Tlacotalpan - María de la Candelaria

The present day started quietly and, oh wonder, without a noise. A young *Fandango* group rehearsed some pieces together with their teacher. That was excellent! Marian devotion began in the morning at five o'clock in the chapel. However, I was still in deep slumber. The actual ceremonies did not start until lunchtime, so I had a little leisure time to briefly tell why this small town was included in the World Heritage. So far, I had not had time to do so because of the rushed events.

It is called "the forgotten city" or "pearl of Papaloapan" (butterfly river). The arcades of brick-faced houses in the center painted in delicate pastel colors in an indefinite variety of combinations are picturesque. This city used to be rich when it was still a trading port for the back country, but after the construction of the railway the town became unimportant and somehow it was forgotten. Since then, hardly anything has changed on the cityscape. As a result, it acted as the venue for several films. That is why many traditions have been preserved. All year long it sinks into a slumber with its 6000 inhabitants. The festivities of *María de la Calendaria* awaken it with all the intensity and brutality of tourism. The city ends up bursting at the seams with people, such as I have experienced in Europe only in Rome for Easter. The city administration is making enormous efforts to master the logistical and sanitary problems. Mobile toilets are set up everywhere and they are thoroughly cleaned twice a day. The garbage collection starts working early in the morning and there are numerous large unmistakable dumpsters set up. The street cleaning service is constantly busy, and the mounted police ensure that no riots occur. Fortunately, there are few drunks on the street, although tequila is not far away. In a German newspaper report I read that *Tlacotalpan* has set itself the goal of becoming the cleanest city in Mexico. They are on the way to doing so if you apply Mexican standards. The rich history and

97

prosperity of the town meant that the town had its own theater, schools, a hospital and even a tram from early on. I am sure you can find even more information on the Internet; I did not want to merely copy my travel guidebook.

At around eleven o'clock I made my way to the chapel (main church). I thought with an hour's head start I might get a seat for the Bishop's Mass. I was mistaken, because the church was crowded with believers who wanted to have their candles and pictures consecrated and offered baby Jesus in all possible cheesy variations to the Mother of God. With goodwill I tried to settle down with a chair in the side entrance. But after getting all sorts of body parts, relics and handbags in my face, I hurriedly took flight. I beg the pardon of *Virgen de la Candelaria*. Do I really have to stand on a pedestal for two more hours to get the necessary view of the procession?

After a lunch at home with fresh pink *gambas rebozadas* and the rest of my chilies, I reluctantly left again. The dogs were left out for a short time because the annoying shooting started again. As I sat on the platform, the sun came out and beat down hard. I had to get a hat from somewhere. For a hundred and thirty *pesos*, I bought some colorful (pink) headgear. There was a lot of noise on the *zocalo*, two music bands fought a duel, which could cause the eardrums to burst. How do the ears of Mexicans survive it? Do they suffer from deafness?

I passed the river and saw free seats next to the decorated ship, and I settled down next to a nice couple. Maybe it was not bad here either, but at four o'clock I left and walked back to the church. I had no idea which way the procession would go, and I wanted to miss as little as possible. Therefore, I looked around and I saw again an elderly woman who I had already noticed in the morning. She was still sitting in her seat. Ok! I was now in the right place! Right! *María* was carried on time to the main gate, amid many bells and accompanied by white Mariachi musicians. Joseph had to stay at home! It was not his day...

She was carried right past me and then took the curve to the river. Down to the water! Many, many heads blocked my view of the ferry. Oh, well, I thought, you can't have everything. I was looking for a free spot where I would at least have a view of the river to see *María*'s boat passing. Many small fishing boats were moored, with a few passengers on board. I had to try it. Great, for eighty *pesos* they took me with them! How fortunate!

Now I was able to follow the procession by the water and did not have and did not have to stand all the time. It was one of the experiences that I will never forget. The many colorfully decorated ships, the pink ferries, cheering and applauding believers, the vegetation, the silent butterfly river, the mariachi music on the main boat, it all just came together! And I was in the middle of all the friendly Mexicans! I could not believe it. Just like I cannot believe my trip to the Yukon and Alaska some time ago, but it was a fact! Here all sorts of old boats had been pulled out for the event. Many tourist companies were advertised on the life jackets of the passengers.

We sailed under the protection of Our Lady and two orbiting military helicopters. What could possible happen? I gave up on the return of the Madonna to the church and the accompanying fireworks, I had left my dogs alone for too long. Now they needed my presence and comfort during the rest of the "concert". As much as I had been impressed by the three days here in *Tlacotalpan*, I was so glad that I could escape the crowds again and disappear from the line of fire.

It will take time for my mice to regain their balance. One more night and then on to a mountain lake! We will stay a little longer there on a good campground and recover from the stress of the past days.

 *personal notes*

Maria, protect our boat, big or small, new or old!

 *personal notes*

Tlacotalban
Maria de la Candelaria

 *personal notes*

February 3ʳᵈ /4ᵗʰ
Some rest is good.

The past two days can be told very quickly. Yesterday morning we drove the eighty kilometers to **Catemaco** in "just" three hours. This time it was not so much considering the road we took, but we had a truck in front of us, with a sugar cane load that was twice as high as the vehicle. Since the last half of the way was almost always uphill, its average speed was a maximum of twenty kilometers per hour. Overtaking was out of the question because the road was narrower than usual, and I was wider than a normal car. The regular cars could overtake but I crept obediently behind. That could be annoying for forty kilometers; however, I was safe and had time!

The campsite was fine, a bit far from the water, but with lots of greenery and quiet. A supermarket was a ten-minute walk away, and a *tortillería* just around the corner. I would nest here for a week at two hundred pesos per day, including internet access. I could not complain. This time I had neighbors from Canada and Newfoundland.

We made a first stroll through the quiet village and along the lake under the sun. The area seemed beautiful to me and we were in no hurry. Anyway, it was warm, and you could walk around in shorts.

The volcano lake (370 m above sea level) is framed by mountains and surrounded by tropical vegetation. The city of Catemaco claims itself to be an ancient center of Indian magic. As the filming location of the movie "Medicine Man" with Sean Connery, the village is now known worldwide. It is still famous today as an occult pilgrimage site for the magic and healing arts of the many resident *brujos* (warlocks) and *curanderos* (healers), and especially on weekends and during the holidays, there are many Mexican and foreign visitors who undergo spiritual rites. Let's see, tomorrow is Thursday!

Today, household chores were on the agenda. I had to wash tons of linen and bring the shine back to the RV. The girls enjoyed the silence and lay under the car. They only came out when I was in the kitchen – understandably. *Mañana* we will take a closer look at the place. Hopefully, they won't do any shooting (it's National Day) in memory of the Constitution of 1917. According to, my most recent information, this festival would be celebrated next Monday to guarantee a long weekend.

February 5ᵗʰ
Boring like the weather – day of rest I

We were lucky to be in this corner of Mexico right now. The center of the State and the surrounding States had been hit by heavy rains in the past two days. Seventeen people lost their lives. In one district in Mexico City, the water reached a height of 1.50 m, the administration closed eight hundred schools. I read about the terrible news on the internet this afternoon. We, however, strolled with pleasure along the *malecón*, had a little view of the surrounding mountains and got financial supplies. Again, it had rained overnight, but it was not worth mentioning. The temperatures were in the mid-twenties during the day causing a certain amount of humidity, which was mitigated by a small north wind. For the dogs, the weather was bearable, and for me too. You could leave the door open and work pleasantly on the PC. I was able to take a longer siesta and just do nothing the rest of the day. It was pleasant not to suffer the stress of sightseeing, although there was plenty to visit and enough excursion possi-

bilities available. I was just not up to it and that was proof that I needed some rest to recharge my personal batteries.

February 6th
Sun! – day of rest II

In fact, today the sun was shining. Then it was hammock time! There was a lot to read for the further route. I planned and researched intensively last night. My planned tour split a little bit between the coastline and the interior of the country. We made a wide detour around Mexico City and therefore I had – unfortunately – to cancel some excavations. But it would only have been necessary to include the visit later in this travelogue. I had already seen these archaeological sites on my first tour. The focus was on colonial Mexico in the coming days and weeks.

The campground visibly filled up during the weekend. It was good that I was firmly rooted because now only the dry docks were available. I had reached the climax of my laziness today, but I think I'll be a bit more active tomorrow. Even idleness gets boring after a few days. Dogs run around in a hurry; my Wuschel is undoubtedly the biggest, but also the one who loves sleeping the most!

February 7th
Catemaco Lake

My energy was back! Great! Now it was easier for me to organize. First, I asked the owner for a dog groomer in the village. Here was the best opportunity to get Knuffi under control. Her fur was beginning to smell. In the next few days, she would be off to the barber!

A local dog lover recommended a lady to me and I would look for her tomorrow and find out the opening hours (today was Sunday). It is far to walk so I think I'll treat myself to a cheap taxi, if one takes me with my "mouse".

The pooches had to guard the RV today. I strolled through the covered market and checked the many street vendors. Finally, I landed at the main church. *Virgen del Carmen* was a popular place of pilgrimage. I watched a few pilgrims and saw Christian faith Mary with pagan customs. The Mother was undoubtedly worshipped. And she was also blessed by the touch of the protective glass. Many believers had a bunch of flowers with them that were passed over their whole body or the body of a partner or child in a very specific spiritual way in order to draw out evil powers and transfer them to the plants. Then, the "evil" could be thrown away once it had been transferred to the plants.

The *curanderos* also do their work: through the ritual of a *limpieza* (spiritual cleansing) of *malos aires*, which disturb physical and mental harmony, and deprive the body of its power, causing illness. The negative energies can be transferred in this way to another medium. It does not necessarily have to be flowers. You can use eggs, certain stones, frogs, or sour limes, which come into contact with any part of the body. Skeptical? Oh, well!

It was getting sunnier! That was the day for a boat trip on the lake. Instead of keeping my money this time, I dropped into an art store and bought some lightweight local souvenirs for home. Now it was time to scrape together every peso! Was there enough money for the two-hour round trip? No way! I still needed to pay for the entrance to the nature reserve. I regretted my decision and wanted to postpone the boat trip for tomorrow. But he did not agree to that, as he had me on the hook – so to speak. Therefore, he reduced the entrance fare. He probably thought: "A customer in the hand is worth two in the bush!" I had exactly five pesos left in my pocket, which later were just barely enough for the *sanitarios* (washroom).

The sky was still blue, but clouds were slowly coming over the mountains. The ride was pleasant as the boat belonged to me alone. Chief Agustín stopped at every point of interest and throttled the engine obligingly when I pulled out the camera. We

108

drove past several beaches and stopped by a dealer for healing earth. She was disappointed that I did not buy anything, but I was as poor as a church mouse. It was exhausting to filter out the Spanish explanations not being able to understand much. Sometimes I simply nodded to please him, and he looked worried – I guess he realized I didn't understand. On the weekend he sailed tourists through the area, during the week he worked as a fisherman.

We docked at the ecological reserve Nanciyaga. This was a piece of leftover rainforest, which was now marketed touristically and demanded an entry fee for its maintenance. I got a friendly English-speaking guide and he led me through the spiritual facilities. The company was introduced to the use of natural healing and beauty products and I was able to admire copies of divine statues. The originals were in museums from New York to Los Angeles. Did they belong there? Or did they rather belong to the country whose culture had produced them? (Just a side idea). For this kind of adventure holiday even an attractive website was created – to be found under its name, better not to make surreptitious advertising!

After registration, it was also possible to take a pre-Hispanic incense scented sweat bath, to consult a professional *curandero* for 150 pesos, to get a free rub with healing clay or to taste the mineral water. Despite all the hygienic dangers I tried the latter, because I liked the drinking vessel, which was a large leaf.

After forty minutes the tour ended, and I did not have one peso left to tip the young guide. However, as it was possible to drive by car to this area, I duped him that I was interested in more treatment and that comforted him. My God, how ashamed I was of this white lie!

With Agustín I went to the monkey island. Like all other islands in the lake, it was also protected. The island, under the supervision of the biological institute of the University of Veracruz, was the house of a few monkeys originally imported from Thailand. In fact, we saw some (even though a little hidden) of these specimens. Now the two hours had already passed and in no time, we went back to the native port. It was a good thing, because by now the sky was completely covered and the batteries of my camera were used up. I promised to return to the captain in just over two hours (to pay for the entry and tip the guide). Did he believe me?

After lunch I kept my promise and ran down to the lake with the dogs. There they could bath, and I paid down my debts. In addition, I instructed the *señor* to deliver a certain amount to the student in the reserve. Fortunately, I knew his name. Did he really do it? Anyway, I could clear my conscience; these people are dependent on tips and I did not want to be a cheapskate. We arrived at four o'clock to the park and I was relatively tired from our walks. There, Wuschel and Knuffi once again romped properly with a handbag-dog.

Now both are tired just like me. Soon I will follow their example and lay flat. Despite sun blockers, my arms and face have gotten a bit more color. (Otherwise no one would believe that I had been in Mexico!) I got the addresses of my neighbors in Canada and Newfoundland; they leave tomorrow and in half a year they will wonder if I'll ever come knocking at their front door. What a great distance! What a huge continent! How many miles and people in between!

February 8th
Day of rest III

Quiz question: Who moved more today? The dogs, the Hammock or me? The answer I'll save for myself. Today is humid and next to the necessary grocery shopping and a date with the vet tomorrow we did not do much. I only paid the equivalent of one euro for a taxi ride into the city. Why run and sweat?

February 9th
A new dog for 150 pesos!

We were on time at the vet for beauty care this morning! Her assistant wanted to lock Knuffi in a cage and move the appointment to three in the afternoon, but I did not agree to that. I would not leave my little rabbit alone in strangers' hands, without language skills!

Somehow, I convinced him to start working immediately and in my presence. The vet came around at ten o'clock, as arranged, and Knuffi accepted her fate. The vet was a sensitive, friendly and competent woman, but nevertheless, I had to force my nervous dog to stay calm – as usual. The lady worked professionally, with mask and headgear. I was not used to that at home. After a good two hours I had a pretty dog again and not a mop on four legs. With all sorts of gestural efforts, we could agree on the "hairstyle" because her English was like my Spanish.

Nevertheless, she could tell me that a German couple lived in the immediate vicinity. During a breather I heard Spanish on the sidewalk with a clear German-Bavarian accent. I could not resist telling her something– and a bridge was built! I was invited to a chat at Katharina's in the afternoon and I accepted. Our wavelength seemed to be right! Elisabeth (the vet) still took pleasure in perfuming Knuffi and putting little ribbons in her hair. I was not keen on accessorized dogs, but it made her happy. Wuschel at home was a little surprised by the unusual scent of her mate. Since I could make out a lot of black dots(!) in the coat of Knuffi, I treated both ladies with a flea treatment at home. That probably happened more than often in this country!

In the afternoon we arrived for the visit and were welcomed in a nice pink house. Katharina had said goodbye to the old continent and now operated a recommendable guest house in Catemaco, with tasteful rooms at an affordable price. The house was called *casa rosa* and could also be found under this name on the internet. (Just in case someone is looking for a nice place to stay in this corner!)

Back home, my PC scared me. It did not react! It could not start anymore! What to do? I hit all sorts of buttons and sent a prayer after prayer to heaven! So far, I had not secured any of my reports or my footage this year. I was scared that I had lost everything. After some time, the device seemed to show mercy at my despair and switched on as usual. Phew! Now I will catch up with my backup copies. That won't happen to me again!

The camper is now ready for tomorrow's departure. I would like to leave early, because it will take me five to six hours to get to the next destination. We also need fuel and food. That and the many *topes* cost time! Therefore, *buenas noches*!

Campsite Catemaco

Catemaco

 *personal notes*

Nanciyaga – sauna cabin and drinking bowl

personal notes

February 10th
Good brakes needed!

Three hundred kilometers through the Isthmus were ahead of us today. Which road conditions would we have? We left early. At nine o'clock I already had my groceries and filled up my fuel. According to the map, the road led straight on through the area. According to the map! First, I had to leave the volcanic cones behind me. The nearest major city was **Acayucan.** For those ninety miles I needed two hours. Not so much because of the road condition, but rather the numerous *topes.* Each village of three hundred people had at least three to five of them! And for the most part they were not marked! I had to be hellish attentive and to watch the traffic carefully. My brakes were fully operational! Finally, we reached #185 south.

We crept diligently through the mountains. In the State of Oaxaca, the road became increasingly miserable. There were government improvement works everywhere – that could have been going on for years. The authorities were probably as poor as the people I saw on my trip.

On the way I found a military checkpoint and, of course, an American car was pulled over. When I explained to them that only the car was American and I was of German descent, a friendly grin went straight over the officials' face. The policemen were very friendly, even shook my hand and asked to see the papers of my dogs. The European dog passport looked very official! I was convinced that none of the three law enforcement officers understood even one word that was written in the document, but it was thoroughly studied to give the appearance of a serious check. Finally, they stopped all the trucks and let the *alemana* drive off with a friendly wave!

It would take two hours to reach **Tehuantebec,** according to the information they gave me. But it took me three hours to find the park in the book. It was away in a small village called **Santa**

Teresa, not shown on any map. I drove past it twice until a friendly boy finally pointed out the right path. Should I go down there? I was warned by the description in the book.

But it got worse! A real adventure! From the former sugar farm there were only a few ruins left. In the driveway, which I did not recognize as such, I saw a simple oxcart. In the former toilet facilities, a family had settled down: the alleged security guard with wife, child and pet. Goats, horses, donkeys and cats roamed free. The dirt could be seen under pines and trees. Although there were some fluorescent lamps in the branches, I couldn't find a power connection anywhere, never mind using any sanitary possibilities. No thanks! But where to go now? It was early although we had been traveling for over seven hours.

When I was looking for the unmarked "RV Park", I had to go through the village square and almost got stuck there. And then it came to me: I asked a gentleman if I could stay there for the night. No problem, he said. Here it was clean and even. Of course, I was the sensation of the evening for the children. With my remaining sweets, I tried to keep them from begging. But far from it! The bravest had to knock on my door again and again at the behest of the cowards. When I set the dogs on them and they started barking, peace returned.

In the village square there was a small library, a "health center" and the municipal administration together with the church and the fountain. But how can I describe the dwelling of the family that I talked to? I did not want to shoot any pictures at that moment. Maybe tomorrow would be a more casual opportunity. In any case, at nightfall the cattle were there, where the family had previously sat together to eat. An absolute coexistence of humans and animals. Somewhat in the background I saw a stone building. Was that the outhouse? When the residents saw my two ladies, I immediately had to welcome the four-month-old puppy. Of course, the emaciated thing got a bowl of dry food from me. Full to the brim! A serving as big as Wuschel's was gone in no time!

118

Yes, now we would see what the night would bring. I trusted these villagers because everyone here knew each other. But for safety's sake, I put my vehicle in the direction of travel and slept in a tracksuit.

Unconditional Addendum: After taking another walk with the Wuffis before bedtime, I saw myself (with minor exceptions) returned to the peasant middle ages. One had (almost) forgotten to let the clock tick by. The family slept or swayed in hammocks in the palisade hut, over mashed clay soil and in the faint glow of light from the village square three cattle and a parked oxcart camped outside. Everything was open to the outside so that the air could circulate. Even the palm leaf roof was covered only loosely so that the heat would escape. The only annoying elements in this "past" were the TV in the corner of the porch and the cars in the small village square.

February 11th
Sweltering heat

The night's sleep was a bit restless, as it was always interrupted by a dog choir. Of course, my little one had to keep up with that. But when absolutely nothing moved any more on the village square, peace returned to the yappers and we were able to sleep until half past six this morning.

Outside, I heard a rumble. Was the farmer already on his way with his oxcart? Too late! When I leapt outside, dressed in makeshift clothes, only his wife was present together with three cows. I asked the *señora* if I could take some pictures. Fortunately, she allowed it. Thus, I was able to convey without a guilty conscience an authentic picture of how many Mexican families are still "living" this way.

 *personal notes*

 *personal notes*

After **Salina Cruz** we switched to the Mex #200. The curvy road took us to the west. The sun was bright and at eight o'clock we had already recorded about 25°C on the thermometer. At noon it was 33°C in the shade. If we could, we would cross *Tangolunda* out of the program and go straight to *Puerto Ángel*. The road had half a million turns and a million *topes* (called *retardores* in *Oaxaca* State), but it was well developed, although it only had two lanes. Accordingly, a heavy truck could bring the ones behind him to despair in the many climbs and descents. There was always a chance to pass – thank God!

We could only catch a glimpse of the **bay of Tehuantepec** every now and then. Most of the route was in the mountainous coastline. Everything was dry! The trees were brown and the rivers sandy. From time to time, however, there were pretty splashes of color on the roadside in form of flowering trees, bushes and tree-high cacti.

At lunchtime we arrived to **Tangolunda**, we could see the RV Park and took a break there. The sanitary facilities were fine (you had to pay fifty *pesos* to use them!). There was no electricity and the permanent guests were dependent on solar cells or generators. The path to the beach went through a small grove and the shore was steep and fairly populated. However, it was enough to cool down my mice. Otherwise I was not very convinced with the location. It was rather more of a parking lot than an RV park.

It was seventy kilometers to **Puerto Ángel**. We would cover that on the left ass cheek – as we say in German, I thought to myself. But it took us another two hours to get there.

We landed at **Zipolite Beach**, a quieter beach than *Puerto Ángel* itself. The beach was an alternative to *Puerto Escondido* or *Tongalunga*. It was also one of the few beaches in Mexico where you could show all your skin. That did not appeal to Knuffi and she barked at a naked male angrily. Many young people with heavy backpacks were strolling around and some of them had camped behind the restaurants on the beach. I had chosen a better place (*Hotel Rancho los Mangos*) and got the last spot for my

123

high carriage. The parking maneuvers were a bit problematic with all the lampposts and trees. But then we found a very shady place for three hundred *pesos* a day, with electricity only. I could postpone water and disposal until departure. It was not cheap, but we had Wi-Fi and a wall around the hotel with well-maintained parking spaces. The beach was a few minutes away with strong waves, which was especially popular among surfers. Swimming itself was discouraged, as there were many undercurrents, but we had a nice big pool in the park anyway. The bay itself was framed by picturesque rocks.

After I some fun with my dogs at the beach, I immediately decided to stay for five days (six nights). Actually, I only wanted to stay for four days. But most of the guests were Canadians and I once again attracted a lot of interest as a German with an American RV. Today, I did not do much small talk. After all, I'd been up since eight o'clock, with two hundred and twenty kilometers of coastline behind me. (Hopefully, Wuschel does not have to go out too often tonight due to the saltwater!)

February 12th -17th
Mexico under mango trees

Day 1: about thirty degrees, pure laziness, got a cold (from wherever), met couple from camping Zorro (Costa Esmeralda) again, hammock, swimming pool, tired in the evening (for whatever reason), enjoyed the beach, talked to people in Mainz and Munich...

Day 2: even more exhausting! In the afternoon, my Dutch neighbors invited me to the Mexican specialty *ceviche* (originally Peruvian) = chopped scampi, marinated in onions and lime juice, mixed with coriander, chopped tomatoes and chili paste for seasoning! Delicious and spicy! No housework today either... Mañana! In the afternoon I discovered the two Canadians of Costa Esmeralda on a fantastic beach. The place was unsuitable for me because my vehicle was too heavy and threatened to sink into the sand …

We dined together in the nearby tiny restaurant in the evening. Great and tasteful! Usually the guys finished at five o'clock in the afternoon, but they cooked a little bit more for us and worked for an extra hour. I was back at ten in the evening. My dogs were our security bodyguards; we were absolutely safe. This was not a place overflowing with tourists – amazingly comfortable and with a lot of flair, even at night.

Day 3: What a stress! Disco noise until three in the morning! At five o'clock the park's own rooster crowed loudly! Rested after two hours of sleep? Light clouds, which was bearable for the Wuffis and nothing to do until the afternoon. Then we met the Canadians for dinner in a nice nondescript pub on the roadside, there was not much choice, but it was good. We had a lot of fun together – a well-traveled couple with open eyes and seemingly a bigger purse than mine, but they did not show it. They were very sympathetic people. In the evening, a short dip in the pool. Ready for it!

Day 4: Today was market day in **Pochutla** – I had the opportunity to go there with my neighbors. This was a small town, ten kilometers to the north, which offered larger shopping possibilities. I gladly accepted the offer and at half past ten we left. I got two hours to stroll and take pictures while Ellen and Richard were doing their shopping. Part of the "community" met again at the market, as the Franco Canadians of the park did: Rita and Pierre from the beach. It was a feast of the senses and faces. I stocked up on vegetables for the next few days, the fish was not to my taste. No problem! Tonight, we would go out to eat together again.

Day 5: housework done, 28°C in the shade, sweaty, swimming pool, beach round, RV prepared for departure. Tomorrow will be only seventy kilometers to Puerto Escondido.

 *personal notes*

 *personal notes*

Colorful market events in the province of Oaxaca

 *personal notes*

Delicious meals from the beach bar

personal notes

February 17th
Departure to the west

Farewell, beautiful park! I would like to have stayed! But we wanted to meet other good friends and see new things! In addition, urgent shopping was needed, because we were running out of dog food, drinking water and non-alcoholic beer. The latter couldn't be found in small places. The day before yesterday in *Pochutla* I asked the camping attendant, who accompanied us, if he knew where I could get that stuff. He looked at me, flabbergasted. Now I'm disgraced for good! "Alcohol-free beer! A cultural shame for Mexico!" was written in his eyes. I gave up and did not ask again.

My first stop was not far away. On a miserable road we went to the Bay of **Mazunte**. There was the Mexican Turtle Center. In open-air pools and aquariums, it was possible to see land, river and sea turtles of all sizes and species, including all seven species (out of the world's eight) of the coastal waters of Mexico. The place was devoted to nature conservation, as the main source of income for many coastal dwellers used to be the capture and marketing of endangered animals. Today, the residents of *Mazunte* (translated: "I ask you to lay eggs".) earn their income with tourism and are supported by the revenue of the center. Thus, they should leave the turtles alone and no longer collect their eggs. Nevertheless, in critical times, the long beaches are protected by rifle-armed soldiers from turtle egg (aphrodisiac) collectors. In 1990, the Mexican government issued a general ban on fishing.

Mazunte was a still sleepier village than *Zipolite* and supposedly cheaper. Apart from a few beach restaurants and simple accommodations there was nothing. However, you could go fishing with the fishermen and let them earn extra money.

133

The last small fishing village was **La Ventanilla**. There was a boat tour through the mangrove lagoon for those interested. The revenue of the excursions also benefited the residents of *La Ventanilla*. Again, this project was designed to prevent sea turtles from being hunted and killed as an income source.

Now it was really time to say goodbye to these beautiful bays and devote ourselves to a larger tourist center. Our destination, **Puerto Escondido**, was seventy kilometers away from my old location. Late in the afternoon we were at the only accessible pitch of this coastal town. It was not particularly praiseworthy but had everything we needed. A few Canadians next to me had settled there for some time. I would have looked for something more pleasant and well-kept! But for one night it was ok!

Now it was time for shopping! From my previous neighbors, I followed the advice to stay in the RV park and to make the purchases by taxi, since *Super Che* only had underground garages. I went to the center with a *colectivo* (shared taxi) for 4.50 pesos. I did not know that you had to push the buzzer in the back seat if you wanted to get out. Therefore, I unintentionally got a small city tour. I jumped off around somewhere and then landed right in front of the supermarket.

It was damn humid today! The sweat ran down my back, but in the *supermercado* the air conditioning was running at full speed. Apparently, there were cheap tomatoes and watermelons. The Mexicans were hoarding them. And I hoarded *cerveza* without alcohol! Who knew when I would have a chance to get it again? That's how it was in Mexico: grab it, when the opportunity presents itself! Piled high and loaded with countless bags, I flagged down a taxi. The young guy helped me loading and unloading and got a good tip for it. At home I missed the turkey pieces and a pack of beer. Could the boy have needed it for his family? It seems I had been robbed for the first time in Mexico! I was just too trusting and had not checked the trunk myself. Well, he would be annoyed with non-alcoholic beer!

About half an hour later the taxi came back! The driver brought me my supposedly stolen turkey! Shame on you, Monika, for your suspicious thoughts! They had somehow slipped under the cover! Only the pack of beer was still missing. But that was not the end of the world!

Although I did not feel like it, I went with the dogs to the beach. *Zicatela* beach was a surfing paradise and many "penguins" surfed in the water. The beach had high waves and strong current, so in all descriptions I was warned to use this section only as a skilled surfer! My four-legged friends got their shower and happily moved off to the camper. I was glad because there was still a lot of homework to do and then tomorrow's drive. Since the afternoon nap had failed, I felt tired despite the short drive. For lunch there was *papas con guacamole* (small potatoes with avocado paste).

Addendum: The purchased paste was so spicy that it made me sweat, my nose started to run, and I voluntarily switched to butter! I needed to dilute the spiciness!

February 18th/19th
243 topes / 354 kilometers in 8 hours

That makes a *tope* every 1.5 km or a road barrier every two minutes! You can imagine how exhausted I was when I arrived at **Diamante,** south of Acapulco in the evening. It was my own fault! Really, I wanted to drive the route in two days. But I was always too early to stop for the next night. The choice was a nice small hotel on the road or a clean, but stinking Pemex gas station. Thus, I dared the marathon of eight and a half hours driving time with two short breaks.

I started in *Puerto Escondido* at nine o'clock in the morning and arrived at my destination at half past five in the evening. The only good thing was the cooler temperature, because it was cloudy and a bit rainy from time to time, but it never got so bad that it was unpleasant. Consequently, we had won a rest day in **Acapulco**.

The *Diamante* RV Park was a Mecca for the Franco-Canadians. Here I was able to handle French better than any other language. The Canadian accent was horrible: *Matäng, biäng, demäng, ... - päng!* Some permanent guests had established proper houses, with a paved anteroom and fitted kitchens in the open air. I did not want to know what such a place in the area cost for the whole year. I was convinced that most residents flew in at the beginning of winter and disappeared again when it got too hot or the rainy season began. Did they know much about Mexico? As I mentioned before, I left Acapulco to the left (in the truest geographical sense). The city was too touristy, too hectic, too Americanized. In addition, I needed cooler areas again.

Since it was written in the guide that the trip did not have much to offer and was boring, I started counting the *topes*. In fact, the route was almost always inland and along the mountain range. At the beginning it was quite curvy, but later it got straighter again for several miles. When I had to cross some bridges, I noticed the many colorful "flags" in the wind. There were still women washing and rubbing their laundry in the river and hanging it up to dry. You had to watch out for roaming cattle, like pigs, suckling pigs, donkeys or goats.

In a small village (?) beautiful round brook shingles were offered near the river. Where otherwise women offered vegetables and fruit, here they presented the stones in big colored sacks. You could get any size. The bags had to be extremely difficult to transport. With a wheelbarrow they brought the stones and they were later sorted and selected by hand.

I had just settled in my corner and was walking with the dogs, when I heard a well-known voice: "Hello! Monika!" Pierre and Rita from Montreal were my neighbors – they had arrived

136

yesterday! The pitch had over a hundred and seventy possibilities and we found ourselves in the same neighborhood again! Of course, there was a long chat in the evening, but by ten o'clock I was absolutely ready for bed. That night, in my dreams I stopped and accelerated constantly. Can you imagine why?

This morning I was busy with a lot of writing stuff (Attorney affairs! Dreadful!). The dogs lounged under the car and I stayed in the camper, hiding from the scorching heat. My thermometer showed 36°C at three o'clock in the afternoon.

Once Rita and Pierre had left in the morning, well-known people from *Puerto Ángel* occupied their place. How small the (camper) world is! Although the park had a small swimming pool, chances of getting a swim were exceptionally low. As in Bad Füssing (a German thermal bath) one stood close to each other in the whirlpool and chatted with fellow sufferers.

The next week will be internet free as I will be in *Cuernavaca* and in the mountains. We set off tomorrow. There are 300 km/190 miles ahead of us. This time I'll use the toll highway. I'm already fed up with *topes*. It will probably be a five-hour drive. Then we have cooler nights again and probably a daytime temperature of "only" 25°C to 27°C. This is not only pleasant for the doggies.

February 20ᵗʰ
677,00 pesos that paid off!

At nine o'clock we left for the Mexican hinterland. It was already warming up again (28°C), and we had to reach an altitude of 1540 m above sea level. In my opinion tonight would be pleasantly cool, if not cold. We had to overcome two mountain ranges. God bless this highway! From time to time I saw a part of the national highway. I gladly paid the high toll – I would probably have needed three days to master this mountain route of three hundred kilometers! Some sections climbed up steeply.

Some trucks had to give up because of boiling water in the coolant and my car also started to sweat. But I remembered an old trick of passionate trailer drivers: drain the heater with heat! Since the side window was totally open, the escaping heat bothered me a little, but it worked, and I did not have to give up.

Due to the high price, the #95D was not busy and I could drive my 100 km/h – if it was straight or went downhill! The road was very well developed and was constantly undergoing maintenance. Various smaller construction sites slowed down the traffic again and again. The route was a beautiful scenic one that again and again offered great views of a new mountain range on level crossings. The vegetation changed, the green became lush and different cacti grew up among the trees. I had missed these plants so far. They were not so common on the coast.

In the first major city I urgently needed refueling. I was not completely confident about the service, as I was not sure if someone had conned me at the petrol pumps. Allegedly, the fuel gauge jumped back by itself and was full only for 35 *pesos*. Since I only wanted to refuel for four hundred anyway, we stopped at 365 pesos. If so, this sum would not really kill me. I only noticed the grin of a colleague. Under their breath I'm sure they were saying: "She fell into the trap!".

Before *Cuernavaca*, the volcano *Popocatépetl* (5452 m) and its partner *Itztacciuhatl* (5286 m) shone bright white on my right hand. We had a magnificent clear view of both mountains. On the left-hand side, I saw another white snow massif, but for the time being it was not possible to identify its name on the map. The 800,000 inhabitants in the city of **Cuernavaca** received us with dense weekend traffic. In theory, it was a popular destination for Mexican capital residents affected by pollution. From here it is still ninety kilometers to the 25-million city with suburbs. Unimaginable in our European conditions! I hoped I would find the hotel, which only had five parking spaces! After shopping at the Walmart, I hurried there to arrive early.

I was the only guest! A pitch cost a hundred pesos a night, a room with a hot shower a hundred and fifty pesos, so I chose the hotel room. That why I needed no disposal and I could save my water. It was an old hotel and seemed a bit dilapidated, but everything was clean, and I took my own bedding inside. For a little bit extra, I got power for the camper and was able to cook my own food. Now I had two "apartments" for three days. The car was safe in a walled garden and the bus to the city drove right past the front door. The center was fifteen kilometers away. My dogs could run free in the garden and I could take them with me into the room. The facility was surrounded by a large back garden with a swimming pool, so it was ideal for my four-legged friends. I did not trust the water of the pool, but I let my feet hang in from time to time. I had no parking problems, knew my ladies were in good hands and was able to devote myself (without worries) to the historic city center.

February 21st
Cuernavaca

The city was highly praised in all books: city of eternal spring, popular destination with colonial charm, flower city...but I didn't see any of that myself. Only a small part in the center looked like and corresponded to this cliché. The bumpy ride to the *mercado* by public bus took about half an hour and cost me seven *pesos*. Around the market hall there was a big hustle and bustle! There were a lot of suppliers and the streets were crammed with all kinds of cars and wannabe vehicles. It was hectic everywhere! Here you could also find the central office for the buses in the surrounding villages, so we suffered their stench and noise. The market was off the agenda today, I wanted to go to the museum and to the cathedral. In the morning it was 12°C outside. Half an hour later, I quickly took my jacket off. It was starting to get warm!

Again, I had overlooked the altitude during my tour. I had to switch back a few gears when walking to catch my breath. It was always uphill and downhill, and I went from the market to the regional museum, the small *zócalo* and the cathedral. Thank God there was a lot of shadow everywhere. *Cuernavaca* had not woken up yet in this corner. The street vendors were only beginning to spread their hodgepodge and only the military played their wake-up call in front of the government palace.

At ten o'clock the *Borda Garden* opened. A much-praised park, which did not convince me too much! The rich silver king of Taxco, José de la Borda, had it laid out at the end of the 18th century. Emperor Maximilian (the puppet emperor) and his wife Charlotte had their Mexican summer residence here.

I wanted to be in the cathedral at eleven o'clock. Supposedly, they played mariachi music in this place of worship. But that was wrong! Apparently, it was not in the program anymore! Well, then I'll go to the Robert Brady museum, just around the corner. The American artist and collector lived in *Cuernavaca* for twenty-four years. His private home was part of the monastery grounds of the cathedral. I was interested by this museum because I wanted to see a self-portrait of Frida Kahlo and several Mexican masks.

Cuernavaca and Museum Robert Brady

"The Last Supper"
Mexican interpretation

This building was a surprise to me. That's how you could live in Mexico when you had money in the years of Josephine Baker: I tried to visit another church with mariachi music at half past one but *again*, I was misled. There were three guitar players on site, but not mariachis! I thought about my two doggies in the camper and whether they might get too hot. So, I apologized to God and made my way home. This time I grabbed a taxi for convenience for which I paid four euros! Not the end of the world!

In the camper it was still tolerably cool, and everything was ok with my two ladies. They headed immediately for our overnight accommodation, because here the temperatures were even lower! I cooked a little, had a long siesta, and let both mice romp in the garden.

February 22*nd*
ßschotschikálko - Xochicalco

"Place of the House of Flowers" – that was my tour today! The night was pleasantly cool again, almost cold. The temperatures dropped to about 10°C at dawn. And then woe! the sun came and then it was time for shorts again!

At ten o'clock I took the swinging bus back to the *mercado*. One of my written guides informed me that there would be a bus to *Xochicalco*. I had written my desired destination on a piece of paper, because for me this place was unpronounceable. I was sent five times from Pontius to Pilate because of my poor language skills. I gave up and stopped a taxi. For two hundred *pesos* he would drive me straight to the ruins. They were thirty-five miles south of *Cuernavaca*. Two hundred *pesos* were actually twelve euros! (Let a taxi driver hear that in Germany!) He was already hired, and we drove back a part of the route, which I had traveled. But today I had more time off to look at things. Many better situated apartments and houses were seen at the foothills of the mountainous city. Here I could imagine living. The air was clean, the street noise far away and the surroundings rural. Now I understood why *Cuernavaca* could be a destination for American retirees with some credit.

Xochicalco doesn't get a lot of visitors although it is an impressive ruin site characterized by different Mexican cultures. It lies one hundred and thirty meters above a wide plain on a hilltop. People know almost nothing about the builders of this place and the excavations so far show influences of several high cultures. The history of this place is one of the big riddles in the archaeology of Mesoamerica. The most significant building is the pyramid of the feathered serpent. On the walls you can see flat reliefs of eight feathered serpents entwined around hieroglyphs and seated people. Of course, there are also other Indian institutions, as in every place of ritual. For instance the Acropolis, dance hall, observatory, steam bath for ritual purification, about twenty altars...

I was most impressed by the geographical location of the shrine next to the stone carvings. You had a wide view of mountainous Mexico. The *Popocatépetl* shone clearly although without a tangle of power cables over the temple complex. The volcano seemed to float, because the mountain foot was invisible through the haze and only its snow-covered part shone in the sun. Even his idle partner *Iztaccihuatl* could be made out. You could see all the way to *Cuernavaca*. Now I also knew the name of the third snowfield. The taxi driver identified it as *Nevado de Toluca* at 4690 m.

The museum and the complex were built and furnished according to the latest standards. The excavations were vividly presented in appealing rooms. For a small fee, there was an audio guide – even in German! I was excited!

Since the ruin site was remote and the actual village with public connections was relatively far away, I asked the taxi driver if he could come back. No problem! He would wait for me at the back of the museum in two and a half hours and return with me to *Cuernavaca*. Agreed! Why should I expose myself to the bus adventure when I could have it so easy? He would drop me off right in front of my hotel. It also saved me time, because I did not want to leave the dogs alone for too long.

At the beginning, the excavations belonged to me alone. A school class joined later. That was the whole number of visitors. I was just busy making good use of the time! During the last half hour I checked the museum.

My chauffeur was punctually in front of the building. Whether he had been waiting for two and a half hours, or whether he was enjoying himself in the meantime, I cannot say. He took a different route back to my "residence". Of course, the fare was a little higher, because the trip was a lot longer. But spending an extra three hundred *pesos* was ok with me, if I considered the convenience and time.

In the afternoon we would rest. I intended to cool down in the pool, but I only made it to the hips! After all, we did not live in Acapulco and the nights were cold! That's how the water was: chilly!

Tonight, I will once again enjoy the TV in the room, although I understand next to nothing. The warm shower did not work, so this morning I had to use my own RV, since cold showers at 12°C outside were still too Spartan.

Excavation findings from Xochicalco

Xochicalco
„Place of the house of flowers"

 *personal notes*

Xochicalco – Temple of the Feathered Serpent

 *personal notes*

February 23rd
What a day!

We left early at nine o'clock. Since the exit from the hotel was bumpy and narrow, I mounted the kerb outside. Now my side staircase is bent, and I cannot extend it anymore. It was not the first time it had happened! The last time it was a tire part on the road, which I couldn't avoid hitting. Well, for such cases I had a lot of stools in the car and they were a good emergency solution!

We needed to do some shopping at the *Pelikan*. I got a better car atlas and bought a microwave for just under eight hundred pesos. The current one had almost given up the ghost. At ten o'clock we finally found *Cuernavaca*. We were driving constantly upwards on the toll highway. You had an incredibly wide view of the plateau with its volcanic cones. The exit to *Toluca* was so badly signposted that I could not slow down to take the exit. I had to drive ten kilometers until I could turn again. I did not want to go to Mexico City! No way! I came across a pass with a height of 3100 m! Twenty kilometers for nothing! The good news is that I saved the toll, because I saw no toll booth on the exit.

The curvy road went through the interior (so to speak, because it was an unnumbered trail along the northwest). It couldn't even be called a street because it was very narrow and it went up and down, up and down! The only advantage was that you didn't notice any pothole. I had to choose this route because there was no other alternative to the big city. I left a thick dark cloud behind me. My diesel had its problems with the thin air again. Me too! Like a mountaineer, I had to breathe deeply again and again to get enough oxygen.

Following winding paths, we arrived in **Toluca**. Even on my atlas it was difficult to find the one village I was looking for. It was like Christmas! There was a surprise behind every corner.

149

The signposts were poor – I had to ask for directions several times. Thankfully, the Mexicans gesticulated when explaining so much that you understood them even without language skills.

Well, now I had finally reached *Toluca*. Here destiny struck! What did *Toluca* have in common with *Tempico*? Not only the "T" but also the corrupt police. In search of the Mex #15 two uniformed men pulled me over after a turning maneuver. Since I was aware of no guilt, I pretended to be stupid. That was not difficult for me, because I understood nothing of their verbiage anyway. I tried to tell them again and again that I just wanted to find the way to *Zitacuaro*. Somehow, I heard something like "driving permission" out of their gibberish. No idea what they wanted. Later, I found out that *Toluca* is part of Mexico City's emissions zone and they ban multi-axle cars in urban intercity at certain times of the day. The city is notorious for RV drivers, the police even set up false signs and get their cash illegally. Consequently, I had not violated a driving ban, but this wouldn't have happened if I had studied my travel notes more carefully!

I pretended to be stupid and in a friendly way I asked the two officers if they could show me the way to Mex #15. Surprise! They drove ahead with blue lights and I followed them. Friendly people – I thought to myself.

Shortly before an important turn, they pulled me over again. They wanted to see "cash" for my "mistakes". Five hundred *dólares*, then everything would be fine! Slowly I guessed what it was all about! *"No pesos"*! – they said. If I wanted to pay in *pesos*, then I should shell out a thousand! I demanded an official form with names, service number, sum and receipt! I insisted. The other option was going to the police station. This responsible office would be in Mexico City. I could not really believe that. Since I was not sure about the number plate and the last number on it (certain numbers are prohibited on certain working days), I traded them down to five hundred *pesos*. I would not pay a higher amount unless they gave me a receipt. They returned my papers and slipped the five hundred *pesos* in their pocket (grinning). I put these thirty euros on the imaginary donation list. Modern piracy! Horrid gang!

Now it was time to find *Toluca* through many construction sites. This industrial city is the highest city of Mexico, with 2680 m above sea level and over one million inhabitants. That's why there was heavy traffic! Since I had already been there, I looked for a taxi to show me the way for thirty *pesos*. The taxi prices seemed to adjust to the altitude. In *Cuernavaca* I would have paid a maximum of ten *pesos* for the ride. But my desperate expression probably drove up the price.

Finally, we were on the right way to *Zitacuaro*. By now it was almost three o'clock. The first part of the road was well developed, the last part was a little bit of a disaster. I decided to take the new *cuota* (toll road). It was only ten kilometers, but it saved me thirty kilometers of bends in the mountain landscape.

At five o'clock we could finally check into the hotel *Villa Monarca* Inn. We had stopped here five years ago with the organized group. Thus, I knew the place, but the owner was different. I got power (last minute decision) and was able to give my three large laundry sacks to a *señora* for cleaning. Tomorrow evening I would get everything back fresh and clean!

Conclusion: Seven hours drive (with police intermission) for 165 km around the *Nevado de Toluca* with snow-covered summit and nearly five thousand meters in altitude. I estimated that we had our pitch at about two thousand meters. Good God, I was done! I did not even enjoy my daily beer. The icing on the cake: My old microwave was working again! Probably it only was the weak current in *Cuernavaca*. Now I had two!

February 24th
Butterflies

We needed to turn on the heating this morning. The outside temperature was 4°C and 10°C inside at seven o'clock. The temperature climbed until lunchtime with almost 30°C. The heat was easier to handle at this altitude because it was not so tropical and there was constantly a refreshing breeze blowing.

As already mentioned, I was here five years ago with a group and on that occasion, I gave up the long program in favor of my dogs. The leader wanted to combine the visit of the nature park *Mariposa* with a hike. That was too exhausting for me and too long when I thought about my four-legged friends. This time I grabbed a taxi at nine o'clock and was lucky with my chauffeur. He was a friendly young Mexican who would drive me for the same price as in *Cuernavaca* and cover the route mentioned before. Agreed! Why had I not come up with this idea five years ago?

Why was I so interested in this place? **Ocampo** (an impassable way for camping cars) leads to one of the rare – and the only officially accessible – wintering areas of the monarch butterflies. Millions of butterflies fly in from Canada and the north of the US each year in November and leave this 3000-meter-high coniferous forest again in April. On their long flights, they travel up to 140 km per day. Officially, there are more than 35 million butterflies in three areas of this region. A fascinating natural event that is unique around the world. Due to the bad road or the doubtful tire quality we had a flat tire and it had to be changed. As a precaution, a spare tire was tucked away in the trunk.

Today I can only advise everyone not to drive this road from *Ocampo*. It was easy to master up to the place mentioned, but around the *zócalo* it got pretty tight! Then the four-track runway was made of cobblestone/gravel. You could get out of lane very easily! In addition, at that time they recorded several avalanches, which came from the storms I already mentioned. At least the small village had had no casualties, but unfortunately the neighboring *Angangueo* didn't share the same luck. The small river was

152

swollen to a huge current and tore earth, boulders and the simple dwellings with it into the valley.

Now we had finally arrived. Since the young man did not want to wait alone, he joined me and helped me with simplified explanations to understand the most important things. It was fascinating to see thousands of butterflies fluttering in the sun. In many cases it looked like falling autumn leaves from a distance. Some sat on my arm and in my hair. Yesterday I was right with my altitude estimation: mountain peaks 3600 m, lower valley 2700 m – my hotel was just below this last village. You got out of breath in the ascent.

An old woman had spread her needlework in the street. Why should I not buy some embroidered butterflies? She demanded twenty-five pesos for each doily. I picked two and pushed a fifty into her hands without much bargaining. Then something happened, which even now still touches me while writing: she took off her headgear and thanked my purchase with a sign of the cross! That almost blew me away!

I was able to "persuade" my chauffeur with some extra *pesos* so he would stop at other places on the return trip and give me time to take pictures. Of course, if he had to wait, for *tortillas* or similar he would get additional *pesos*.

The center of the village *Ocampo* had a very well-kept appearance, considering the housing situation of the rest of the population. I urgently needed some change and fled to a café, which was more of a *Lonchería* (for small dishes). There I finally succeeded in taking the picture for which I had waited a long time: mother with child in the *rebozo*. Baby carriages are known only in places like Mexico City. Each mother carries her offspring until they can walk. The frequent physical contact probably creates an extraordinarily strong bond with the mother.

At around one in the afternoon this wonderful trip finished. That was good, because the temperature was hot by that time. In the camper it was pleasantly cool for my loved ones. My driver opened the trunk and as a farewell he put a butterfly in my hand. Well-meaning! It was a male. These die after mating anyway. The animal seemed already dead, so I dropped it off in the car. Wrong thought! The small beast hid itself and was probably sitting in one of the many corners to face his death. Could my evening light lure it out? Otherwise, I would find him at the end of the journey when I did the general cleaning.

The afternoon was relaxed with lots of reading and a great opportunity to fill my gas tank at a reasonable price. In the evening the young woman came with my laundry. She demanded a hundred *pesos* for her effort. If she knew what her labors at home would be worth …! I appreciated that, because how many women did I see doing this hard work at the well or in the river? Now she would have some more money in her pocket!

Tomorrow we will go 220 km west to *Pátzcuaro*. Hopefully I can meet friends there and settle down for a comfortable week. The lake is 2000 m high and is praised in one of my guides as the most beautiful lake in Mexico in wooded hills and amid extinct volcanoes. Let's see if the book is right!

Zitacuaro – Butterfly
Santuario „Mariposa Monarca"

 *personal notes*

 *personal notes*

February 25th
Hope dies last...

250 km, if we take the detour on the motorway – but 210 km if we drive over the mountains, which register some 3000 m passes. I opted for the longer and more expensive option. Up to the last ten kilometers, the road to the highway was passable, but then it was in direct competition with the Alaska Highway and was a little stressful. It took me two hours to get to the Mex #15D and cover almost seventy kilometers. From then it went on quickly, but I couldn't make up for the time lost.

Morelia lured me with the signpost "*Pátzcuaro*" into the center and not around, as I had intended. I prayed earnestly that there would be no driving ban in the city center for two-axle cars, which would again cost me endless discussions with police officers. As expected, it was close to the *centro histórico*. Many people were on the way. I hoped to find a public transport connection from *Pátzcuaro* later to get here.

Finally, I left the city center without any obstacles and hoped to meet my friends soon. The road to **Pátzcuaro** was well developed and had two lanes. I almost immediately found the camping. But no acquaintances were to be seen far and wide. The place was fully occupied. By now it was almost half past two and I had not gotten a bite between my teeth. We tried it at the other pitch, the *Pozzo*. A lot of free space, but no Karin and no Klaus! I could not stay here, because within a few hours a caravan group of over twenty campers would arrive. Crap! Five years ago, our group also spent the night here. When I saw the gate entrance, Helmut's high box came to mind. No chance for the next days either because the group would stay for a week. The other camping was also full.

Well, maybe they were back in **Quiroga,** about twenty-five miles away. I had mentioned this location in one of my mails. Wrong! I was absolutely alone in the pool area. The driveway was only big enough to be able to pass. Where else should I search? Let's stay here. Maybe there would be a new chance later!

From somewhere I got power, but the water had to be started first. Disposal was planned "nowhere". The young Mexican was immensely proud of his English but for me it was as he were speaking Chinese. If my Spanish was that bad, I would keep quiet! But people showed patience again and again, so I also gave him my full attention. The dogs were able to jump around freely in a big terrain and that was worth a lot.

Ok! Not the most beautiful lake in Mexico, no friends, no relaxation, no internet, no *Morelia*, no browsing in the many craft shops. At least I got a glimpse of the city. A beautiful colonial town with a huge cathedral, sumptuous buildings and a nice *zócalo*!

If you could not stay here, what to do? More than likely I would drive the Mex #15 tomorrow in the direction *of Chapala* Lake. That was 280 km of road, again over the mountains! Pure stress! Estimated driving time seven hours! We will manage it, ok? And if not, we will use a Pemex on the way for overnight stay. I was frustrated with the many efforts for so little success. At least we had a safe place for the night, even though we did not get to see much. The neighborhood was undoubtedly rural. The young Mexican slept on the grounds because of us and so we were well protected!

February 26th
Reversed!

After recovering a bit from the exertions last night and putting my frustration on paper, my brain began to work again.

What's wrong with me? I have the most beautiful walled space for me and my dogs, the heated swimming pool is just for me, electricity and water are available, toilets and hot (?) showers as well, buses run every half hour to *Morelia* and taxis take me cheaply to any desired destination. For eighty *pesos* the night! I only miss a little company. Nothing is perfect!

The decision is made: we'll establish our operational base here! Why the pressure? This morning, the young gentleman got the money for the next three nights. He had some problems multiplying 3 x 80 and adding last night to the final price.

The morning was a bit cold and for the first warm-up I had to use my gas heating and later, to keep the temperature, I used the electric oven. In addition, I decided on the in-house shower, because 8°C outside was not my preferred bathroom temperature.

Walking around with the four-legged friends in the village was not very pleasant because of the many stray dogs and so I put them back in their hideaway and set off alone again, armed with the camera. I liked **Quiroga.** Here I had my typical Mexican small town. Not overrun by tourism like *Pátzcuaro*! Pretty and well-kept restaurants! Life took place on the street. A nice church and a shady market. Two pretty *plazas*! I would start another photo session in the afternoon, because now, at noon, it

was 26°C in the shade, which was outstanding in this breezy altitude.

It was true what I had read in a book: the Mexican eats always and everywhere. At ten o'clock in the morning, the first breaded peppers and fish were sizzling in the oil, soups were served and tortillas filled with various ingredients. At this time of day there was already a feeding frenzy. I also had the impression that the Mexican preferred to let others cook than to stand in front of their own stove. Even breakfast was often taken outside. How else could the many vendors that you saw in front of every house and street corner survive?

With some help, I had spotted the departure stop of the buses to *Morelia*. This will be my destination tomorrow. My little Spanish is not so miserable after all. We stood well in the shade on our meadow, and my two ladies could stay alone without me for a little longer. The employee had taken off the covers from the pool for the coming weekend and fresh lukewarm water could be enjoyed. Apparently, he expected weekend guests. The swimming pool was public, but the RV park was separated from it.

162

At half past two, the first teenagers came for a fun-filled happy hour, so, my two ladies had to go on a leash! But only until six o'clock, then the pool was closed. I was free to go in and out because I got a key for the side entrance, but I didn't feel like using it anymore. It was so cozy in our corner! However, some beautiful figures made from papier-mâché had summoned me, so I had to go check them! Both dogs  had to guard the house again for a short time. I was back on time to feed the predators, though.

February 27ᵗʰ
Morelia

Bright blue sky for visiting the capital of the state of *Michoacán*. **Morelia** has retained the character of a distinguished Spanish colonial town to this day and its center was declared a cultural heritage site by UNESCO in 1991. I dared the "adventure" public bus and the first connection left under my nose. But twenty minutes later, the next bus came. Cost for thirty-five kilometers: twenty-three pesos. Unfortunately, Mexico always relied on mouth to mouth information, as the stops were either random or signposted, but without direction or timetable. Thus, finding our way around for us tourists was always difficult.

The end station of my line was *Morelia*, far out of town and I had to grab a taxi to the center. The locals knew which of the *colectivos* they had to use. Not me! That would have saved money,

163

of course. I was dropped right off in front of the cathedral and could start my city stroll.

The most beautiful buildings were along the main street. This stretched a long way from the sweets market (*Mercado de Dulces*) to the aqueduct. The day before yesterday I had been incredibly lucky that no *gendarme* caught me. It was forbidden for heavier vehicles to cross the city center. The only law enforcement officer who had seen me probably closed his eyes.

There are many museums, as well as churches and well-preserved aristocratic palaces with beautiful manicured courtyards. The mighty cathedral made of brown pink rock was the central point together with the *zócalo*. I let myself stroll with the help of the map until I landed in the walls of the church and the convent of *San Francisco*. There I discovered the *Casa de las Artesanías*, where a variety of first-class regional folk art was exhibited and sold. Of course, that was the right "food" for me and my camera. Better than any museum, as it presented the craftsmanship made by the locals, grouped by location and region. Of course, I stayed exploring this place for a long time.

Then I dragged myself (it had become warm again!) along the main road to the aqueduct, which today had no function, except for being a picturesque highlight next to the small square. It was one of the landmarks of the city, with over 1.6 km in length and with 253 round arches.

I had to walk back the whole distance, and stumbled several times, as I had focused my eyes more and more on the beautiful facades than on the sidewalk. The library in the church *La Compañía* and the sweet market should be my last two visits. Then I wanted to go on a search for the bus home. The library was closed, but you could look into the beautiful reading room. Unfortunately, the glass panes were so dirty that I couldn't take any pictures.

The market next to it had not only a lot of goodies, but also the usual tourist kitsch. I had a collection of candied fruit put together, but offered it to the *hombre* at the pool, because the treat was so sweet that it had a bitter aftertaste.

I needed a taxi back to the departure point of the buses. The chauffeur offered to drive the route to *Quiroga* for two hundred and fifty *pesos*. I managed to lower the price to two hundred and decided on his offer due to the time and convenience. I was done with running and I was able to free my pooches much earlier than if I had been on the regional bus.

With a growling stomach, I arrived in front of the swimming pool at half past two. Now I had to cook. It was soon half past three when we sat down to eat. The day had gone by for me. A short siesta and now my "homework". As warm as it was during the day, in the evening I needed my heating, because from seven o'clock on the temperature dropped rapidly and at night reached values of five degrees at most. One advantage of this climate: you could sleep, and mosquitoes wouldn't annoy you.

 *personal notes*

Morelia
Capital of the state of Michoacán

167

 *personal notes*

*Arts and crafts
in the
Monastery of
San Francisco*

 *personal notes*

Colourful market in Tzintzuntzan

 *personal notes*

February 28th
Tzintzuntzan

Sounds pretty Chinese, right? But that's not the case: **Tzintzuntzan** (Place of the Hummingbirds) is the former capital of the *Tarasken* Empire and lies seven kilometers south of *Quiroga*. From there the missionary work of the Franciscans began under *Vasco de Quiroga*, who has made a name for himself as a peacemaker between the Indians and the Spaniards. In addition, this small town is a center for pottery, wood carvings, furniture and handicrafts made of straw. Apart from that, one finds a small excavation site, which is only of limited interest.

Of course, I had to visit this place, if only because of the arts and crafts. I asked for a *colectivo* at the exit of the village and I drove for five *pesos* with five other passengers (!) to the village. A taxi would have cost me thirty-five *pesos*. It was a cheap and adventurous alternative!

On the way there I passed the *zócalo* of *Quiroga*! I think the whole place was there to eat at lunchtime. One fried pig (*carnitas*) next to the other was offered. I could try and take pictures, but there was no free space left and the people sat to eat on the edge of the fountain or the stairs to the arcade. We all were entertained by a guitarist and people in costumes. These figures performed the *Baile de Viejitos* (Dance of the Old Men). This dance was created to commemorate the victory of Hernán Cortés over the people of the *Tarasken*, after the *Tarasken* prince disguised as an old man before the conqueror arrived. The dancers wore masks and at first, they made a very fragile impression, then they accelerated their dance movements and at the end they turned out to be young men.

There was a second interpretation that I personally liked better: that this dance was originally dedicated to the god of the ancients and the fire and was danced as a mockery of the Spanish *conquistadores*.

In *Tzintzuntzan* I enjoyed a market with all the colors and peculiarities of Mexico. It was a feast for my camera. The old Franciscan monastery was very impressive for me with its huge atrium. The green areas were refuges of the shadow seeker. Cool spots were provided by a lot of olive trees, which were rarely found in Mexico, as the Spaniards had forbidden them (why?) in their colonies.

Going for a walk and looking for souvenirs ate three hours in a heartbeat and a *colectivo* brought me back to *Quiroga*. This time I could not resist the *carnitas*. I was ravenous and the meat smelled so tempting. I also wanted to take with me a little of the *salsa mexicana* – freshly made from tomatoes, onions, green chili and *cilantro* (chervil), marinated in lime sauce. Tasty and very spicy!

The swimming pool was busy today so I kept myself discreetly in the background with my two ladies. Tomorrow I wanted to go to *Pátzcuaro* by bus, taxi or *colectivo*. Consequently, my two darlings will have to stay a bit longer without me.

Quiroga at lunchtime

 *personal notes*

Month of March
1800 km/1125 miles

West coast to Teacapán
(State of Sinaloa)
West coast to Álamos
(State of Sonora)

 *personal notes*

March 1ˢᵗ
Continuation of the journey

After returning from my trip to **Pátzcuaro** this afternoon, I sat down to prepare the next destinations for March. I was in doubt whether I should go all the way up the coast, or if I could once again turn inland. Everything was not possible. I would skip a few colonial cities of the program: *Guanajuato*, S. *Miguel de Allende* and *Quertaro*. **Morelia** should set an example for the others. The detour would have been too far and too exhausting. The Copper Canyon also fell victim to the considerations because the political situation and the drug rivalry in *Chihuahua* seemed a bit critical to me at the moment. A woman alone should not take risks! This canyon has been there for so many years, that it will be possible to come again. (Never say never!)

I want to cover 1,600 km/1,000 miles until my birthday, with many long stops along the Pacific. Therefore, there will never be more than 150 to 200 kilometers between each destination. After all, we will not see any ocean for a long time after crossing the border. We will spend Easter far in the north. The chosen place has the funny name *Huatabampito*. I hope that by this time many migratory birds will have left, and more parking spaces will be available again. In mid-March we will go back to the coast. Thus, our further "ordeal" should be understandable.

I dropped a few *pesos* in **Pátzcuaro** today. I could take the bus for eleven *pesos*. As it did not drive to the center, I got off on the way and stopped one of the many *colectivos*. The distance from the lake to the *zócalo* is unpleasantly long. I saved my legs for five more *pesos*. There was a lot going on in the town today. Too bad that they had totally torn up the main square and the place was under renovation. There were construction sites everywhere! The beautiful palace buildings around were not affected. Very well-kept restaurants in tasteful courtyards could be seen, and beautiful private terraces and tantalizing arts and crafts too.

179

Of course, I stayed in one of them longer than usual. I liked the colorful tapestries. The prices were affordable, considering how much work was in such pieces. I was particularly impressed that the owner of the shop made his own objects. All pure hand-made! Good that I had picked up more *pesos!* In another work-shop I found a mask to which I could not say "no" for three hundred *pesos*. Now I did not need to drive to another place to find a mask carver. I had my dream object and hoped it would look good with the one I already had at home from *San Miguel de Allende* from an earlier trip.

The public library was housed in a church. Interestingly, it looked like a monumental painting of the history of this state, worked with great attention to detail. Here I checked my emails to be updated. Too bad, the missing friends were not far away, but not being able to communicate was a disadvantage! I got her message too late! Well, maybe further north! They had to cross the US border at about the same time as me!

At least I could take a quick look to the lake. I did not find the pond that special! The water had a dirty color: it was gray-brown and uninviting. It was evidently not suitable for bathing. I had no desire to sail to the exploited island for tourists or even check its monument. After all, I already had four differently sized tap-estries and a wooden mask! For fifteen *pesos* I preferred to drive back to *Quiroga* with a *colectivo*.

On my way back to the swimming pool I stopped briefly to get some *carnitas*. That gave a nice lunch with my remaining noo-dles! As already described, I spent the late afternoon with all sorts of plans. The next stations were called *Mazamitla, Villa Co-rona, Tequila, Santa María del Oro* and then my favorite: *Playa Amor* at *San Blas* in the middle of the month! Tomorrow 190 km/120 miles of country road through the mountains are ahead of us. We should be able to do that in four to five hours even if we have miserable conditions.

March 2nd
There is another way!

As usual, before a long drive, I slept uneasily last night and was up at six o'clock. No worries! Then at least we would leave early. At half past eight we were ready to go. The boy from the swimming pool was nowhere to be seen. So, just in case, I dropped the keys in the box office. He will probably find them. The gate was not locked from the inside and with a lot of maneuvering and hitting the wall slightly, I came out of the narrow entrance. After these struggles, I was already bathed in sweat in the cool morning hour! At least I did not have to go through downtown anymore.

The road went upwards, into the morning fog. Consequently, I overlooked a *tope*! Oooops! Luckily, the cabinets stayed shut! Only the thermos flask rolled on the floor! Slowly, *señora* Monika! We have time!

I needed a whole hour for the first five and a half miles. The sun came out and the trip was like a tour through autumnal vegetation. The brown of the winter had not gone yet.

Zamora was our next hurdle. The city was located in a very fertile high valley and was known for its strawberries. Its signage was less famous. After I got lost first, I just took the direction indicated and landed next to the unfinished cathedral (the landmark of the city) right in the center. I was stopped by a policeman. No, not again! But he was very friendly and drew me a sketch to help his explanation that indicated how I could get out of the maze to the Mex #15. When he saw my doubtful face, he drove ahead. This time without any thoughts, friendly and helpful! (See headline!). Finally, I was on the right way, but had lost an hour in the city of 150,000 inhabitants. The road was well developed. But what does it help if it goes uphill and a bump comes up suddenly? *Paciencia*! Slowly but surely, I could cover less kilometers than I had thought. I had to stop for a moment and get exercise, because after all we had already been on the road for four hours. A police patrol stopped next to me and a policeman asked in English if everything was alright or if I needed help. When I said no, the police drove on. (See heading!)

We found the campsite near **Mazamitla** immediately and were greeted friendly by a Mexican/American couple. The place looked neat and well-kept but with truly little shade. We could hide behind the camper anyway. Since we were back at about two thousand two hundred meters of altitude, a pleasant cool wind was blowing. We had to slow down our movements so we wouldn't run out of breath. At night it could be cold as usual. I was greeted warmly by my neighbors. The woman was from Regensburg/Bavaria, her husband from northern Germany. They met in Canada and have lived in London for 50 years, in Windsor, Ontario... The owner of the RV Park invited us on a tour to **Mazamitla**. About ten people accepted his invitation. It will be a fiesta. But what a shame! The celebration was postponed. To compensate, we went for dinner in a well-kept restaurant. Again, I got into conversation with a couple from Newfoundland. It turned out that they were close friends of the people I had met at Lake Catemaco. Now I had their address for the future. Since I had had lunch at three o'clock, I was a bit skeptical about the size of the serving. But I did not have to force myself. It tasted wonderful!

Mazamitla was one of the many *Pueblos Mágicos*. This meant, that it has many places of cultural interest and is frequently visited by tourists. But today it was quiet in the village. The architecture of the houses was exceptional for Mexico. The people used a lot of wood, which gave the impression of a European alpine village – just like it said in the description of the book! But I suspected that no one of the authors had really been there!

Near our camping there was a lake. We'll visit it tomorrow by car. Therefore, I did not unpack much today. For the time being, we would settle down for three nights, to wash the bedclothes again and to clean the RV. The dashboard had a lot of dust piled up as well. The only problem was that there was no Wi-Fi. That's why my loves must wait a while at home, even though I had been missing for a long time. In return, they will get a lot to read when I get to write to them!

March 3ʳᵈ /4ᵗʰ
"You can't escape!"

Last night I was too tired to write anything in my diary. Over the past day I thought that there was nothing special to report. With thin air and lots of sunshine I got busy in the camper to deal with the accumulated dirt. In addition, I was finally able to wash my sheets and do other small household chores. After the curvy top ride yesterday, I had absolutely no need to do anything harder. When I woke up from the siesta, I checked my laundry and I discovered a new RV next to me. I looked a second time: that was the "Minnie" of Klaus and Karin! Coincidence? Fate? I think both. They had left *Pátzcuaro* later and I had set up my temporary station here. The same had happened on the *Baja California* in *Mulegé*. Mexico is huge! The world is small! I was so glad to see them both alive and kicking after such a long time! The last time I saw the two guys (I think) was before leaving Germany for the States and their planned Alaska tour. The dinner together was followed by an extensive conversation and therefore I went to my sleeping corner later as usual.

Having gone to bed so late affected my sleep. I got out of bed relatively late the morning after. I had a relaxing breakfast and then the camping car was prepared for a short trip. Before I did that, I decided to spend another day at this friendly place and go on a little trip tomorrow. My friends joined us as well. Thus, we could spend some nice hours together, before our ways separated again.

The reservoir of **Valle de Juárez** is not particularly big or exciting. Probably its water supply for this valley is necessary for survival. Its cleanliness leaves something to be desired, so I would not even wet my toe in it.

Well, the dogs should get their coveted wet belly and we took a relaxing little snoop walk along the tiny *malecón*. Later I went to the town for a few errands and a little stroll around the *plaza*. There it was pretty and pleasantly shady. Simply comfortable!

After a short lunch Klaus took care of my snarling steering wheel. We could not find the filler cap for the goo. Thankfully, a Canadian came and discovered the object. All that was missing was the liquid. The owner of the campsite had some stuff in stock. Hopefully, the next few kilometers my *coche* will work again without noise and I can save myself some repairing expenses.

March 5th
Manzanilla de La Paz

Because of today's trip, I had extended one more day. The hosts and the guests wanted to visit a small village and then go for a trout lunch. I could not miss that! In the morning tour, my mice made a dark-eyed angry look at a Canadian "enemy". They could not accept his grumpy expression and barked at him terribly. Since he then stomped after them, instead of behaving calmly, they became even more furious. I kept them short on the leash, but we had one less friendly neighbor!

At half past nine we set off. I could ride with a Californian couple in the car of the host. Klaus took care of his RV and Karin was one of the party. The little village – see name above! – in the mountains was small but very appealing. The streets were unusually clean and the *zócalo* cared for. We were especially pleased with an old *hacienda*, which had been converted into a tasteful hotel. But there was much more to see in a local small "hotel". Countless picturesque corners! Here I would want to live immediately, although everything gave a chaotic impression.

184

The woman had converted her parents' house into a hostel, for one hundred and twenty *pesos* a night per person with a TV!

In a small chapel dedicated to *Virgen de la Guadalupe*, I was able to light a few candles for the onward journey. Here they were not electric. I hate that, even if it is understandable because of the fire hazard! We had lunch in a nice eatery on the way back. The specialty was trout. If you wanted to and had enough serenity, you could catch your own fish. Some of the participants in the group tried it out, but at some point, they gave up resignedly. Only Sel (the campsite operator) was patient enough to fish a large trout, which was met with deserving applause. It tasted fantastic and everyone was happy with the appetizers. My friends were happy about my return. They were not alone, because Klaus always took care of the group with a few nice words. But he was not the master!

Since tomorrow there are only a hundred kilometers to the next destination, I can save myself packing today and I can clear everything tomorrow. Somehow, I have no desire to leave this friendly place, but the distance and the miles to be handled speak a word of power.

March 6th
On a recovery trip

With a sad heart, I said goodbye to the pleasant RV park. It was half past ten when I got on the gas pedal. Well! I'll probably meet Karin and Klaus again before crossing the border. From now on it would be pleasant to drive. There were

hundred kilometers to cover today. We made it on the developed road (Mex #405) in about two hours. It went down, clearly! When I reached **Lake Chapala**, I was about seven hundred meters lower than on my last pitch. That did not just affect the temperatures. For quite some time we went south of *Chapala Lake* along Mex #15.

This water is the largest natural lake in Mexico. It is 82 km long and 28 km wide on average. Like all the lakes of Mexico, it does not necessarily have the best water quality, yet it is used for water sports. Because of the favorable climate, Americans and Canadians settle on its banks to rest. The agricultural economy also benefits from the climatic conditions.

But the lake was not my destination today. I passed two campsites I had information from. The waters of **Villa Corona** attracted me, thirty kilometers to the west. That I skipped **Guadalajara**, should be understandable because we visited this city on our first trip to Mexico. Therefore, a detour was not necessary this time. I think this metropolis is worth seeing, though.

The thermal springs of the water park **Chimulco** feed different sized swimming pools with warm water. Every evening, the basins of the bathing area are emptied and filled up the next morning with the natural thermal water. There is a fully developed RV park with all amenities.

Finally, after a good two weeks, I once again had the opportunity to go online. But before that, I did not just let my legs dangle in the 39°C warm water. Refreshment didn't happen at an outside temperature of 28°C. But it was nice and wet! Of course, as it was Saturday it was a bit busy. Tomorrow should be the same. But in the evening the noise will be gone, and I'll be able to bask in a pool until ten, which is filled especially for the camping guests every evening. But today I did not feel like it anymore. The pitch price of 230 *pesos* was not too high, considering that the use of the pool was included; the regular entrance fee was ninety *pesos* and you had full access to all the services. For my dogs there was a lot of greenery around and we could walk on the shore of another lake. To downtown **Villa Corona** it was a half an hour walk.

When I came back from an exploratory walk, someone sneaked around the car with a wiper and cleaning rags. Did I want to have it washed? Of course! Certainly! I had waited a long time for this favorable opportunity. For two hundred *pesos* (twelve euros) we came to an agreement and the *señor* came at about six o'clock with his colleague. Now my "American Wuschelmobil" shines like new again! The mire of thousands of kilometers has disappeared! Rainfalls are no solution in the long run.

For the time being I have paid for three nights. Maybe I'll add a fourth night to visit the market on Tuesday. We'll see. Anyway, today I'll be ready for bed early, because I had to have a few pills to treat itching. Was it the water or my budding sunburn? I don't know.

March 7th
Sunday ambience in Chimulco

Even before breakfast, before the regular bathers arrived, I enjoyed the fresh water of the pools. That was pleasant: on the outside, the cool morning temperature and in the water it was warm. The sulfurous water bothered my skin. Now I knew where my itching was coming from last night. But after a thorough shower at home and a lot of lotion, everything was fine.

The day was filled with frustrating letters and emails to various fools in Germany. That was annoying, but unfortunately it had to be done. In addition, the bathing fun was limited with all the visitors, so I waited to do that in the evening.

There was a sizzling noise and food smell in all corners. Many even brought their own barbecue. the ingredients and paper plates were brought in huge baskets. At noon there was no free seat. You could stand in a corner and watch the whole thing and be amused. A big family had organized a mariachi group. Of course, I had to pull out my camera. Pretty lads and gals, wearing their impeccable cute costumes! I liked this spirited music. But they also played sad songs in their repertoire -a lot of heartache!

In the late afternoon I went to the village for a walk. A sleepy nest! Ninety percent of the inhabitants were probably swimming somewhere! I went around the *zócalo* and visited the interesting sandstone church. Quickly, I did a few essential errands and then it was the pooches turn. In the evening I decided to enjoy a thermal bath under the Mexican night sky. Are we feeling well? Yes, we are!

March 9th
Tequila

Let's forget yesterday's day! It was cloudy, listless and insignificant. Was it the water what made me so tired? No idea! Yesterday (Monday) only a basin was filled since there were hardly any people there. It was cool this morning, unusually cool. I canceled the bathing pleasure and took off. At nine o'clock we were on the road to the West. Shopping was necessary. My fridge

gleamed with yawning emptiness. Most of it was used up. Could not remember the last time I had properly shopped. **Tequila** had a supermarket along the road. Maybe would I end up in town if I followed that road? In need of a taxi? I certainly did not want to drive into the center with my big box. The connection to the Mex #15 was not famous but had to be handled with a bit of caution. The state road was narrow and filled with many bumps and holes. We were now in the area of the famous *tequila*, the national drink of the Mexicans, extracted from the heart of the agave. Everywhere you saw wide fields of agave, which formed a green-blue contrast with the mountains. Sugarcane was also grown, and I finally got a shot of one of these huge trucks with their high-pile cargo. When I was driving, pictures did not always work.

Small Agave Remarks: In the time before Columbus, the Indians used the agave as food, for clothing, paper and – with their spikes – as a torture instrument. Although there are over four hundred species of agave, only one (the blue maguey agave) can be used to produce tequila. After about twelve years, when the plant can be harvested, its heart has reached the size of a water ball and weighs about fifty kilograms. Then the prickly leaves are chopped off by hand, the heart is crushed and roasted. For about three days, the manufactory cooks the heart until it is soft, then it is sliced and juiced. The resulting honey-water is distilled twice.

In the Mexican way, you must drink the liquor as follows: Usually you sprinkle the back of the hand (between thumb and forefinger) with a pinch of salt. Now you lick up the salt, gulping the tequila all at once and then bite into the lime – the drink soon shows its burning effect. So much for now! Of course, there is still more to tell. But there are innumerable sources of information open to those interested!

In any case, I liked the town. There was a cheap car park just ten minutes from the center. But hello! Today the sun was heating up again! I was traveling at lunchtime and got thirsty and hungry. That's where the *mercado* with its small restaurants came in handy. I still had to taste the *birria,* a specialty from the state of *Jalisco.* This was a ragout of sheep and goat meat, similar to a hearty goulash soup, served with fresh onions and limes plus nice hot tortillas! It tasted great! I strolled around the area for two hours, visited the local museum, enjoyed the colorful houses, admired the flowers, and took a glance at two of the most famous distilleries of the place.

At about three o'clock we set off for our RV park. It was located south of **Magdalena**, not far from *Etzatlán* and was easy to find. Without the detour, I would have arrived at lunchtime from the other direction. The road was quite bumpy and poorly developed. The park had two surprises in store: First, it was pretty, quiet and well-groomed; second, I met the Californian couple from *Mazamitla* again. They came directly from there yesterday.

I will stay here tomorrow and enjoy the leash-free environment for the dogs for 150 *pesos*/day. The owners live in a small house in the property and call six dogs their own! There is something going on! I enjoy the few (with me three) guests and look forward to a quiet day tomorrow. Maybe the swimming pool is open in the next neighborhood.

March 10th /11th
Nothing is perfect!

Spontaneously I extended another night in this nice place. The extra day here was a bitter need, because on March 10th it was necessary to bring order to my castle and use my cooking skills. On the other hand, on March 11th I needed to get back at my computer for a lot of writing. The problems with the German troublemakers found no end. Since I had an unexpected Wi-Fi signal, I had to check and answer the important mails immediately. Unfortunately, on that day, I had to turn down an invitation for a trip that would have taken me to other hot springs in the area. I had the whole park for myself. Only the dogs of the owners were around, as they hoped for more treats. At least I had a cozy evening meal yesterday with Cathy and Mike, the two Californians. I had so many leftovers in my fridge, that we three were sufficiently full. Bonnie (the owner) also came along and brought us two beautiful white lilies (the flower of Mexico).

Tomorrow I will start going towards the coast. It is two hundred kilometers away, of which at least half are paid motorway. I hope we can do that in three to four hours. Then we will be in *Playa Amor*, south of *San Blas* and *Mazatlán*. That is our next Pacific stay, unfortunately without Wi-Fi. See you sometime again!

March 12th
Playa Amor

A pitch the way I remembered it. Nothing has changed in the last years. But stop! The toilets had been whitewashed (some time ago!) and the "love" (sign) looked less cool. It would need a new coat of paint! The same magnificent views of the Pacific, few tourists and many pelicans, spectacular sunsets, and slightly higher palm trees. The second part had just been rebuilt. I suspect they will construct a new sanitary building. Years before I was able to let my four-legged friends romp there off-leash. When the workers were gone, that worked too! We also had the beach and the waves. My two ladies could play in the water as much as they wanted.

Now, the tide is rising, and the sun showers down its last silver rays on the waves. A light, refreshing wind keeps the mosquitoes away from us. The temperature is still around 30°C in the evening. However, it is relatively sunny.

191

What can you do? One of my books gives in one word, the most appropriate one: hang out! And we'll do that here next week. Hang out and enjoy because there's nothing else to do. In theory, according to the prediction, the weather will stay warm!

Where is this charming and somewhat neglected place? A few selected readers know it. Check **San Blas** in online maps, two hundred kilometers South of **Mazatlán** and go fourteen kilometers south in the coast, until you find the small town of **Aticama!** Arrived! For 180 *pesos* the night on the railing or 160 *pesos* further back in the meadow, with a small week discount. Memory and reality match for once. That rarely happens.

We found it difficult to leave "Delia's" this morning. We were adopted by Bonnie as if we had been family members for years, not just staying for three days. The farewell from the Californians was difficult. Our paths will probably not cross on this route anymore. But we have the internet.

On the bad road, we needed almost an hour to get to the *autopista* with refueling. But then things progressed quickly. The highway was very well developed and led through a beautiful mountain landscape. Here one of my book guides was wrong, describing the surrounding as boring. I did not think so. It went a lot downhill, but also pulled a few stretches uphill, so I had to use my trick with the heating again. Each new bend brought a new picture of the mountains. In addition, we had the blue sky, a beautiful contrast to the lonely and barren environment. We came through volcanic area. The lava rocks laid around every-where from eruptions. In the distant past, it must have been vi-olent and bubbly here in Mexico! I took *Santa María del Oro* out of the program in favor of *Delia* and *Playa Amor*. Doing so we could stay longer at the Pacific. The only major city on our way was **Tepic**, a pure industrial city. The town offered a serviceable two-lane bypass. We did not have to go through the center. Thirty miles and then the turn off to **San Blas.**

The road was as narrow and winding as I remembered. These were traffic lanes on which you could lose side mirrors because the branches hang so far into the street that you have to drive over the middle of the road to avoid scratches. Attention, on-coming traffic! I still had my three expensive side mirrors from the US!

Right! There was the departure point for the mangrove tour! In *Aticama* we saw the many open street restaurants that we once took a stroll through. Then the somewhat neglected invitation: **Playa Amor**! Arrived! After four hours driving time and 315 *pesos* motorway toll! It was two o'clock and I opened our "tent" and we ate outdoors, on the parapet overlooking the ocean! Heart, what do you want more? But yes, my dogs had to get a wet belly first! They really deserved that after their abstinence! … and now I am waiting for the sunset to take some impressive pictures.

March 13ᵗʰ
Hang out???

They all left this morning! *Playa Amor* belonged to me alone! I considered occupying the parking space next to the stairs. Then

193

I wouldn't be far from my hammock under the palm trees, on the opposite side. Thus, I moved for the next half hour! I had time, because in **María del Oro** we changed to a new time zone. Now we were in mountain time and we had a time difference of eight hours with Germany. This hour, therefore, I used for the change. Walking on the beach was not possible since the tide had not gone back yet.

As soon as I was installed under the round arch, a big Mexican family arrived with five cars from *Guadalajara* and made themselves comfortable with a million toddlers around me. The tents were built up noisily, music was played from the car radio, food was prepared for the entire workforce, and so on. At first, I did not feel like gathering my things again and fleeing. But who can fight against at least thirty people, including grandmothers and infants? I pulled back again and entrenched myself in the farthest corner of the square. Not bad, now I stood with my broadside to the water and looked through my side door on the Pacific. With the hammock, I followed the advice of the site operators. Let's see if I could hang it up again on Monday. With the dogs I wanted to search for the nice beach restaurant, which we had visited on the first tour. Because of internal disturbances I had to leave early.

The water of the Pacific was extremely warm and offered barely any refreshment. During the afternoon, the sky became cloudy. Hopefully, no rain! The weather forecast had already predicted short showers a few days ago. Never mind, then I would have no reason to postpone my PC work.

By the way, today I let myself be tempted to a small calculation task: Since my start in Oneonta NY, we drove pretty much 8,250 miles to here. If I did not calculate wrong, these were about 13,200 kilometers. There were about 4,510 kilometers in Mexico. We had about two thousand kilometers to cover in the remaining four weeks until we got to the US border. But we must cross Utah later and go northbound! Now calculate …!

The rest of the day was dedicated to walking, reading and dozing, so it was not exciting. Unfortunately, the pelicans' flight

194

squadrons could not be screened. They were too quick and too far away. We preferred to follow the crabs on the warm rocks!

March 14ᵗʰ
time problems

What time is it? Mountain time – one hour earlier? Mountain time summer – one hour later? Mexican time – one hour earlier? Do we have to change to summertime? I tried to find the owner of the place. He confirmed me (in contrast to the laptop) that it was four o'clock, instead of five o'clock! No summertime in Mexico – not yet! America had switched today, and so did my notebook. Clear? I did not want to be late for my date for dinner! Next to me, a nice couple from British Columbia had arrived. He came from Baden/Germany and she was Canadian. Friendly people, on the way south! So, there was a German-English mix going on around the table. At the age of twenty, Horst hitchhiked across the States to South America, met his wife and got stuck in Canada. An interesting life story. I had the impression that you encountered more interesting people on such journeys than you would expect. You just must dare to contact or accept. We tried to find a small restaurant to eat together. For this reason, "hanging out" was not possible today.

By accident we landed in the restaurant that I knew from my first trip. They have built a new hotel. The business must have boomed. We sat on the terrace, with loud music and had garlic prawns for dinner. Unfortunately, the conversation suffered a bit with the booming bass. The Mexicans were loud.

The next morning, I gave them information about several camping places. In the afternoon I plunged a little into the water at low tide – suspiciously eyed by my two ladies, wondering whether I would come back again or not.

I must take care of my skin. It is slowly starting to react. Tonight, I got some cans of cold beer out of the fridge to calm down the spots that did not respond to my medication. It will probably be the only substitute to anti-itching-pills – say: "Antihistamine"!

For some reason this weekend was longer, and our campsite was over-seeded with big and small tents, happy teenagers and countless barbecues. Let's see how long this extension lasts. I couldn't find any holiday in any of my smart books.

March 15th
A day at home

The cloud cover had spread. My neighbors left late in the morning towards the South. I spent most of the day in the camper. Wuschel had saltwater problems and I had my sun allergy! Or the pustules were a result of the tiny, invisible sting-flies, called *jejenes* – "you do not see us" (freely translated). No idea, anyway, it itched awfully! My cortisone ointments were running low! Therefore, I had been diligently correcting my "Gravel Roads I". I was almost done with the first and second book block. I felt great in my little villa on the Pacific. With the door open, I heard the waves crashing, pelicans flew in formations over me, small fishing boats sailed on the water, almost the whole complex belonged to us alone. Why do I need a real villa on the sea having this? The sunset was red to purple due to the cloudy atmosphere. Presumably, the allergy tablets were to blame for me retiring soon. "Good night! *Hasta mañana!*"

March 16th
Poor like a church mouse!

I was broke! Since I spent almost all my last *pesos* at the dinner yesterday, there were only two hundred left. It could not really be considered a fortune. I decided to take the public bus twenty kilometers to **San Blas**. Here in the countryside you can look for a cash machine or a bank branch in vain. As a precaution, I pocketed a few dollars for direct exchange. You never knew if the machine would really accept the card. No idea how, where and when the bus left. You could just stop the vehicle by flagging it down on the road. Official stops were searched without success, the same happened with *colectivos* and taxis. So, I walked slowly towards *Aticama* this morning, looking around at every sound, to see if the desired vehicle was finally approaching. That was especially pleasant in the sun. There was nothing until **Aticama** (two kilometers). There I saw a gentleman in waiting position in front of a little store. Yes, the bus would stop here. At least it was shady. I stood there for a full hour and photographed the opposite fish restaurants with their offers. I was forced to be patient because the balance of my cash register demanded funds.

Finally, the crunching vehicle came. The ticket was fourteen *pesos*. I could just afford that. **San Blas** has seen better times. A castle still testified that this fishing village was once an important Pacific port for the Spaniards. At that time, the city had 30,000 inhabitants, unlike today. The bus stopped at the *zócalo*, where I would take it again for the way back home. Departure time was at about eleven o'clock. So, I had an hour to find my ATM and buy some fresh vitamins. The first of the existing ATM was broken. The second I found only on the second attempt. I had overlooked it. However, I spotted the "currency exchange" sign. Yikes! It was probably full there! How many Mexicans wanted to exchange *dólares*? I got my money and was able to save the other currency. Now I felt better again!

At noon I was home, dropped off by the driver right at my "front door"! On the way back we made a stopover in another village. There was not a lot left to arrive to the camp and I would have ended up among cows again like in *Tehuantepec*. On the last kilometers of my journey, I did not consciously encounter this poverty. Or did I miss it because I was already used to it?

197

I spent the afternoon on the beach, reading and lounging. The dogs did not want to go into the water. It was probably too sunny for them. They preferred to doze in the shade under the car. My God, how could you spend your daily life with so much sleep? I would like to take them as my role model! The temperature and the air outside were now pleasant (half past eight in the evening), but very damp due to the rising spray of tidal waves. This, together with the light, attracted the little buzzing beasts again. That was why I pulled myself back to my villa for writing.

Now we have two more lazy days, then we continue north. I'm not sure yet how far. In just over a month we must cross the border! Then other adventures will be waiting for us.

March 17ᵗʰ
The expulsion from paradise

After my night's sleep was interrupted several times by itching and new spots on my skin, I decided to pull back from *Playa Amor*. The perpetrators were these small, nearly invisible white flies that attacked my exposed body parts in the dark. Blisters formed where I had been bitten by them and took almost a week to disappear. The only thing left to do was to escape! Our last visit had been at the beginning of December. At that time, the beasts were taking their winter sleep, I guess.

At nine o'clock in the morning everything was packed, and we were ready to leave. A pity, I would have liked to stay two more days here. Well then, we would discover new shores, further north! To get ahead as quickly as possible, I chose the toll road. Sinfully expensive! For nearly a hundred and fifty kilometers I had to pay five hundred *pesos*. The road was only two lanes. But due to the low traffic volume, there was an opportunity for overtaking in an emergency.

198

It went through fertile plains, along the border mountains. The main cultivation was tobacco and millet. The brown-red color of the plant shone in the fields. Later, the arable land was transformed into salt pans, which to me seemed to be very dry and not working. **Escuinapa** was our exit. I wanted to go to the sea, to **Teacapán**. Since it was a tongue of land, like an elongated peninsula, I drove thirty kilometers back and jerked two kilometers on a dirt road to the coast. There I exchanged one paradise for the other, for the same price.

We are located on a spacious beach, have excellent Wi-Fi, a large swimming pool and a few guests. The pool has a pleasantly refreshing temperature and is suitable for swimming. As a precaution, I have the dogs on the leash, but I see many running around freely. Since my little one has her seizures again and again, I prefer to keep her close.

I could not go shopping alone. To do that I would have had to go back to *Escuinapa* because of the one-way streets. We will have enough food for the next few days. In any case, we'll stay until we either run out of dog food, food, drink or toilet paper. There is still plenty of everything on board.

On our evening walk on the beach, in the setting sun, my two ladies kept sniffing around. Knuffi first because she got the smell better. Both were staring into the distance with care. There had to be something. But what? Then I saw it too: not far from me, perhaps fifty yards offshore, a flock of dolphins frolicked in the evening light. We stood for a long time and watched their lively game until they disappeared in the vastness of the water.

March 18ᵗʰ
Five months of gypsy life

True, almost six months ago we landed in New York City. What can you see and experience in five months? What does one see and experience at home? You see, that's why I love traveling! That's why I changed the daily routine for a camper.

I have not finished my journey here on the continent, but there is already a new project in my head. But I'll tell you more about that later! Last night, I slept miserably. I felt guilty with the lawyer problems at home. After three hours of sleep, I tried to talk on Skype, but no one was available. Eight hours time difference was cruel! I fell asleep again and jumped out of bed at half past nine to wake up in the pool. The expected rain took a long time to come; so, we went down to the beach for a long walk. A paradise for my two (and for me)! The water shimmered soft emerald green, contrasting with the white-breaking waves. Nothing like water and a maximum of five persons ashore.

The rest of the day was unspectacular. **Villas Ornac** (a few kilometers north of *Teacapán*) was a small bungalow complex with many good pitches, some right by the seaside. The number of visitors was low and would become even lower in the next few days, as several Canadians and Americans were heading home to reach their homes at Easter. Should be ok for us!

March 19th
"water rats"

The day consisted of a constant switch between swimming pool, beach and RV, in bright sunshine. With some cunning, I found someone to drive me to *Teacapán* for shopping to ensure my survival. Today I renewed for another three days, which meant we would definitely stay over the weekend and on Monday. I was almost out of food. That was it for today! There can't always be so much to tell...

March 20th
Teacapán

Hoping for some restocking and seeing the emptiness in my fridge, before breakfast I grabbed the opportunity to defrost and clean it. This was urgently needed. I couldn't go into the pool, because it was too early and the first morning walk with my ladies was quickly done.

A nice gentleman examined my dripping steering fluid but could not help me. Now I will repair the leak in the States at the next round-check and always fill before driving on almost empty. As far as it lasts beyond the border. I was also told where to get the gear oil in *Teacapán*. At around noon, Jean, a friendly pudgy American, came and drove me with Darlene (painter from Vancouver Island) to the nearby village. In this small village you could not get everything in the same place. You must know where, what, and how to find the most diverse businesses. Fruits and vegetables were there, bread next door, *tortillas* around the corner, meat behind bars, engine oil (three bottles!) next to it, dog food in the pharmacy, lunch in the pub, drinks close (non-alcoholic beer anywhere!). So, it took up a while on the dusty streets until we got everything we wanted. The bakery was worth seeing. Everything was baked in a furnace, on ancient sheets. It was amazing how many delicious sweets could be made from such an oven. We only had to wait for the bread rolls. Good, we would come back later!

There was a short sightseeing tour by car after the pub and a short snack. *Teacapán* was located on a river mouth with hardly any tourists. A homely place that had an attractive *malecón*. The boats bobbed up and down in the water. Some offered a small tour in the mangrove area. Pelicans rocked on or beside fishing boats, to grab something to eat. Life proceeded in comfortable roads. Only a few streets were paved. The dust covered the drought. Behind the entrance arch, at the end of the village, you could see a few pretty villas and bungalows. We visited two other campgrounds but had to confirm that ours was by far the best. It was late in the afternoon when we got back. First, the dogs exercised with a beach walk, then it was my turn with a long visit to the pool. Unfortunately, a cool and strong wind came up; that's why I retired in my four walls despite the sunshine.

201

At some point, Roy (one of the Canadians) arrived, he was dragging something heavy inside a towel. "I have something for you, what you are looking for in vain" and then six cans of alcohol-free beer rolled out of his makeshift carrier. "I do not like it" – he said. Almost like Christmas for me! A little later Jean came over with a can of beans and two sausages! …. "so that you have enough to eat!" My God! Did I look starved? I must add that the Canadians were people from BC and not from Eastern Canada! I'm speaking from experience: that would hardly happen among French Canadians.

My final departure is on Tuesday, because otherwise the route is too long and exhausting. In addition, I must remember the Easter holidays, where all Mexicans want to be by the sea. That means booking a place in advance, so I don't sink in the sea of tents.

March 21st/and 22nd
Lots of departing

Anticipated: We are only three campers of my size on the kilometer-long coast. Why? In the last days gruesome rumors about raids, kidnappings and other acts of violence have been circulating in *Mazatlán* and in the wider area of the campsite. Especially a married couple shared the fear of the rest of people. Following the motto: "Have you heard?", six big RV buses left to the north yesterday and today three big trailers and a couple in a minibus with children did the same. "... they are getting closer!". As if the war front was advancing!

Should I join the general mischief party? How dangerous is it really? I have neither precious nor other valuable goods on board and my RV does not look like wealth! The coming Tuesday was scheduled for departure day. Why be overcome with fear now? I agree with the determination of Jean, and we do not believe in a hasty departure. They will stay as they expect families from the States over Easter. And me? One day more or less will not change my fate. So, I will stay as well. In a caravan

202

group, one is more noticeable than as a lone fighter – my opinion.

Although today the beach and the swimming pool were for us alone, I dedicated myself to cleaning the living room. Whole sand mountains were to be cleaned as usual. I hid my valuables in the most different corners of my motor home (you never know!) and wrote down the hiding places, otherwise I would never find the money again! After all, I had some nice cash on board, because the dollars from the States and my remaining euros were still there! I put my pepper spray at hand and a sharp pair of scissors was within reach of the driver's seat! Honestly! How would the dogs and my "precautions" help me against rifles if it really came to an emergency? Despite everything was I a little affected by the general hysteria?

We will continue watching tomorrow. I'll drive the toll *autopista*. The road is safe because there are no official exits without toll booths (I thought!), and it does not lead through numerous villages. But that is illusory too, because the corrupt police are no help at all. I suspect that the bandits are more active when

Teacapan – Villas Ornac

the Easter holidays start, and a lot of people are on the way. It may also be that they want to wait for the return trip wave of the wealthy Americans and Canadians back from the coasts to their home country for Easter. (The Mex #15 is just the connecting road to the south.) Who knows? My overnight destination is 350 kilometers from here, away from the big route and big cities. In two days, I'll probably settle down in *Las Glorias*, two hundred kilometers away. There I'll spend, if I like it, the Easter holidays. If not, I'll drive to the place with the ineffable name *Huatabampito*, south of *Los Mochis* – in the state of *Sonora*.

I have just come back from a happy hour. Just like I thought! The rumors had been spread by one person who disliked traveling alone. So, the gentleman told stories that happened either a long time ago or were exaggerated incidents that had to do only with the drug mafia. In this way, they fueled the fear among the campers, causing their premature departure. Good, that's their problem! They would have gone home soon anyway. With their fearful prejudices they made the young couple with the two children cancel a two-week stay here in this beautiful location! They felt responsible for the children. So, the gossiper got what he wanted, shame on him!

March 23rd
Made a good choice!

We left at around nine o'clock. As we needed to refuel, I drove the Mex #15 *libre* to *Mazatlán*. It was well-developed and little traveled. We made 140 kilometers in two hours, which was a good average on a country road for Mexican conditions. Far and wide no *desperado*!

In **Mazatlán,** shopping was needed to replenish my supplies for the next few weeks. I'd set up my camp far from any civilization. Thankfully, some major hypermarkets were right next to the bypass. There I couldn't sell my second microwave – no Pelican supermarket!

Two hours highway to **Costa Rica**. No stop at *Celestino*. I was too early for that and tomorrow the saved miles would benefit me. At kilometer 180, I left the *autopista* and went through an agricultural area to the previously mentioned small town. I just had to drive straight ahead, then I came to my desired street, the one I saw yesterday on Google Earth.

At four o'clock we reached our destination: the bathing area **Cascabeles**, on a small shallow lake. The pitches were very pretty, with a small covered *patio* equipped with a table, a bench and a night light! The sanitary facilities were not inviting but I had my own. The area with a pool, a go-cart, boat rental and toboggan was fenced and closed in the evening. Even though I was alone there, nothing could happen to me. Logically, I excluded piracy from the water side, as the lake was too shallow for that. Wuschel ran out a few meters and was wet to the belly at most. We took a long walk to explore the area and had a magnificent sunset over the lake. After a few clean-ups, I could enjoy a full fridge and a stocked-up freezer again. We had enough drinks on board and enough dog food too.

Now my two ladies are waiting for the bones to cool down, they deserve a treat. However, the world is unfair: my two mice crack each bone effortlessly, but I broke a tooth today! Just because! Now I must look for a dentist somewhere, I have not figured out where. Maybe in *Guasave*? I'm staying there longer. Happy Easter! That's forty kilometers from the coast! Then the holidays are still pending. I'll have to take care of that in the next few days! Crap!

March 24th
¾ paradise for twice the price

This morning at six o'clock I was completely awake and well rested. Right! So, we started earlier than usual; we were on the way at a quarter past eight. Mishap in the early morning! When checking my steering wheel fluid, the greasy lid fell into my gear and I could not get it! What a nuisance! Despite sliding and jerking with a pole, the thing was stuck. Would it be dangerous to drive without that lid? I headed for the next Pemex, filled the tank, and asked for help. A young woman was on duty and rolled under the car. No success! A truck driver saw our unsuccessful efforts and got involved. He, too, pushed himself under the car and (indeed, decorated with oil) pulled the darn thing to the surface. He spoke some English and I could at least thank him. Since he liked my Mexican belt very much – the item was lying somewhere in the camper – I gave it to him! Exactly his size! Thus, one hand washed the other – as we say. I was happy about my cover and he was happy about his new strap. So, no *desperado* but helpful Mexican hands!

From **Culiacán** I switched to the *autopista* and at half past eleven I was at the exit for **Guasave.** Narrow streets along to **Las Glorias**. Giant tomato fields everywhere that were being harvested by an army of hand pickers. Sh... work in this heat and constantly in a stooped posture! The workers were dressed like Foreign Legion soldiers in the desert. No wonder they were out all day long. From now on I will enjoy every tomato with a little more respect!

The RV Park **Mr. Moro** is located directly on the kilometer-long beach and has a large pool. Unfortunately, the cars are close to each other, but we have a nice place, almost on the shore. At present, a few Canadian camper groups seem to be my neighbors, because the predominant language is French. When they are gone in the next few days, the three-quarter paradise becomes a complete one. (I'll be glad, as I no longer like to be exposed to this group pressure!) The price is higher in this park than in the others I had stayed at before. I'm paying 1650 *pesos* (275.- *pesos*/night) for six nights (seventh free), a hundred *pesos* a night more than in the last paradise. I'm next to a nice restaurant with a decent menu. I was able to pay my fees in dollars, which left me some *pesos* for extravagances.

Unfortunately, today it is so windy outside that we all prefer to stay in. Maybe the stiff breeze will settle towards evening. My awning will hopefully be able to resist!

Oh, my half tooth! As it causes no pain and it is just annoying, I will save the drive to *Guasave* and delay the treatment a bit. Maybe I'll get used to the little blemish.

We will spend a week here and for the Easter holidays we will disappear to *Álamos* (northeast of *Los Mochis*). According to various reports, the holidays should be a nightmare. Therefore, my escape is scheduled for the day before Holy Thursday (31.03.). I hope it will be quieter in this town, as all Mexicans are on the beach somewhere.

Internet is not reliable here. If I'm lucky it works, but it fails most of the time. The best is still the written message on Skype, unfortunately not the phone, but I don't have as many contacts on that app. Pity!

PS: I have just come back from the *palapa* restaurant, because they are supposed to have the best Wi-Fi signal. That's right, but Yahoo is on strike here on the coast. For an hour I was harassed by mosquitoes before I could send my reports. No chance! I do not like it anymore! I'll be grateful even if a couple of mails are sent!

Forty RVs are leaving tomorrow. As already suspected, two large groups filled the place, but, as I expected too, they all want to be home by Easter! Then the following days will be relaxing. I met the family with their children and the green minibus here again. They drove off and therefore were already here two days

earlier. They were installed two spaces away, so they are at a small distance from my two racks. Knuffi has always barked at the kids if she did not like something. Now everything was fine again!

March 25th
Almost like Robinson Crusoe

At half past eight, I was alone in this place! I felt like a modern Robinson Crusoe. Only the helpful Friday was missing, so I went by myself to the stove and cooked ahead for a few days. Now there were bread dumplings, goulash soup and rice with meat to eat. Do not ask me all that I cooked that morning because I don't remember anymore.

Since yesterday I've been watched by six eyes. The dog of the owner hasn't left our side. Last night, he slept under the RV and accompanied me every step of my way. No, it wasn't my own two "mice" who interested the poor animal. It was me! After all, there were treats for everyone and therefore there were no jealousies. In the afternoon, at four o'clock, several RVs arrived. Whether they came together or not, I could not say. All were Canadians on their way home. Let's see how long they stay! The internet worked for a short time and I was able to "post" a little and answer emails.

Now the connection has already disappeared. That's why I can get on with the planning for the remaining days. It won't be long until I have to cross the border, then pretty much three months of Mexico are behind us. An exhausting, but also unbelievably impressive ride with several highlights and relatively few lows. And there is still so much more to see!

March 26th
Taste of Easter

The weekend is around the corner and the beach will fill up. Although the RV Park is quiet, a lot of young teenagers cavort on the beach. That

208

would be acceptable, but with their whizzed-up cars and beach-combers, they dash up and down the long stretch of coast, turning loops in the damp sand, blowing it everywhere, and indulging in dangerous races. It's not so nice to go for a walk with the dogs with all that going on. So, we spent the day quietly around the camper and the one writing this, jumped into the pool a few times. Will the hustle and bustle slow down on Sunday, or will the holiday rush seamlessly pass into the next week? I can also escape on Tuesday (the day I didn't pay for) and I will only lose one night. I can handle that.

March 27th-29th
Well-guarded!

We have had three more wonderfully lazy beach days. Now it's time to do something again. I'm not the type who can bask in the sun all the time. Despite a fantastic beach and constant sunshine, the time is hanging heavy on my hands. Slowly the feeling is creeping up that I will miss something. Well, I can do a lot with my travelogues series. In addition, I'm intensively studying our next destinations in the States, but for now I want to visit a few other interesting places before finally crossing the US border. Will I be given the chance to visit this beautiful and interesting country again? There is still much to explore.

The last few days I was well guarded. The resident house dog (female) had joined my two other watchers. She followed us to the beach, slept under my motorhome at night and could not stay too far during the day. This morning she even ran after me into the shower, and she accompanied me to the pool. She did not seem hungry, because the dry food was never completely eaten. The goodies, on the other hand were appealing to her! It was interesting to see how the little animal dared to interact more and more. At the beginning she was lying on her back and neither of my ladies could persuade her to play. A walk in the waves was out of the question. Now she scraps with Wuschel for a while and hops with my companions through the rolling waves. The snap on the leash has become her favorite game. No fear! But I have to leave my "foster child" in her own house! God forbid – Three dogs traveling? No, thanks!

You can tell the holiday season is coming. On the beach, the quads frolic and it is advisable to keep my friends on a leash when they come with roaring thunder. Most of them are youngsters with their attractive *chica* on the back. But toddlers are also placed on the handlebars of these fat vehicles. It's a special fun game for my *protégé* to hunt these chatterboxes, and the reaction of my Wuffis is to bark at all of them. I can't fix the "little one". People closed entire areas on the beach to have a little piece of the Pacific Ocean of their own – like claims at Alaska's gold rush times. Some tents have been put up in the hotel area; on the RV-camping I'm alone. In the morning the beach is still almost empty.

Yesterday (Palm Sunday) there was a healer on the grounds who tried to drive evil forces out of the visitors. This was accompanied by drum rhythms and meditative flute music. Next to my *villa*, someone came along with a lot of eggs (raw or cooked?). Oh yes, Easter, I thought! Was it time for an egg hunt? No, no! The eggs were needed to absorb the negative energies from the bodies. The participants stood reverently in a long line waiting for the master and holding flower bunches to be embraced by him. At that point he stroked the egg over their body and then threw the "soiled" egg and flowers in a bucket. The whole ceremony reminded me a lot of *Catemaco* on the East Coast and its miracle healers.

There was every kind of audience, from young couples to parents with children, pregnant women and people my age or far beyond. Here on the west coast, faith also seemed to be able to move mountains. Maybe that kind of treatment would be good for me as well? But if there is no faith...

210

March 31st
Just in time!

Yesterday I totally missed the date of my birthday and forgot it! It does not matter! We were ready to start this morning at eight o'clock. Since I expected at least four hours driving time plus shopping time, I did not want to arrive too late at the destination. When cleaning up, I got into conversation with a worker. He also saw my departure as an escape. This afternoon, the beach and the whole area would fill up. The little *Las Glorias* turned into an inferno overnight. Last year, up to 60,000 (!) visitors were in the region for Easter. The first signs of the mass onslaught were already visible: mobile toilets, scaffolding for public address systems, countless (still empty) food stands, stages for music systems...

He told me that there was little difference between day and night, five nights without sleep and not just the noise of the numerous music bands – add to that the thunder and howl of the pimped quads and trucks. Thank you, no more needs to be said!

Guasave surprised me with two supermarkets, one of which was a generous Walmart. In *Ley* they did not have one can of nonalcoholic beer for me, so I had to go to the second location. I almost cleared the shelf empty. Now I have stock up to the limit! But does that mean I am an addict?

I had to pay about two hundred *pesos* for the section to **Navojoa**. It was four-lanes and the quality of the road was a bit so-so. When switching to the state of *Sonora* we met the fruit control! Crap! All my shopping was clearly visible on the back of the bed. Cunningly, I said nothing about my big dog when the officer wanted to inspect the camper. As expected, he stopped outside and respectfully risked a quick glance: "Any fruit?" "Not really! Only vegetables"! I could shamelessly confirm, and he waved me away in a friendly way.

Anyway, we stopped at two o'clock before *Navojoa* on our detour to **Álamos**. The highway was boring, but now during the last 50 kilometers, the country road went through an interesting mountain landscape. The lane was well developed and went uphill!

We are the only guests at the local camping site. That does not bother me at all, as I can leave my girls alone now and then and go to the city. It's a ten-minute walk from here to the first *plaza*. Tomorrow I'll look at the terrain. Maybe I'll ride my bike for four days. The pitch is ok, although from a higher price range with a price of 250 *pesos* per night. The shower functions perfectly, with nice hot water and strong pressure! We are staying under shady trees and have a concrete forecourt.

I have to say that yesterday's cleaning was "carrying coals to Newcastle". The loamy sandy bottom of the park was gray and crumbly again. Two hours of work for the cat (no recompense) – as we say! Since I had to stow away the shopping today, it was soon five o'clock. In the absence of other goodies, some bones had to be cooked for my ladies. The sun was gone by half past six. Thus, I had no need to go to the city today. We would be here for five nights and the next four days offered ample opportunity for strolling. According to the Internet, the weather will keep and promises a daytime temperature of around 32°C and higher. At night the temperatures will drop (hopefully) to a pleasant 14°C. Here we don't get the refreshing breeze of the coast. Behind these walls it should be quiet. Exception: Knuffi sees a cat! Then the nagging starts in the middle of the night!

Month of April
2700 km

Alamos
Border USA (Lukeville)
Arizona 1300 km
Lukeville to Oatman/Kingman
Arizona 1400 km

 *personal notes*

April 1st
The whole day on my feet

If you went to bed at ten, you were awake at six o'clock. In addition, a uniformed employee was already active, collecting leaves with a rake. Never mind, I had some plans.

I left shortly after eight, armed with a camera and some *pesos*. You never knew! It was still dawn in the town. The market had opened and offered breakfast to the still sleepy Mexicans. I strolled and photographed without end, wandering around. Here a pretty lantern, there a decorative portal, an interesting doorknob, flowers in front of a window, house fronts, cacti and agave, courtyards...The ambiance reminded me a bit of *Tlacotalpan* on the east coast, but there it was more original. In **Álamos**, the influence of wealthy Americans was more evident. Many houses were for sale. Prices seemed to be well above average, as many American pensioners had bought some homes. Now, it looked as if *Álamos* was going to be empty again. The American "occupation" was only seasonally.

I walked around until half past ten. Too bad, I would never make it to the viewpoint by foot. Too steep and too far. Then at the tourist office I was advised to wait for the *Ligo*. That was an exceptional means of transport that went to the *mirador*. I encountered the decorative and special vehicle on the way home, so I used the opportunity. No, I did not want a round trip for a hundred *pesos*, but fifty for the view? That's where we got into a deal!

Guys, that was a jalopy! Blind mirrors, holes plastered with glue, parts smeared with putty and cement, ignited by a short circuit with two cables above the steering wheel, a Mexican tune instead of a horn... it was a treat! Just for the way it was painted it was worth paying fifty *pesos*! Imposing and extraordinary! Nobody would have permission to drive people around like that in Germany.

with "Ligo" uphill to the Mirador!

Ligo delivered me back to the museum with much "honking" to draw attention to itself. I started on the way home. By the way, now I had a bird! A colorful cockatoo was in my camper (over the bed) and will sit at home on the hammock! I bought it in an "artist/craft-grocery" (rather a flea market) together with a very expressive and inexpensive sun mask. There were also rare figurines made of paper-mâché. This time I was able to slow myself down! They were so difficult to pack! In addition, I already owned four pieces from *Tzintzuntzan*! On the way home I wondered about the car caravan which invaded the city. Where would everyone find parking? Now the impression was completely different from this morning.

Tomorrow I'll be on my way when the streets are not so busy, in the morning. At home, work was waiting for me. I wanted to wash my dirty clothes before Easter and wipe down my camper – see yesterday! Knuffi made the cleaning decision easy for me

216

when I noticed a stain on the carpet. Unfortunately, she had not passed the dryness test today. Apparently, the morning meat soup had been too much and the time of my absence too long, consequently her "water heater" had become leaky.

I was done after five machines of laundry. In addition, five dryers! Every half hour I had to go back to the laundry room. At four o'clock all was stowed away, and the bed had fresh sheets and cover.

By now I felt my legs only halfway down. My hundred pictures of *Álamos* were sorted in the box, the travelogue was written, and my dogs and I needed to be fed. I was so tired I postponed the evening stroll for tomorrow before the silent procession would start for Good Friday. It was only ten minutes to the first *plaza*; so, no reason to unbuckle the bike.

April 2nd
Good Friday in Álamos

"Nice" to hear that it is not warm at home. Here, it is about 30°C in the shade under a bright sky at around two o'clock local time. The dogs like it better in the RV than outside! They did not quite get along with this accommodation, because the free space to run was too tiny. Small disposal rounds within the walls, a bit like in a sprawling prison yard. *Guaymas* is not far away and once there they are doing better again. For me, this place has the advantage that Wuschel's intestinal flora regenerates from salt water and the flea powder can be applied. They should not go into the water for two days after this treatment.

As planned, I strolled into the city a bit later today. There were still not many people out at ten o'clock. When will they be active here? Probably at midnight? That's when the music jumps from the *zócalo* over our walls.

I just came across a living procession on Good Friday. There weren't too many believers there, but all those present followed it with fervent devotion. The heavy cross to be carried must

217

have weighed some kilos! Jesus Christ was painted theatrically bloody, so that all his torture could be vividly imagined. The more blood, the more pain, I once read. The Mexicans just love it, in every respect.

At around noon, the visiting caravans began to invade the whole place again. I thought that many day trippers were visiting the backcountry for a picnic, because the nature reserve of *Sierra Álamos* was not far away. A visit to the local museum completed my walk. I could also still buy a few pretty *sarapes* (women's scarves) as a souvenir, because unfortunately I was too thoughtless in *Tzintzuntzan*. They were a little more expensive here, but my only problem was that the selection was a bit more limitated. My Mexico days finally coming to an end and I had to profit from what the country had to offer.

I did not want to stay away for too long, first because I had an evening program and secondly, I had discovered that, surprisingly, the office of the parking lot had just got a free Wi-Fi reception. I wanted to try that. And it worked out great. That's why I could send my last daily reports earlier than planned.

The evening walk to the artists *mercado* just outside the village proved to be a flop. Too much junk! This was the location where the silent procession started at seven o'clock. But wait over an hour? That was too long for me. So, I turned around and went to the *zócalo*. There it was wonderfully comfortable and informal. I wanted to be home before the night fell. I had too much respect for the uneven pavement, the high curbside and the poor lighting. So far, I had brought my bones safely over all walks. At some point, the procession would pass in front of the trailer park, but now I had lost the desire to run to the entrance again and again.

Tomorrow will be a quiet day in my four walls, because nothing happens in Mexico on Holy Saturday. Another stroll in another direction? Let's see what I feel like doing.

April 3rd/4th
Easter weekend

Dead pants in *Álamos*! The bustle had died down the day before yesterday. The guests of the motel were reduced in number. The excursionists had taken off. The heat increased – we reached 32°C yesterday, which restricted your movements. I took care of a few errands in the village and quickly pulled myself back into the shade of my accommodation. Thank god for a little breeze every now and then.

Now I'm looking forward to the sea again. Tomorrow we will continue north. *Guaymas* is two hundred and fifty kilometers from here. That's easy to do, but enough even so after I take down my tents in the morning.

It was quiet tonight! Relaxing after the noise from yesterday! I was bone weary hanging on the ropes all day, even though I had made up for some sleep in the morning. For that reason, I worked diligently on the PC and wrote the introduction for the second volume. My improved project is taking shape little by little. In the backyard colorful flowers bloom. Probably the Mexicans have taken their cheerful and strong colors from nature.

According to the announcement on the church notice board, there should be an Easter service in the main church at twelve o'clock. I wanted to visit it, but there was only a collective Easter baptism of about fifteen children, from babies to two-year-old kids, all neatly dressed in white, with a lot of godparents and godmothers.

I followed the ceremony for a while, but I finally took off. Phew! It was so hot! A small market was taking place on the dry river, not particularly worth mentioning. When the rain-season is at its peak here in the summer, lots of rain is likely to come from the sky and turn into torrents. I calculated it from the height of the river spans and the curbside.

219

In a *tortillería*, I bought a mountain of hot *tortillas* for ten *pesos*, so fresh and hot that I could not eat one on the way, I would have burned my fingers. It smelled wonderful! I spent the afternoon with my ladies in the shade. But soon, Wuschel was at the door again asking to get in. A real mamma's girl! And the little one right behind! I couldn't feel lonely, right? At last the telephone connection worked out again. So, today I spent a lot of time talking about this or that via satellite. But there was not much new going on in Europe.

April 5th
A worthy graduation of Mexico

This morning I was surprised by a message on the Internet: magnitude 7.2 earthquake in northwestern Mexico! Thank god we were not affected. The forces of nature displayed their power in the northern part of *Baja California*. The outbreaks could be registered even in LA and Phoenix. We have slept peacefully. Thank you all for the anxious inquiries over the Internet!

During the drive to **Guaymas** we three had no problems. Only my "marbled" cockatoo (made of plaster) fell from its pole at a *tope* jump and broke its neck. Let's see if I can fix it tonight. He is so cheesy, and I do not know if I will find a similar one in the next markets we visit. That's what happens if you don't pay attention to your animals!

The two hundred and fifty kilometers were boring, and I could dwell a bit on my various thoughts and plans. By three o'clock we had reached our luxury hostel. From our first tour I was familiar with the hotel, with its beautiful facilities. I also chose the accommodation to have a pool again and my dogs an uncomplicated beach.

The main building dates from 1936 and was built as a railway resort. Its style resembles a venerable *hacienda* and its lobby reflects wealth. There are impressive cacti in the grounds, probably older than the building itself. Maybe I'll dare to visit a dentist in *Guaymas*. I have time, but not the corresponding "courage".

First the dogs went swimming, then me! That was a pleasure after the days of abstinence in *Álamos*. I took advantage of the Wi-Fi offer in the lobby and checked the weather for the coming days: the prospects were not bad. The sunset in this bay was a poem like years before, and it is even praised in the Baedeker guide, page 212. That's why I was running fast to catch the last rays!

April 6th
With the courage of a lioness ...

... or the art of finding the right dentist in *Guaymas*.

I started looking for a suitable expert this morning. Under no circumstances would I let them extract my fiend! I wanted to get an opinion first.

For five pesos I took the bus into the center of *Guaymas*. But where, in the eternally long *avenida* could I find the doctor recommended by the hotel, if I did not have a house number, but only the phone number? I asked in a pharmacy. They might know. The nice gentleman did not know, but he phoned for me. He got no answer. But just around the corner there was another *dentista*! I went to the doctor's office. He was "only" a *dentista* of the simpler category, a craftsman. For my case I would need a skilled professional! He gave me an address, at the other end of the city. So, I grabbed a taxi because it was too far to walk.

The doctor's office at the given address did not look quite trustworthy. Pretty grubby from the outside! In Mexico, you should not necessarily make a judgment based on the look of the buildings, though. Often, they are tip-top inside! "A good

221

dentist?" The taxi driver could recommend one. I was curious and trusted him. Nice, clean little house, well-kept gentleman, mask, ordinary practice, some English skills... I decided to give it a try. No chance to replace the broken thing directly. I had thought about that and was not surprised when the doctor offered to make a bridge by the weekend. Now he could only fix it provisionally. Extracting the culprit would not be necessary. I just had to wait a bit. Later I was reassured in the tiny waiting room (three chairs) when I saw the diplomas hanging on the wall proving that he was a trained dental surgeon. Well, at least that was something!

Then he worked on my teeth for a whopping two hours and I felt he knew what he was doing. Hopefully, the result will be satisfactory. Well, my provisional solution was not the finest, but it was ok for the moment, and my broken tooth was covered. Now I must wait for Saturday, until I can afford to smile again.

I got for 450 dollar – about 300 euros – three beautiful new porcelain bits. Incomparably cheaper than the prices in America and Europe! Thus, I have saved some money on my health insurance because I got no receipt! When I thought about our dentists...no wonder that many Americans, especially under or uninsured, indulge in Mexican dental tourism. And the German ADAC health insurance knew why dental treatment was not included in its foreign protection! The doctor's office was modestly furnished, only with the most important instruments, but everything was available for a clean treatment. For me, that was just like waiting for Christmas!

I called the previous taxi driver for the drive home to the hotel. A slap in the ears! Since he could not give me any change (or wanted to, I thought) I agreed to this fare. Of course, I did not get anything back. The price would have been okay for both trips! Well, he should keep it, even if it was a little more expensive! After all, he had brought me to this dentist, so there should also be a commission included!

I spent the afternoon quietly by the pool and with the two dogs on the beach. Recovery from the "stress"! As I still had a numb mouth from the anesthetic, I allowed myself a long siesta. The spots were still reacting a bit to the procedure, but hopefully that would not last the whole day!

April 7ᵗʰ–9ᵗʰ
Waiting for the bit (not Christmas!)

The days here in the hotel were quiet and pleasant. I worked a lot on my corrections, logged out the Internet, went swimming every now and then with the dogs in the bay, otherwise I had my legs up and relaxed.

Once I took a trip to the city to search for a new parrot (!) at the *mercado*. Lucky strike! I found a sales booth with the same objects which were even more kitschy! Now my new bird may swing in the camper until we leave the continent. When the time comes the bird will leave the unrepaired copy behind. Maybe I'll take it with me to Europe safely, like some other things I cannot send by mail.

Of course, I strolled around the harbor and examined the few buildings worth seeing, such as a church and the town hall. When it got too warm for me, I made my way home. On the bus, a young American resident in Mexico told me that the same hustle and bustle took place here during the Easter Week at *Guaymas* and *San Carlos*, as it did everywhere along the coast. The city had an average of 200,000 inhabitants but in this special week it had 700,000. That meant half a million visitors! Inconceivable!

On Wednesday, a medium-sized sea lion got stranded in our bay. Unfortunately, he was dead and polluted the air around him, but the local managers were not in a hurry to remove him. That was work! In the meantime, the animal began to stink more and more (let's see who's faster, the authorities or the vultures).

223

This luxury hotel cannot afford such a stink for long. At least the animal was not dead in the pool.

Karin and Klaus arrived today, and we had a very comfortable evening together with all sorts of new ideas and plans. That made me think again before falling asleep. For the dead sea lion, there was a third (hotel) solution: it was sprinkled with lime and buried with sand. At least there was less of a stench. Hopefully, the tide won't be too high at night, otherwise the lion will be exposed again!

Saturday will be really Christmas for me because I'm looking forward to my new "biter". I have Sunday for testing. If problems really do arise, I can hang on for a day or two.

April 10th
A new smile

Prostheses need some time to get used to, especially if they affect the chewing molars. The gap is closed, and the broken tooth is bridged. But I must get used to speaking with the foreign body in my mouth. From the outside it looks good, much better than before. Well, it will be alright, but Christmas presents usually leave a better impression!

Today I was able to explore the technology and interior of a pickup truck with a friendly neighbor from the state of Washington. I would like to have such a thing! Amazing how much space is available inside. You can leave the "house" somewhere and drive the truck through the area (even through you'll find narrow streets or gravel roads) without the extra "load". I will save this experience for my next life! For the present one, I don't have enough cash in my wallet.

Now there is a dinner together in the "Minnie". I'll stay until Wednesday and then drive straight to *Santa Ana* for the last stopover to avoid the bans on forbidden things in the RV.

224

April 13ᵗʰ
How time flies!

I could not believe that we had already spent nine days in this beautiful place. The past days had been lazy and yet they had evaporated in no time. Karin and Klaus also decided to stay until Wednesday, which provided sufficient entertainment. In order to get rid of all the food that we were not allowed to take over the border, we always conjured up new dinners with imagination and creativity with the existing things. The situation reminded me a little of our gourmet dining on *Baja California* with Chris and Sabine.

My new chewing tool was still causing me problems. I did not know if the permanent headache in the evening came from it, or if the constant wind had settled in my skull. Let's see if we are further away from the sea on our next destination!

There will be an overnight stay in *Santa Ana* and on Thursday I hope to easily cross the border to Arizona. Despite the visa, there was always a certain amount of uncertainty, as the border guards had absolute authority and could reject the entry even without justification. Maybe the officer would not like the nose or the perfume...

Our route then will lead directly to Phoenix to let "Camping-world" carry out the necessary repairs and maintenance work after the five thousand kilometers in Mexico. It is eight hundred kilometers distance from here. Then I will plan further. The Internet is unlikely to be available until then, therefore: So long! I'll see you in the US!

April 14ᵗʰ
... only two remained!

The race began at half past nine. I was on my way at that time, but K&K started later. Up to **Hermosillo,** it was a 140 km long four-lane road through fallow land or through a desert-like landscape. The grass on the roadside was brown and dried out, the earth dusty because of the drought, only some cacti bushes were blooming occasionally and, in the background, the bare edge mountains. Somehow, I got an appetite for a dark green, lush forest again.

On the way to the Pelikan in **Hermosillo,** a truck on the right lane came too close to me. Or did I overlook him when switching? Anyway, now I got the proof that buying my reserve mirrors was legitimate! Totally destroyed my right one! Twisted and faceless! Slowly and carefully I made it to the supermarket without changing lanes. Now I needed screws. I already gained this experience on the *Baja California,* where I lost three mirrors within a few days. But first I wanted to see if I could sell my second microwave, which had been on the front bench with me from ancient times in *Cuernavaca.* It was taken back without any ifs or buts and the cashier gave me cash. That was more than useful because my *pesos* were tight. We still had to pay the toll, refuel twice and then the camping fee. Now I had a little leeway. The repair proved to be more difficult than expected, because the screws on the broken mirror were rusted on the one hand and bent on the other by the impact. One of the brackets had lifted off its hinges. My delicate fingers could not do the job despite having the right tool. I needed someone stronger, so I looked around the parking lot and asked an older *señor* who was assembling the carts. He proved to be extremely helpful and provisionally fixed one of my three reserve levels as well as he could. Now I was not completely blind! The piece was not quite suitable and now I had a bizarre rear view when driving. But better than nothing! For this reason, I will try to get rid of the other "fake" mirrors at Ford, because it was not possible to return it to another Ford dealer – only where I bought them.

The route from *Hermosillo* to *Santa Ana* was just as changeless as before. I made it in less than two hours, because the road was well developed and had four lanes. At the **Benjamin Hill checkpoint**, they waved me generously through, while behind

226

me the trucks stood for miles and before me a caravan was thoroughly checked. One less thing!

The RV Park of **Santa Ana** was right at the town entrance and was ok for an overnight stay. You could not expect much luxury for a hundred and thirty *pesos*. Apart from me, on arrival only a couple from Colorado was there. I could choose my place. A little later I would have been unlucky, because seven French Canadians arrived and filled the small square completely. Now they squat together in cliques, making noise, laughing... and growling. Like at the Oktoberfest!

Once again, a negative example from the province of Quebec! I'm curious whether they behave the same way at home, or if they are different. I would not be surprised, if more and more parks ban this type of people from entering. There are camping grounds that have a "Quebec ban" at the entrance – a crossed out "Q"!

I was lucky with the couple from Colorado. We went together to the village for dinner. The pitch operator took us to a nice and good place. There was meat cooked over charcoal, *tortillas* so big that you could have used them as a tablecloth, with lots of chili and cheese. It tasted wonderful and for almost seventy *pesos* with drinks included we were completely full! A nice ending for my last Mexico night.

Edgar, our host, found a mechanic who bolted my loose mirror back in place and put new screws in the rack. The view was still not one hundred percent, but with these dowels I could safely drive over cobblestones and gravel roads. He demanded only a hundred and fifty pesos for just over an hour's work, which I rounded up to two hundred without thinking. I had my little reserve!

Now let's see how long the folk amusements last next door and, if possible, they will drop off relatively soon, since we got up comparatively early, I slept miserably, and the siesta failed.

April 15th
Through the Sonora Desert

Last night, the Canadian sessions were not as long as feared, and I was able to go to bed at around eleven o'clock. I collected our meager remains of dog food, fruit and cheese and gave it to the groundskeeper. Although it was only half past eight this morning, we were the last in the starting hole. I intended to drive to **Lukeville**, about halfway to **Phoenix**. All the other neighbors wanted to cross the border in *Nogales*. To the car border authority, about thirty kilometers south of the border town of **Sonoyta**, the roads were good. However, we had to endure a few miles of gravel roads, as they intended to expand the continuation of the road. The last part was the old country road.

For us Europeans the route was so flat for miles, that in the morning you could already see who was in the house for lunch – as we say in German. Joking aside, it was a dreary and not very varied ride and it went on for two hundred and sixty miles. Desert and cactus landscape, cactus landscape and desert and vice versa. Only shortly before the border authority did it become a bit more mountainous and more varied for the eye. The landscape began to bloom. Yellow bushes on the ground, some colorful cacti, and the bright red flowers of the ocotillo. It was hot! I think we reached 35°C that afternoon as well.

The clearance of the camper was easy, we went through customs from Mexico easily as well. We just returned all the papers we owned and got our cancel stamp. The transfer process of us three into the States took a lot longer than usual. The border man in the shack wanted to send me back, as I had come here three (!) days before the expiration of my permit. I got silly so he sent me to the immigration office.

There were many ifs and buts until my next six months were approved. The smart officer just wanted to send me back to Germany, then they gave me only three months (by mistake) but

228

finally it was half a year. My argument two years ago was convincing, when the California K... (Officer – see elsewhere!) told me that you could extend an extra visa a second time for half a year. The official here had not heard of it yet and first had to interview his supervisor. Everybody says: "That's the law – that's the law!" But every border official knit his own law or has no idea of the right one. It takes a lot of patience with the bureaucrats and a submissive attitude, otherwise you are right out the window. Ignorance?

With all the discussions, they had completely forgotten to look into the camper or check my things. Thus, I got rid of many things in vain. But you never know! I did not even have to show the dog passes. Finally, I had my white "paper" (in English: residence permit) in the passport. Now we were ok until October of this year. Once you were in the country, no one asked for the document!

The following campsites on the route did not meet my expectations. We couldn't go to the place at the Organ Pipe National Monument because of my stupid fridge needing electricity. In addition, we were well on time. So, we drove through **Gila Bend**, about a hundred kilometers west of Phoenix. That would save us a lot of time tomorrow.

The landscape was so nice I had to jump out of the car and take pictures for my memories. This desert here with the blooming cacti is simply unique. A gift for me, as I intend to spend a few days in the park at the weekend (if the repairs allow it).

I was wiped out in Gila Bend. I could not drive anymore and checked in the local RV park. It was in the middle of the desert, with a nice view to the northern mountains. The location had over a hundred spaces, of which a maximum of a quarter was occupied. Many snowbirds had already moved back north. On the pitch we had a lot of freedom of movement, so even when fully occupied, the neighbors did not step on our toes. The prices were higher than in Mexico. Here I paid twenty-four dollars for the night (about eighteen euros), but with full hook-up (water, electricity and sewage) and free internet access, which worked great.

Lunch, coffee break and dinner happened together at four o'clock. We were eight hours on the road with the various interruptions and drove four hundred kilometers. Hopefully, it will stay clear overnight because a starry sky in the desert is extraordinary.

April 18th
What was the next?

As it was scalding hot, we retired either in the shade or in the ventilated camper. The doggies were dozing, barking at passers-by and I was busy with the plans for the next few days. At night I left my "apartment door" completely wide open (of course, with fly screen in front of it) and flicked flies away only with the broom. Since the gate to the camp site in Mesa/Phoenix was automatically closed in the evening and you could only access the campsite with a numerical code, you are comparatively

230

protected against "raids". Besides, I had my two werewolves in front of the entrance – of course inside, to avoid problems.

This afternoon I turned the air conditioning on for the first time on this trip. That means something! From 36°C inside, I was able to reduce the temperature by 11°C in one hour, so we'd be ok until the cooler evening. However, as soon as I gave the device a little rest the temperature went up again immediately. The next few days promised, according to "online weather", to be more moderate again. Not bad if we have to hang around in a workshop!

April 19th
It can only last hours!

Today I got up at the crack of dawn: half past five to start at seven o'clock. I had an appointment at Ford exceedingly early. In about twenty minutes we arrived easily despite being in the outskirts. The vehicle was delivered and then we waited expectantly for our camper during the next four hours. In the meantime, the employee surprised me with the message that the car urgently needed a new oil pump. I had no choice but to believe him. I must expect to pay around seven-hundred dollars with all the other services (oil change, etc.). Gulp! But it was inevitable, thinking of the route that lies ahead. I cannot complain, because this was the first repair in half a year (not bad after what I had experienced in the last tour and after having been in Mexico with its road conditions). If I thought about the previous trip, I had already had this problem in Alaska. But not everything can be seen in a negative light!

So, we waited patiently until noon. I was bored to death! The pooches were laying comfortably in the visitors' area and did not make a sound the whole time. But they received all the pats and praise possible from the other people waiting. Then a shock at lunchtime! The built-in new pump did not work. They had to remove it and replace it with another one and they wouldn't be done until around four o'clock. More waiting! Great! It's because of the RV's age – after all, my old mill was sixteen years old and matching spare parts in the States are rare. In addition, the mechanic later explained that the installation was a huge problem because there was not enough workspace and he could not use his tools. Much had to be fixed with physical strength and manual skill. What did an official know about pig-breeding – as we say in German? All the technical English expressions did not help either …

Thankfully, I had my notebook with me and could pass the time correcting the old travel reports. Who can read the same book for eight hours?

Now, as I am currently working, the inevitable burger for lunch rumbles in my stomach and the cold coke promotes my digestion. The television is on tirelessly and brings the same news repeatedly about the volcanic eruption in Iceland and the economic impact for the USA due to the decommissioned air traffic. The air conditioning is running and makes waiting easier. Someone plays "Patience" to pass the time. You don't believe how many older and much older people are waiting for their car here. I am not sure if I would drive an RV in this late autumn of life – if only out of consideration for my fellow human beings. I hope for positive message in about two and a half hours. In the meantime, I'm mentally going back two years to the southern states. See you later!

It is half past five! The car is ready and my nerves are on edge too! No wonder if after waiting for nine hours, you're in a bit of an emotional crisis. But I was still under control! What else could the mechanic do? But now the ladies quickly jump into the RV! I cannot praise them enough! They were sitting in various corners and barely spoke up, except for when thirst or guts overwhelmed them. Patient girls! Hopefully, the repair of the fridge will be faster and cheaper!

April 20th
Dreamers

No, not us! My alarm rang for the second time in a row at half past four. I wanted to be on time for the appointment at eight o'clock at *Campingworld*. We made it, despite massive professional traffic on #60. "Sorry Madame, we've moved you to one o'clock in the afternoon!" Sorry? I couldn't believe it. Why did we get appointments if they were not respected? I was more than annoyed and expressed my anger verbally. That's perhaps why I was promised to be serviced earlier than they said! Fingers crossed!

In the waiting time I tried to get rid of the fake Ford exterior mirrors. Heavy plastic bag and two dogs on a leash would have made even an oven sweat! It was a failed attempt and I learned again that "Ford" was not equal to "Ford". I could not buy an article and return it elsewhere, as in Walmart or Mega (see microwave and its journey through half of Mexico!): the branches were independent. There was nothing to be done. That's why I marched back home with my weighty mirrors. I just spied my RV disappear around the corner. They would not…? I saw a mechanic unpacking tools.

We sat in the visitor's room with a lot of hope, but it took them a long time to come back to us. Once I asked how they were doing, and I got the information that my bill had not arrived yet. So again, back to the waiting room to my patient ladies. I made some purchases for the camper and saw that the refrigerator was working properly, the entry level was straight, and the responsible mechanic was under another car. He might have given the bill to the cashier long ago. So, again back to the counter looking a bit furious. They took care of it immediately and found the paper somewhere in the workshop. I could have waited hours if I had not protested. Nah, today I had had enough. I didn't want to waste our time here because of their sloppiness. With a few critical words to the people in charge, I said goodbye and drove three hundred dollars lighter to our port "Maverik".

Under a blazing sun we quickly disappeared under the bushes. I scraped a few more quarters (25-cent coins) and just had enough for a machine wash and dryer. With this heat I urgently needed the blouses and shorts most! The other things could wait. So, I dealt with homework in the afternoon. I got my car polished for forty dollars. Even the roof of my RV was cleaned. I did not want to know what it looked like up there. The windows were shiny again and there was no dirt left in the awning. You did a good job, guys!

April 21st
Arizona - Picacho Peak State Park

We were in no hurry that morning. It was still sunny, but the weather forecast had announced cloud cover and thunderstorm for the next two days. That should not bother us, rather it would cool down the temperature a little. We set off at half past eight in the morning because I was already awake at six o'clock this time. What the hell?

We drove the already known #60 direction **Phoenix** and took exit 179 on the highway (country road) to the south. The country road was good! Phoenix and suburbs spread another twenty kilometers to the south. And the construction activities were never ending. Administration and people conquered the desert in a hurry.

There was a strong wind from the west, whirling sand and dust in the air. You had to drive with the lights on because the visibility almost bordered on fog. After having my annual passport for all National Parks and Monuments, I did not want to miss the nearby ruins of *Casa Grande*. My navigation guided me correctly. To my astonishment, I learned that we were in the

234

National Park Week and the admissions were free. This was probably true as well for the Organ Pipe!

The relics of the *Hohokam* Indians date from the 12th century and further back. They gave their name to the present branch. The dusty place in the vast plain itself seems to have sprung out of nowhere. The "Great House" has probably been used for the purpose of astronomy as well as food storage. The area is not big and can be visited quickly. Not very attractive, but high roofs were probably inevitable to protect the four-store building.

Forty kilometers separated us from the day's destination. From afar, we saw the striking *Picacho* peak out of the plain. To-night, we would sleep at its feet. The mighty saguaro cacti were taking over. These giant plants towered majestically towards the sky and some greeted the visitor with outstretched arms. Happy season! They and their other cacti siblings had just had their seasonal heyday. The campground was surrounded by this unique landscape and even offered electricity for twenty dollars a night. The sanitary facilities were good American standard.

235

The area offered lots of trails through the park, from easy and short to difficult and long. For today we can do without it, except for several smaller walks on the road. The clouds became denser and it was raining lightly. This was good for us after the murderous heat of the last few days. I had to be careful that my ladies did not move too far from the path, because they could easily suffer a treacherous sting.

The most malicious plants were the Teddy Bear Cholla, which grew in groups. Their knobby ramifications reached out like the arms of people who wanted to be caressed. Woe to those who succumbed to this temptation! The devious hard spines of this Opuntia were studded with the finest barbs. Even the softest contact was enough to have them in the skin or in the coat – with no chance to remove them. I even know of a case where they had to be surgically removed. These botanical teddies loved bulky clothes that could be grabbed in passing. Some hikers had already taken off their jeans to free themselves from the caress of these "bears".

While the Teddy Bear Chollas were at least still standing upright, some of their insidious allies were creeping across the desert floor, patiently waiting for careless backpackers or curious dogs, whose trouser legs or fur they could stick to with sharp spikes. Such a thing once pierced the sole of my sneaker! Hard as nails! So, dogs! We stay on the road! It's a deal!

In the evening, the campsite, which also offered a wide view of the valley, filled up. Let's see if we leave tomorrow or go for a longer walk. The weather will decide.

236

April 22ⁿᵈ
Rain in the desert

After an unbelievable sunset last night and fantastic light conditions, I woke up a little traumatized at half past six. Phew! That night my subconscious was active again! But the beautiful morning compensated me for all my nightmares. According to the weather report, we would get massive rain today.

There was no sign of it yet, so I went for a longer walk with my two mice after breakfast. We took the first stroll of the park: it was longer and the road usable (see yesterday!). Afterwards I put both ladies back into the camper and used a little bit less than an hour to take pictures, this time on the trails. The landscape around the *Picacho* Peak was impressive and unique. Unfortunately, the I-10 looked like a flashing tapeworm in the valley and the parallel train with its loud whistle (even at night)

237

bothered me too. This reminded me again of the proximity of civilization in the desert.

Yesterday I decided to make a stopover in Saguaro National Park, west of Tucson. The Gilbert Rey Campground is beautifully nestled in a rich cactus landscape. It is sixty kilometers from here. Let's see how the cactus blossom is getting on there. Consequently, my trip to the Organ Pipe National Monument will be cut slightly. But we have time!

We drove south into a bad weather front. The first rain since my "crossing" of Mexico at the isthmus. When was it? I enjoyed the cooling after the long hot period. I did not mind throwing on a sweater and slipping into long jeans. Even nature was in urgent need of refreshing water. The temperature had fallen rapidly to 10°C and besides a hot cup of tea, my little heater had to work – two days ago it would have been unthinkable! A short time ago I could not walk with the dogs because of the heat and now today because of the rain.

As the morning progressed (just like the internet had said), there was some clearing in sight and the black cloud above us had already disappeared.

The landscape in the **Saguaro National Park** is different from the last one. The mountains are less dominant and less oppressive to the park, the variety of cacti is interspersed together in a narrow space with many more yellow-flowering shrubs. The blooming has not started yet. The buds are only at the beginning of their season. But after the rain, maybe...? On the park we are well protected and guarded by a giant guy in a large parking bay. There is plenty of free space on this large campground and no neighbor bothers the other: there is always

238

a lot of space in between. It is isolated from technical progress between two Indian reservations and the actual national park.

The amusement park "Old Tucson Town" a few kilometers away does not disturb us. This amusement park has a one hundred percent film western backdrop. In television series such as the "High Chaparral" you can see the background of the "Three Sisters" (mountain range).When you have seen it once (or 200 times), you have seen them all!

The weather became more friendly in the afternoon and I immediately went out with the ladies and later on with the camera. However, looking up in the sky, the next squadron of black clouds was not too far off. So, the mild sunbeams helped us speed up our pace!

April 23ʳᵈ
Organ Pipe Cactus NM

During the night it rained like in a well-functioning shower and in the morning the world in the National Park was gray on gray. Not even the Three Sisters could be seen. I drove the #86 through the Indian reservations.

Anyone who thinks of poverty as being only in Mexico should drive along this road. Rich America? Forget about it! The situation of deported indigenous people is still shameful in the US. Far away from the thoroughfare, on dusty, expansive terrain, there are poor dwellings that are in no way inferior to the corrugated iron barracks of many Mexicans. It is also no excuse that Mexico is only a stone's throw away.

The mountain range that accompanied us to the south also belonged to the neighboring country. The road went miles straight through this part of the Sonora desert. A huge plain with lots of shrubbery. Sometimes you saw isolated saguaro cacti; other times, piles of them. They all rose straight up into the sky like standing tombstones, some up to four meters high or more. It looked like the Greeks had forgotten their pillars there.

I could explain why last night and this morning were so cold when I discovered snow on the mountains. In fact, I had plans to drive to **Kitt Peak** to the huge telescopic antennas: didn't get to do that on my first trip. Again, the drive up to the mountain made no sense because the telescopes were wrapped in cloudy cotton.

The farther we moved east, the sunnier it got. The air and visibility were usually clear because it had just rained. The sky with its bizarre cloud formations reminded me a little of home and our national colors. Before the turnoff in **Why** I refueled at an Indian casino (always relatively cheap) and found that "Golden Hasan" also had a RV park on offer, which was not listed in my directories.

Five miles from the Mexican border we found the visitor center of the **Organ Pipe Cactus National Monument** (the official name). Due to the park week, I saved the entry fee (would have been in the pass anyway!) and only had to pay the fee of twelve dollars for the night. I think it was so cheap because there was nowhere to get electricity and no hookup.

240

The location of the park is unique. I love it especially because it is so isolated from any civilization in the desert. Let's see if the last clouds disappear and we get a starry sky. We have a waxing moon. Here, apart from the voice of the wilderness, there is absolute peace and quiet. No whistling of trains (*Picacho* Peak) or the lights of a nearby big city (Tucson).

We were there for lunch. It took me three and a half hours to drive the two hundred and forty kilometers. After lunch and a siesta, I went for a walk with the girls, always careful on the street as the dangerous "teddy bears" were common. I saw some offshoots up to a meter away from the mother plant. Extraordinarily strong hops! Then I walked alone, only accompanied by my camera. I remembered a path that went up the surrounding hill and offered a fantastic view of the countryside and mountains. Searched and found! The walk took about an hour or more, depending on how often I stopped to take pictures. On the hill, with visibility to Lukeville (border crossing), the wind whistled and in the late afternoon it got increasingly cooler. We did not reach twenty degrees today. With a considerable number of pictures, I went down the valley again to my waiting ladies.

If I looked at the opuntia cacti, I marveled that a whole bouquet of yellow roses grows from each of the numerous ears. The flowers of the Saguaro cacti already had thick buds, but they had not bloomed yet. The organ pipe cactus had just started to bud. Its blooming will come next month. It was amazing to walk through this colorful variety of flowers, but always with a look on the floor to avoid falling into the trap of a little "teddy bears".

241

 *personal notes*

*Cactus
blossoms in
the NP*

 *personal notes*

April 24th
Nice neighbors

No cloud in the sky when I opened my eyes at about seven. A cool gorgeous morning on our first walk! The panorama of the surrounding cactus garden was simply perfect! A small woodpecker tapped wildly into one of them. If you looked closely, you could see that many of these saguaro cacti were dwellings for various kinds of flapping wildlife.

Cleaning the apartment in this weather? No way! The few dust balls on the floor could wait! I tried my deployable solar cell for the first time on this trip. It worked and fed my home battery with the necessary twelve volts. I did not need more. I secretly charged the laptop in the campground toilet. There I had the only power source. Just had to watch out if the cleaning staff came by, because that was forbidden according to park rules. During the next hours no one looked at me and my office was ready for action again until tomorrow. In this way I didn't have to use the generator: it made a lot of noise and used a lot of propane.

Überraschung vorprogrammiert ...

My "great" solar panel fascinated the young neighbor from Wisconsin. He was chugging around with an old trailer and truck – he was about half my age. Trailer or neighbor? We got into conversation and he carried a box of informational material about Utah and the national parks there. He had completed his second service in Iraq and was now enjoying leave before joining his boys in his unit in the army again. According to the stories he had reached a certain grade level.

245

The talk was so nice that we also had lunch together. If a thought of cleaning had lurked somewhere, in these moments it disappeared into oblivion.

In the afternoon, friends of Mesa showed up and they left for a long hike. We would meet again for dinner. I used this time to read and for a cozy siesta again. In the meantime, it had become warm and the dogs joined my company in the RV. Later, when I wanted to persuade both ladies to take a short walk, Wuschel went on strike consistently and in every corner, she pulled me back home. Ok, I would not like to walk in the warmth with a winter coat either!

For our joint dinner I cleaned lettuce and then we ate outside. The two students from Mesa were also very friendly and open-minded. They were good sports fans who were also traveling with kayak and bikes. They had a young two-year-old boy with whom my ladies soon became friends. He was now the "hero" in the pack!

Our session lasted until it got dark. Now I have retired to the camper due to the evening cold. Besides, my "homework" was waiting for me. Tomorrow we will pick up everything without haste. There is no hurry because the route is less than three hundred kilometers. I would like to add another day, but for organizational reasons, I need the internet service tomorrow night. That's why I must look for a suitable campsite.

April 25th
A lot of Africa!

A totally unspectacular day! We left at about nine o'clock, rolling the hundred and thirty kilometers to **Gila Bend** and I-8 north, as we had done ten days ago. We sat on the Interstate and then drove a boring hundred and fifty miles through Arizona's barrenness to the west. Not even cacti could grow in this dry country, only low shrubbery, brown grass and lots and lots of dry land. Those who could still bear the situation were the many

American and Canadian migratory birds, but only in well-equipped winter reservations. Most of them had already gone home.

It's quiet in the RV Park. Our night-accommodation is in **Wellton**, 18 miles east of **Yuma**. This resort is in the middle of an agricultural area that offers moderate prices. For 25.- dollars, I have a large swimming pool and free internet access. I need it for technical reasons today and tomorrow. The sanitary conditions are impeccable and clean. Unfortunately, the RV places have not the slightest shade and the white pebbles heat up under the sun like a solar system. When will tires start melting?

In the afternoon we were able to record 37°C outside. My air conditioning worked at full blast. After all, I brought the heat down to 28°C inside, but the constant blow was annoying. At about half past six, I could leave the dogs outdoors for a little while. I tried to refresh myself in the pool twice, but it was warm as bath water. You could stay in the water for hours without cooling off!

Tomorrow, it should be a few degrees hotter again. I must try to get out of bed as early as possible to fill my shopping basket in Yuma. The best way to endure the heat is by driving. It is two and a half miles up to **Buckskin State Park** in Colorado. We should do well until late noon – according to Google Earth, which doesn't have to deal with the heat.

April 26ᵗʰ
Furnace Arizona

This morning the phone rang at half past five! What happened? The time was too unusual! My friend Dee from Davenport just wanted to say hello before leaving for the next three weeks. She was traveling with her little camping car. She had not considered that there were three hours difference. In her state it was now half past eight! I was not angry with the "alarm clock" because the morning sun was already announcing itself with a deep red sky over the distant mountains. Soon it would burn down on us mercilessly.

It was still cool. That's why I was able to get through all the start-up matters without problems. When I went to take a shower at eight o'clock, on the way back I had already started sweating again. That was not a good sign.

The shopping at Walmart was a change of air conditioning indoors for heat outside. I tried to finish quickly so we could get going again. The wind cooled the temperatures a bit despite the fierce sun. We turned on the #95 and went through a ruthless land – we went straight on for miles. The whole area north of **Yuma** was a military training ground in a barren desert landscape. I made a stop to let the dogs poop. Just as we were getting out of the camper van on the side of the road, they were firing guns somewhere in the distance. Therefore, my fearful rabbits quickly forgot their needs and pulled me urgently back into the car. Well, let's move the matter to later! Nothing, nothing, nothing, on 130 kilometers to Quartzsite. But wait! Once a tank crossed my path and somewhere, I also saw a fire truck and an ambulance!

The road was excellent. I could therefore make a good speed, even if it was only two lanes. The traffic was extremely low. I expected to reach State Park at two o'clock. On the way I was a little worried about the fuel gauge. I was in the lower quarter and of course no gas station nearby. Well, I could make it until Quartzsite. Then I must take what comes, regardless of the price.

Quartzsite is the "*Dorado*" of human migrating birds. It is not nice but functional. There are many places in the area where you can stay for little money for a long time, of course, with all the discomfort the desert offers. Currently these spaces are lonely. I came through this area once in November – cruel! The

248

wastewater is drained into the desert and buries "the human disposal" as well. From time to time water quenching trains come and provide the snowbirds with fresh water. In this way, many "Northern Lights" come over during the winter season and they don't have to pay for expensive heating back at home. But this life for five months? I don't know! Of course, there are also a lot of commercial RV parks with better facilities. These are the residents who do not have to count every penny (pardon, cent!).

From **Parker** the route became more interesting. We drove along the California border, through a mountainous landscape. I did not really want to say mountains, because they were more rustic than hills. The deep reddish-brown color made a painterly contrast with the cloudless sky. Occasionally the Colorado river glanced stealthily through.

Buckskin Mountain State Park is worth a visit and I do not regret the detour. The park is wonderfully nestled between the mountains on the Colorado River and belongs to the upper price range of the State Parks with a price of twenty-eight dollars per night – otherwise you don't have any other option! The water is crystal clear and pleasantly fresh. There is, thank God, enough shade. We had plenty of choice and from morning to evening we were protected from the scorching sun under two trees. For now, I paid for three nights. Here we could deal with the heat better. The power supply was optimal, so the air conditioning could work well. Even the dogs could swim in the water at certain locations. That was nice after the dry time!

But nothing is perfect! Unfortunately, the meadows were full of these little prickly ball seeds. I sat patiently with my darlings tonight to take off the beasts. Both ladies had almost taken this "picking" as a caress. With a temperature of 28°C I could now leave the door open at the end of the day and expect some cooling. My fridge was packed again, and I had plenty of drinks too. Except for the heat, we were doing great! God bless the inventor of air conditioning!

April 27th
Ouch!

It was about time! For over six months no finger sprained and no joint twisted! I just wanted to write this into the book of my personal records when I stumbled over our curb last night and got me a blue toe! Good thing I still had my high percentage Diclofenac ointment from Canada on board. This was 10% compared to our maximum 1% ointments. I sat around with a bandage and picked out the biggest shoes. I probably won't be able to check the trail tomorrow, I thought to myself as I had already checked the pictures of the State Park. And that was right! My left little toe had taken on a gorgeous blue purple color overnight. I made it to the shower and made the first slow tour with my ladies. A new hot day was coming. I could not sit here all the time because of the stupid toe!

Thus, I opened the kitchen on board and cooked nine roulades with a pound of minced meat and a pound of beef. This worked quite well because everything was within reach. I just needed to turn around or take no more than two steps. Work and storage room were unfortunately small in my kitchen corner. Therefore, I filled bowls and plates and piled them up. A clumsy rotation and the pile started shaking or sliding dangerously. Meanwhile, however, I had practice catching stuff in flight (faster than that as the dogs were waiting expectantly!). The result from the above-mentioned ingredients were then nine delicious roulades, six stuffed peppers and a huge bowl of goulash soup.

Please do not ask me how, but I always manage to cook two dishes at the same time, I can also divide the few pots and pans, cut all the ingredients and stumble over my dogs. They must be with me with their snout up: something could always fall on the floor, right? Then there is the problem of storage. Did I cook too much, or can I store everything in my small freezer? These

250

are logistical problems, believe me! Everything is packed and stacked as tight as possible. Keep the bags tight, or take the risk that they burst, and have the mess in the refrigerator compartment? Will I be able to separate them later? Is there enough space for my alcohol-free drinks in the fridge in this heat? Many questions must be asked. But by half past two, all were satisfactorily answered, and I could take a siesta with the last dishes drying! Tomorrow I may have to eat two stuffed peppers because I could not squeeze them anywhere.

Until about ten o'clock in the morning, it was possible to keep the apartment doors open. Then the temperatures exceeded the bearable mark and I switched on the air conditioning. Unfortunately, I had to keep the doors and windows shut to get the best effect. It felt like being in a cage of five square meters. Veil clouds had spread and made the heat even more humid.

This will now be the low-pressure area of the next days, which this weekend will touch Flagstaff (our new destination of about 7,000 feet altitude – 2,300 m) with light snowfall (according to the Internet). This is one of the reasons why we spend some time here on the Colorado River. Therefore, I'll dedicate myself tomorrow (inevitably after today's activities) to the overdue house cleaning. Everyone knows how much I love house chores and that is why I keep holding them back!

Although the Colorado River is wonderfully clear, it is not suitable for swimming. Its water from the heights of Utah and Arizona is too cold and as it flows, it does not have enough time to warm up "decently" on the way to this point. However, this does not prevent my ladies from catching sticks for refreshment and then rolling around in spiky grass as if they were in a puddle. So, I am busy again for some time removing all the stinging blades from their fur dress. Because of this it is recommended that dogs are short-haired with a smooth coat in Arizona and South of America!

April 28ᵗʰ
Cool! Cooler! – bearable

Done! My dwelling was clean! In two hours, the RV was spotless. Why did I always hate that so much? It was not that time consuming. I suspected that it was due to my family history and the sterility of my parents' home! There it was extremely clean all the time!

The temperatures were cooler today, which meant that we still had to live with an average temperature of thirty degrees and a bright blue sky. Six degrees less than yesterday made a huge difference, though. The wind from the east was fresher and it cooled down the temperatures. So, you could sit outdoors without problems and read a little.

In the afternoon, despite the thick toe, I managed to walk to the lookout point – but without dogs, because that way I could take my time. From there you had a magnificent view of the State Park, the sparkling Colorado River, the rusty-red mountains and California across the street. Even our RV was easy to spot in the human-empty space.

My pooches were later retrieved with sticks while my twisted toe enjoyed the cool water. That was good, for me and for the dogs! I prepared the next few days and had now hopefully sorted the next routes and stations well. They were not quite compliant with my initial plan, but we had time and we would be able to cut corners elsewhere. I read in many places that mid-May was the right time to travel to Utah. So, I would do it!

April 29th
"The little housekeeping duties...

... are easily done by themselves – says my husband" (famous German ballad). Who will wash my clothes then, please? In the song it sounds nice! But I must find a campsite that has a washer and dryer as soon as possible. It's urgently due, because all my blankets and rugs had pieces of the spiked plants and their remains stuck. The seeds had clung to the surface. You could only remove a fraction of it by hand and the dogs have brought all of them inside with their fur.

I chose a casino with an RV Park near **Bullhead City**. They did not accept me, as Wuschel was too big for the park – only dogs under twenty kilos! Then someone else would get our money! I studied my literature and discovered an RV park (not a resort!) for the same price on the way to **Oatman**. I wanted to go there anyway so I did not care about the casino rejection.

We made a leisurely stopover in **Lake Havasu City** on the reservoir with the same name (Colorado River). After all, as a European I had to walk over the "London Bridge" there. Perhaps England's capital was in dire straits in 1968 when the dignitaries decided to sell this impressive bridge to the State of Arizona for $ 2.5 million. Who knows? In England, the bridge was dismantled stone by stone, transported across the Atlantic, across the United States and rebuilt in Lake Havasu City. That cost another $ 4.5 million and took three years to complete. Expensive fun times! Now Arizona had a true bridge from GB and you could

253

hear the bell tolls of the Big Ben from a small paddle steamer. I marched over it once, back and forth, took my compulsory photos, and when I wanted to take a picture of the bronze statue of the bridge "importers" my batteries went on strike. Ok, I guess I won't, then!

Lake Havasu City was a new city totally focused on water tourism. I did not see too much of it, so I cannot say whether it was nice or not.

Tonight, we are sitting on the edge of the **Mohave Valley** and the so-called **Mohave Desert**. By mistake (exit 1 – detour) I drove along a piece of the historic **Route 66**, which led through a sandy area with little vegetation. If you went off the road you would have to shovel the sand to break free. There were warning signs for sand mounds on the roadside. The temperatures had dropped and there was a strong wind. The weather forecast for the coming days was variable according to the Internet. I could expect temperatures around freezing at night. During the day, the sun would supposedly fulfill its mission. Should I go back to Mexico, then?

April 30ʰ
Mother of the Roads – Route #66

No way, I'm staying here in Arizona for now! We had plenty of time because the day's objective was a stone's throw away. The weather was playful and shifted between slightly cloudy, bright sun and thick piled clouds. Everything was represented. We only had ten miles to **Oatman**. That was right for a morning

254

walk. The way there was a bit boring and went up to the east. That changed abruptly when we reached the **old route #66** and had to cross the ridge. Previously, it was Oatman's turn, the ghost town or the mining village.

Oatman is located at an altitude of nine hundred meters. Of course, as everywhere in America, it is marketed in its past. Somehow, despite all the old wild-west flair it lacked something. This is not due to the wild gray donkeys. Today they are domesticated and eat the carrots out of the hands of tourists. Previously, they were used for underground and outdoor transport. When the gold mines and village were abandoned around 1940, the four-legged laborers were released. From then on, they had to keep themselves alive in the barren mountains. Some time later the village was reactivated and since then they are the tourist attraction in Oatman. Some are a bit aggressive and should not be fed. Because of these "wild" ones they have created a warning sticker with a crossed carrot on the forehead.

From Oatman we continued up the Sitgreaves Pass to an altitude of almost a thousand and two hundred meters. I did not remember the road being so fantastic. We came from the opposite direction with our group several years ago. Today I had time and was able to shoot some pictures, because no daily goal to report about would stress me. I was thrilled with the landscape around me and made numerous stopovers. By chance, I stopped at a rest area because the view of the valley was so overwhelming. There I discovered numerous tomb crosses with personal gifts: here a pair of glasses, there a VW badge, then a spoiled

whiskey bottle and a frayed headband. Somewhere I have read that some people scatter their ashes in the wind here and the simple crosses remind visitors of their existence on earth. This was a wonderful environment for a final resting place. If at the end of my time a little money is left from my many travels, I would be happy to be able to stay in such a nice place – a dream! (… and I mean it!). I would ask for a welded USA map, a dog collar and a toy RV instead of a whiskey bottle as a distinguishing feature! But I don't know if German law would agree to that!

Slowly (using second gear) I drove to the other side of the pass back into the valley. Here the mountain formations were totally different. Some mines still seemed to be in operation as there were mailboxes along the road and small dust roads led into the backcountry. Who else lived voluntarily in this godforsaken but beautiful landscape? We only used Kingman for refueling, picking up dollars and Walmart for a quick lunch break. I had taken much longer than I had intended for these few miles. Well, it was the camera's fault!

Now we were on the slightly wider route #66. I didn't remember it being in such a good condition. We made our way to **Peach Springs** in no time, because I could drive my 100 km/h constantly. We arrived at the Indian reservation of the Havasupai. Many distinct faces met me on the street. Peach Springs was just a small village, but in recent years it had come up with an exclusive hotel and a tourist information office. There I got material for the next days. I planned to head for the simple campground at the **Grand Canyon Caves**, as

256

described in the guidebook, and decide depending on the weather. The campground was available, but simple? It had been powered with electricity since the printing of the book and had a water supply too.

That's why the charge is a whopping thirty-two dollars for the night, without waste. To its credit I must add that the camping is very quiet in the middle of the plain on the way to the Grand Canyon, it gives plenty of exercise opportunities for my dogs and there's a beautiful old yew stock. Even a weak Internet signal is available. The phone is on strike, but I can work with the mail. Big bunnies are loping around the area and most likely I saw a lynx, because the animal was too big for a cat. Both ear tufts were also somewhat recognizable. So, we were surrounded by pure wildlife.

The altitude (just under 1,800 m) is now noticeable. The temperature has dropped to 10°C at 6:30 in the evening and my electric heater must be on. The air is wonderfully clear, and the clouds are starting to warp. Mosquitoes and annoying flies are unlikely to cause problems tonight. I hope the weather will be decent for my next business!

Nostalgic gas station on Route 66

 *personal notes*

Month of May
2800 km

State of Arizona
1250 km
Canyon State Utah
1550 km

 *personal notes*

May 1st
Labor Day – saved a lot of money!

At half past five in the morning I had to get out of the feathers. I had such a calf cramp that I could only relieve it with stretching exercises. As I was waiting for news, I opened my mailbox early in the morning and was called by many people over Skype. Therefore, ninety minutes later, I wasn't thinking about returning to bed anymore. In addition, the sun was shining in a cloudless sky. So, I decided to risk my experiment.

In my sly book I had read that we could take a side trip from #66 to the village of Supai, which was paved all the way for a hundred kilometers. I knew that you could reach the Indian village at the bottom of the canyon by a strenuous walk, by mule transport or by helicopter. I trusted the helicopter. So, I drove a hundred kilometers in beautiful weather and fresh temperatures through a barren, lonely plateau. I did not meet one car. I felt as lonely as on the Dempster Highway in the Yukon. The only difference: the paved road followed high voltage and later normal power lines. An endless view! Hopefully, after two hours – because I kept to the speed limit – I reached the plateau and there I found a footpath that led into the depths. Only a few lonely horses stood around and there were a lot of parked cars. I thought that, because of my vehicle, I would be the only one here!

I had completely overlooked that the 1st of May is also a public holiday in America and thus many had indulged in a long weekend. Helicopters flew into the Canyon only on Fridays, Sundays and Mondays. The lodge down there was certainly fully booked and how could I spend hours on a horse? I couldn't nail my dogs to the rocks overnight! I turned around without success and drove back to the #66 in ninety minutes, regardless of the speed limit. Who sets up a radar trap for two cars per hour? Bad luck, but I saved a lot of money. What to do with the unexpected free day?

I decided to drive to **Williams**. There were some campsites in the National Forest that were in an affordable price range.

On the way I met countless motorcycle freaks and old veterans in lovingly trimmed corvettes. This weekend, they held a "car rally" from Seligman to Kingman in honor of Historic Route #66. Since they all started in Seligman this morning, they all met me. At the caves I was driving at full speed. Good that nobody was following behind me. A lot of vehicles had gathered with their drivers in front of the motel and this was the opportunity to photograph some of these nostalgic companions.

We continued our journey to **Seligman** where we also had our lunch break. I wanted to see what had changed in the last few years. Several old motels seemed to have been abandoned, new souvenir shops added. But the famous "Snowcap" was still there. You really see the collection of curiosities and order a hamburger from the owner. Why? This is be a surprise effect for future travelers! Anyway, the takeaway is worth a stop.

We sat on the I-40: it went up gradually but constantly. We approached the snowline considerably. We could not access the first selected campsite due to flooding of the road. That's why I chose **Kaibab Lake.** The stop had no service, but tomorrow I would empty my tanks.

Dear people! The camping was located at 2,300 m above sea level! The air was getting thinner again when walking! It nestled around a small lake, in the middle of the forest and had a lot of free space around each pitch. That was not important now, because there were only a few visitors! Sure, who would go camping in the cold? Only fearless travelers like us! I pulled out my long underpants and summoned my courage to go with Wuschel and Knuffi for a long walk. Only the water was forbidden for my swimming rats due to the rules – water protection area for the treatment of drinking water.

Tonight, I was on my last legs because the day was so long. That's how I reduced my power consumption a bit. Meanwhile you noticed the days were getting longer and of course, my batteries benefited from this. Therefore: "Have a nice evening"!

262

Snow Cap - Impressionen

 *personal notes*

May 2ⁿᵈ
Gentle flakes...

We had successfully survived the lousy cold night at Kaibab lake: Wuschel on two thick blankets, Knuffi with me in bed and me with a turtleneck sweater, leggings and thick socks. The temperature was 8°C inside and 3°C outside. If these were not extremes in no time...The heating ran at full speed while I was managing the first round armed with both dogs, anorak and headband. It inexplicably went on a long time! I didn't like that!

Thankfully, the heater for the boiler burned without problems (... which was not always the case) so there was first a hot shower to warm up. When I looked out the window, the first snowflakes were falling softly from the sky. During breakfast it snowed more heavily, and the forest soil was slightly sugared. The streets remained free. My old girl had to work hard to start with the altitude and the cold. The RV proved its effort with a huge black cloud after countless times of preheating. After all, my old vehicle managed it by itself and didn't need a chemical remedy (starter spray). Good car!

A quick round in Williams brought nothing because the village was in Sunday slumber when we left. On the I-40 to **Flagstaff** there was not much going on either. We gained some altitude and, in the forest, I discovered a lot of other cleared snow. We left the city on the left and swung south for a short while onto I-17. The clouds broke up.

Therefore, I decided to drive to **Oak Creek Canyon** immediately. On this street (#89 old) there was a lot of leisure traffic and I met more RVs than usual. In a short turn before the hairpin bends, we stopped at a lookout point. Then it went rapidly into the depth with several spectacular curves. We lost altitude surprisingly fast and gained milder temperatures.

The lower part of the canyon was impressive with its bizarre red rocks. There were always lay-bys, where you could stop. The tourist town of **Sedona** was nestled in this outstanding landscape, surrounded by magnificent rock formations. It was a well-maintained new town, probably because it was slightly more prosperous. The buildings were tastefully fitted to the landscape, many with a reddish, ocher color, built in the Adobe style (very common in New Mexico). I really liked it there. I would probably lack the necessary change (money) to live here. We continued downhill on an excellent two-lane road to **Cottonwood**. There we wanted to stay at the "Ranch of the Dead Horse" (State park) for tonight with power supply.

The landscape here in the valley at 1,100 m was not so spectacular, but the temperatures were more moderate, and the place was located on the *Verde* River – ideal for me and my two ladies. I was surprised by the price. Twenty dollars! This was out of all proportion to our last overnight stay for eighteen bucks. I would have even had to pay extra for disposal – but I saved my dollars! A strong wind blew throughout the day and it caused a fast movement of the clouds. Nevertheless, I took a walk that nearly lasted two hours in the afternoon. It was so long because there were many different small and long paths and we had once again missed the right one. Never mind! However, after the march I felt my cracked toe again! I decided to hang on for at least two nights, explore the surroundings for a while, watch the weather and go for walks.

May 3rd
How small is the world?

In a former abandoned gold mine in the middle of Arizona you meet a farrier whose family comes from Bad Tölz (Bavaria/Germany), where I was born and where relatives live. More details later!

266

The night was bitterly cold again. At half past three, I recorded only two degrees outside and eight degrees inside. I quickly started the fan heater and back to bed! The oven had enough to do for the next two hours. With the humming background noise, I could not sleep properly anymore. I crawled out of bed at six, since the dogs were already up. A bright blue sky compensated for the morning coolness. This would be a good day out! I had planned the **Tuzigoot NM** and **Jerome** with its Ghost Town, both not far from here. After breakfast it was too early to start, so I laid down again until nine o'clock, this time without background noise.

The **Tuzigoot National Monument** was a former residence of the *Sinagua* (Spanish: "Without water") Indians, who lived here in the *Verde* Valley between 1000 AD and 1400 AD. For the preservation of the historic site, the structures of the dwellings – only accessible from above by ladders – were reinforced by newer materials. The Indians had used clay, which was heavily weathered. The small museum provided information about their way of life. An unsolved mystery to this day is why they suddenly disappeared without a trace.

The next stop was called **Jerome** and it was on the opposite mountain slope. The place advertised itself effectively as "resurrected" ghost town. It was a not so old abandoned copper mining town that was revived when a mine museum was established and turned into a State Historic Park. The souvenir shops and restored saloons teemed with history-hungry Americans and curve-bike riders. The location of the village with views of the Cottonwood Valley and the distant rocks of the Oak Creek Canyon was unique. Through the snow pits, the two highest mountains of Arizona (which are more than four thousand meters) were easy to spot.

267

A promotional truck got me interested in the gold mining ghost town in the backcountry. I could take the chance if it was only a one-mile detour! I'd take a look! Well, for five dollars admission, I would see enough discarded vehicles and conveyors.

You wouldn't believe what people collect! You could see the old shacks of the miners and their closed mine entrances. There was a working sawmill with a unique operator (an old donkey named *González*), a practicing farrier and lots of junk for photography!

I was drawn back to the blacksmith twice on my tour. There were some original things on his counter. He had converted a horseshoe into a horse's head and wall hook. Fifteen dollars for it. I got it for fourteen because that was the only money left in my pocket! We started talking. He showed me beautiful hand-forged knives and told me that he was selling the objects worldwide. This inconspicuous-looking artist even has his own homepage.

By the way, he told me that his family came from Bad Tölz. I asked twice just in case I hadn't heard correctly! Yes, his ancestors were from there. Great handshake when I confessed to him that the same city would be my place of burial. I got a friendly dinner invitation for tomorrow at his home in Camp *Verde*. Immediately accepted! The place was not far from tomorrow's route and my visits. So, I could get going in the early afternoon and still be at my hosts' place on time after the visits.

Out of love for myself and my dogs, I extended our stay at the *Dead Horse* for another three nights. It was a fantastic State Park. The elevated pitches were very generous and offered a wide view of the valley. Let's see what the thermometer says tonight!

May 4th
Three and a half tank fillings

It was unusually cold again during the night. The morning heated up quickly, so I could use the shower at around ten o'clock. The sanitary facilities had no heating here. Our program started in the afternoon. I wanted to pair a few sightseeing points with the invitation, and as a present I burned several CDs and gave them a little something to spice up. What else would you give as a gift if you wanted to avoid dust collectors?

We walked with pleasure along the stream, splashed around in the lagoons of the park and sniffed the area for two hours. When I started feeling pain in my toe and the sun got hotter, we went back home. It was time for lunch and a little siesta. The latter took longer than we had planned, consequently we only had time for Montezuma Castle on I-17. The building was one of these *Sinagua* Indian residences, like those you could visit in *Mesa Verde*. These dwellings, built into the halls, were inside the rocks like swallows' nests and completely protected from attack. You could access them via ladders. Considering that every drop of water had to be transported up the stream, I bet it was a tedious task!

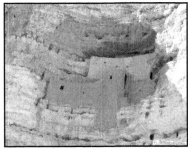

The National Monument closed at five o'clock, so we had another good hour to do something. I was looking for a suitable opportunity for a little walk because we were in an absolutely shadow less and dry environment. We did a bit of a drive through the countryside. Montezuma Well already closed, Montezuma Lake not easily accessible and Montezuma's revenge affected Wuschel. I had enough of Montezuma and headed for **Camp Verde**. At the junction of a side street we

269

discovered an access to the *Verde* River. Finally, I was able to leave my mice in the shadows and by the water. They had to guard the car later because of my host's jealous dog.

I was warmly received by **Ray Rybar** and his wife Heidi. His house was easy to spot, because of the rusty utensils and blacksmith stuff piled up all around the house. The landlord showed me his machines and answered many questions patiently. I had no idea about this craft. He told me that he was at the mine only once or twice a week and that he also works here. I was lucky to come across him!

During the evening, with a good Mexican meal, I was more and more surprised! I sat opposite an unassuming blacksmith who was one of the best in the world. There is an official directory of one hundred and three world's best master blacksmiths and he was one of them! He showed me books that depicted his works. Orders were coming in from all over the world! Fantasy tables masterpieces! Swords with Arabic design, dagger and knife with wrought decoration, Damascus blades...It was an interesting evening and I learned a lot about the manufacture of these items.

At the mine he had offered to sell me a good knife for four hundred dollars. His usual prices were way higher than that and I could understand that after seeing his works. So, now I hardly dared to mention that my limit would be three hundred dollars. He showed me another knife and suggested we meet in the middle. Ok! I thought: That was three and a half tank fillings of Diesel for my RV without considering the price variation of the ones that I had paid and those I would pay in the future. After

all, I had not treated myself with anything for my birthday! I agreed and rummaged through my last dollar cash. I was well worth such a beautiful piece, right? He said that if I met someone in Holland with a similar copy and the same stamp, I should not say for how much I got this!

He also mentioned that he intended to pass his knowledge on to younger people, as he was self-trained. In good conscience, I promised to dedicate him a page in my future book. (Www.rybarknives.com). I think he and his art are worth it.

Soon it was almost half past nine and I had to go home. Road #260 was well developed, and I did not find it difficult to find our State Park at night. I was so excited by the special evening that it took me some time and two beers to get to bed. Tomorrow we will have a quiet day before finally heading for Utah.

May 5th
Bone idle

We got up at seven o'clock. This night was not as cold as the previous nights. After breakfast I got on with my neglected journal entry from yesterday. I was busy with the design until ten. At that time, I got very sleepy. The dogs were taken care of, the temperatures within a tolerable range. So why not lay down again? I slept soundly until noon. Now I could really go to the showers without shivering.

Picked up the book and went out in the shadows to read until I got hungry. Lunch and reading again until about four o'clock. At this time, it still was a good 30°C in the shade, so I had to move with the girls in order to cool down in the stream and river. Walking around for an hour in the heat was enough. My two ladies were dazzling again and my broken toe less painful.

I quickly wrote a short diary entry and prepared the route for tomorrow. That was it already! How was it with God and the lazy day – as we say in German? Somehow, I was tired again! Was it due to the wide range of daily temperatures that the body must cope with? We go from just over 0°C at night to around 30°C at lunchtime.

May 6th
A light breeze

After I had gone to bed early yesterday, I already crawled out of my corner at six o'clock in the morning. The dogs were happy because they needed to get out, even if it was cool. "It's going to be a long day," I thought to myself. "It will not hurt, if we get out early".

We were ready to leave at half past eight. Of course, the early sunrise can make you more enterprising. Arizona had not switched to summertime. On the way I did not find the library to get online but I found a Walmart. I quickly stocked up on my groceries, because from now we would stay in remote places – I thought. I renounced the **Montezuma Well,** the sight was not worth the detour. I wanted to be at the National Forest campsite, which was in the volcanic area of **Sunset Crater**, as early as possible (I saw too many RVs on the way!).

Before that, I headed for the **Walnut Canyon** with its cave dwellings. Within a short period of time and with a tail wind, we went from 1100 m up to Flagstaff (2300 m altitude). The I-17 pulled up nicely and I had to use the heating trick a few times to prevent the car from overheating.

Only a few kilometers east of the mentioned city you find the **Walnut Canyon NM**. In the area of the canyon you can visit impressive relics of the *Sinagua* Indians. A steep stairway with two hundred and forty steps leads to a circular route around a

272

rocky outcrop into the depths of the canyon, which sometimes runs dry. This is due to the dam of *Mary Lake* upstream.

I was tempted to climb into the gorge, I did not want to do the entire 1.6-mile route. I had enough to see. Circular or not, I had to climb up the two hundred and forty steps! So, I balanced my kilos slowly upwards. With the puffing because of the altitude it was a bit more difficult. The dogs had to guard the car. The wind blew right around my ears. This was not a treat for my ladies who hated the wind like poison.

It was twenty kilometers to **Sunset Crater NM**, just behind **Flagstaff**. Shortly before the turnoff, there was a forest fire west of me. Thick clouds of smoke spread in the direction of the National Monument. The visitor center and the campsite were hardly distinguishable. No blue sky came through. I did not like that. Unfortunately – or thankfully – I was told that the camping season would start tomorrow. What should I do? Where could we stay tonight? The possibilities on the way to Page were poor so I inquired at the visitor center. Cameron would be the next option. I would have to drive extra kilometers and instead of the 180 km had planned, I'd have to cover 250 km! I had no choice.

The area around Sunset Crater was unique. You could see rusty-red soil, crumbled jet-black lava, large boulders from an eruption: everything was there. The landscape seemed even more realistic and dramatic because the forest fire could be smelled all over the place. Secretly, I was glad about the closed campground, because this way I could escape a few kilometers away from the fire without a guilty conscience (in these matters I am like my little dog, "a scaredy-cat"). In a similar situation, at Yellowstone West, Wyoming, I took a detour of nearly one hundred miles to avoid having to drive through the forest fire area, although the authorities had no concerns.

Up to **Wupatki NM**, it was thirty-five kilometers north, always slightly downhill. At some point I had a fantastic view of the **Painted Desert**, a color changing plateau depending on the time of day. The view was a bit too hazy for taking pictures, though. The black lava later went over the rusty-red rock, which was the building material for the castle-like dwellings of the *Wupatkis* (around 1100 AD). The first building of this kind, next to which we had our lunch break, reminded me of the location of derelict castles in Scotland. But instead of a lake there was only stone desert all around. The second building, the House of a Hundred Rooms, was imposingly set in a rocky landscape, probably by a stream that had now dried up. The other ruins in the reserve were not spectacular. I was impressively accompanied by a bright blue sky and the snow-capped crests of Humphrey's Peak and its neighbors (12,633 feet), with the cloud of smoke surrounding Flagstaff in the background.

At about four o'clock, when I got to a crossroads that I remembered from earlier days, I discovered a sign for an RV park behind a gas station. It was not overwhelming: it was in the wilderness, but it had all the hookup comforts, for only twenty dollars. It was relatively cheap – I only needed a place to sleep. I had had enough of nature over the last few days. I saw that the park the ranger had recommended, was only two miles away when I went for a walk with the dogs, but I had already paid for this one. What the hell? I was too tired to be annoyed after today. Maybe the other place would be cheaper, but who knows? We were again at about 4,000 feet – an altitude of 1,300 meters. An eternal up and down!

274

The craft shops of the Navajo Indians were not "dangerous" for me this time because I had my precious knife and I also remembered my first visit to the Grand Canyon!

Now in the evening, the strong wind stopped blowing. It had been our companion all day. I had to steer strongly against it, if it came from the side. However, five tons were not easily swept off the road! Since I arrived three new neighbors have come. So, I'm not lonely in the desert!

May 7th
Breathtaking!

I don't know where to start today! The day was so full of impressions I can barely bring them all together. I'll probably continue writing tomorrow. I'm too exhausted now. I just sorted out my pictures a bit and it is already eleven o'clock. I will say goodbye and tomorrow (hopefully with renewed energy) will continue to work on the travelogue. Good night!

May 9th
Time jump

I did not manage to write about May 8th either. I will do that today. I had booked a smooth water rafting tour for the upper head waters of Glen Canyon and Colorado from Page. Unfortunately, the water was so rough that I was told on arrival that the tour had to be canceled. I was put on the list for tomorrow but with the current strong wind, I could vividly imagine that a "Softy Tour" would quickly become a "Wild Tour" and that would be more suitable for the younger generation. There were quite a few companies who paddle down the Colorado in big dinghies. These tours must be booked at least one year in advance and they usually take a week or longer. The price (no idea what that could be) was out of the question for me anyway. Or should I leave my faithful friends with someone this time?

So, with the change of program I'll write the missing travel reports today. If no tour joy tomorrow, I will cancel it with a heavy heart. Well, let's go back again to...

May 7th
Antelope Canyon

Weekend! Many rented motorhomes! A lot of Germans! That did not bode well for a new pitch. I started in **Cameron** at around eight o'clock – absolute record! – and coped with the first hundred and ten kilometers. The road was well developed, and I was getting closer to the rusty-red mountains and rocks of the Colorado River. I drove the #89 north because I wanted to bypass the Grand Canyon this time – or at least try to approach it from the north side. I suspected a slightly higher price for campsites around **Lake Powell** so I decided to go south to **Lee's Ferry Campground** of the US National Recreation Area. With my annual pass I would save on the entrance fees, so I only had to pay the contribution of twelve dollars a night. I had to do without electricity and frills, but the place had toilets, picnic benches, barbecue and lee.

The recreation area is located in a beautiful canyon (the Marble Canyon on the Colorado) on a scenic high plateau. From here, the whitewater rafting boats start going down the river into the Grand Canyon and this is where the "softies" arrive from Page. The journey to **Page** is a bit long-winded – first you must drive thirty-five kilometers to the south and then forty kilometers to the north again, because there is no way to cross the mountains from this broad ravine. But you can cover the distance with an hour's drive on good roads.

276

At around ten o'clock I reserved a place there for two nights with the possibility of extension! We immediately went to **Page**, ignoring the photo opportunities we had on the way. This road was very impressive, right through a massif with wide views of both sides of the pass into the valley! Page or the Marble Canyon were about four thousand feet; the pass, six thousand feet.

Before Page, the road branched off into the Indian reservation of the Navajos. The **Antelope Canyon** was under their protection and economic contract. The Indians offered ninety-minute jeep tours because the canyon was otherwise unreachable. For twenty-five dollars I was one of the many participants of the tour at lunchtime. Allegedly, according to the book, the light conditions around this time were the best. That's what many "Japanese" thought, all equipped with a tripod and a thousand-dollar camera. I had to deal with it, if I wanted to see this particular sight.

The jeep with ten people rattled through the "Sahara" and stopped in front of a cave with a twisted rocky entrance. An older generation Navajo would take a break to meditate before entering the spiritual site. We inexperienced tourists flooded into the dignified cathedral of rocks and light. A devout Navajo must have considered this sacrilege; on the other hand, the unique rock wonder was their only source of income. Our guide regretted this unavoidable situation. In particular, she criticized the recklessness of the Asians. Apparently, she did not like these people at all and hated being pushed and bumped by them to get the right position for the best shot. I had the same impression and even observed a few that behaved like that.

The guide accompanied us through the narrow cliffs and made us aware of special points again and again. Then we could go back alone and look at them ourselves. The lady understood something about photography and put different cameras on the best light conditions, including mine. I have to say, the pictures this time were much better than the first time I had taken them.

277

personal notes

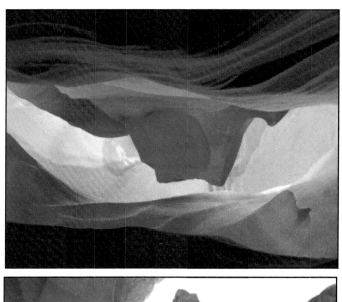

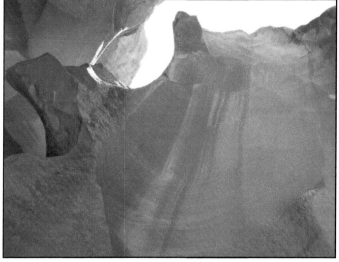

Antelope Canyon bei Page

 *personal notes*

May 8th
Lake Powell

Houseboat on Lake Powell

I forgot to mention that a couple from Regensburg/Bavaria stopped next to me. So of course, last night we chatted endlessly. It was nice to be able to speak my native dialect again after such a long time. For this reason alone, it was impossible for me to write my travelogue.

This morning we saw each other again at some magical rocks in the canyon. Previously, I was grateful when they gave me a lot of stuff and food that they no longer needed because their journey was ending in two days. Although I made many photo stops on the rocks and on the Colorado bridge, I had to be punctual at the resort. I wanted to try and get on the internet there. The chances were good. I also had to take a walk with my ladies, because now they would have to wait for six hours without me.

Nearly fifty people took part in this excursion. I found a good place on the upper deck, all to myself, because everyone else was a couple. I had enough freedom of movement and could capture the landscape in my pictures.

Lake Powell is a flooded canyon (Glen Canyon), from which only the mountain tops can be seen. In some places it can be a maximum of two hundred meters deep. It provides water and energy for the whole area, but has more and more problems getting its water replenished. A water line mark on the rocks shows how much the water has lowered in recent years. If you extrapolate this to the whole area of the lake an unimaginable amount will surely lost. Today it is the water sports area par

Rainbow Bridge

excellence in the States and the second largest man-made lake. Its busy coast-line spans nearly three thousand miles, more than the entire west coast of the United States. They started to fill it in 1963 and the lake reached its peak in 1980. Now the water level is drastically sinking again due to the environmental conditions!

The first two hours to the Rainbow Bridge were the most exciting. Then, when I ran out of enthusiasm, I got tired and I was asleep for almost the entire return trip. However, it was no biggie, because the sky got cloudy and the shots were therefore less dramatic.

May 10ᵗʰ
On the easy tour

No, I did not forget yesterday! But after I came back from Page to our campsite, not much had happened. My tire blocks were gone, and my receipt was no longer where I had fixed it. I wanted to mark the place with the blocks. Maybe someone else needed them? I asked a ranger if he had any idea where they could be. In the trash cans? I did not see anything yellow jutting out. Therefore, I sadly put the items on my "list of lost things". When I was in the middle of writing the last travelogues, a rather stately officer stopped in front of my camper, with my two blocks under his arm. He thought that there was nobody on my pitch because my receipt had disappeared. Great, now I had my tire blocks again.

I spent the whole afternoon writing about the last few days of travel. This time I had to get the necessary power for the notebook out of the generator, because I did not have enough battery.

We could forget about going for a walk today. In the meantime, the wind was blowing harder, which would certainly have turned Knuffi into a UFO – flying object. This light breeze turned into a growing storm by evening and during the night a hurricane swept over us. The camper rocked like a steamer and I didn't get a restful sleep at all. At some point, the gusts calmed down or I fell back to sleep despite the swinging. I didn't have high hopes for the raft trip.

By six o'clock the sky was clean and blue. A beautiful contrast to the rusted mountains. What looked so dark brown was weathered iron, which had deposited in the sandstone many years ago. As a precaution, I called the agency, so I would not have to travel the long distance for nothing. The tour would start at the appointed time today. Thus, I combined the morning with refueling, disposal and internet. It was noon before I knew it, and I had to hurry to be in time at the meeting place. I looked for a shady place for the ladies, took a short walk and then they would have to take care of the camping car for the next hours.

With a charter bus we went to the Glen Canyon dam. From there we drove for two miles through a narrow tunnel into the

depths of the canyon until we got to the water surface of the Colorado river.

The waterway to Lee's Ferry belonged to the actual Glen Canyon. One hundred and fifty kilometers were flooded as Lake

283

Powell constitutes the most exciting water sports area in the US, accessible for cars in very few places. Only thirteen kilometers of the canyon had remained, which we now would sail down at a water level that is calm. The road detour to Lee's Ferry was less than fifty miles. The bee line would be only seven miles.

We were four boats, each with fifteen passengers. I chose to sit at the center of the floating sub-location, because here I was also able to move to take pictures. I would have been stuck on the side wings. It was a leisurely hour on the river, surrounded by seven hundred feet of side rock. The warm afternoon light did the rest to make the canyon look impressive. Shortly before the horseshoe bend, we took a break for lunch. Here you could also admire rock carvings of the Anasazi Indians from the past.

I liked the curious gecko better, it basked in the sun without being disturbed by the folks. We were still on the water for another hour until we reached Lee's Ferry. From here the Grand Canyon began. The ropes with the red ball stretched over the water marked the exact border between the two canyons.

I would have been home earlier, but my RV was in Page with my ladies. So, I climbed wearily into the bus for the return transport and this time I let the driver do his duty. I took a small nap, catching up on last night's missed sleep.

Just after six o'clock we were back at Page. Now I had to go back quickly to the campsite before night fell – that was at about half past eight in the evening. Shortly before the Walmart of the city, I wondered if I should rather sleep there to save money. I thought about my two dogs and their preference for the Colorado. Besides, what should I do here at six o'clock? I preferred the tranquility of Lee's Ferry! We checked in for the night just on time but did not get back to our old place. There was enough selection, though. A walk to the river with my friends and short dinner from the fridge. That was it for today!

May 11ᵗʰ
Inferno

It was windy this morning and a lot of clouds could be seen over the ridge. Never mind, we were leaving anyway!

At **Marble Canyon Lodge** we turned right and drove the #89alt, which is considered to be particularly interesting in my beautiful map.

Shortly after the village we found the rock dwellings (Cliff Dwellers). An enterprising lady who had been stranded in this area due to engine damage had settled here years ago. The imposing surroundings had persuaded her to live in the shade and shelter of the massive boulders. That was around 1930, according to a small board. A photogenic environment!

I saw threatening clouds towards the west disappearing behind various canyons. Of course, I had read that the road to the northern edge of the Grand Canyon was still closed due to seasonal weather reasons. I did not think much of it. Snow in the middle of May? That happens! But remaining snow? I wasn't astonished either when I found on-coming traffic.

Then it started suddenly! After we had passed the Vermillion Cliffs, the snowflakes began to fall gently, but the road was still clear... A few miles further it looked different and the **Kaibab National Forest** was covered in snow. The road was getting whiter and you only saw a narrow lane that the previous car had left behind. No one had told me that I had to climb past Jacob Lake at eight thousand feet (nearly 2,700 m). In second gear and at a maximum of twenty-five kilometers per hour, I drove across the plateau. The windshield wipers began to freeze in the dense snowfall. I hoped that the frozen wasteland would soon come to an end and the road would descend again! But I had to wait a few more kilometers. Thankfully, the other few road users kept the safety distance and were not risky drivers. The snowplow had cleared the other side of the road, but we still had the slippery mess on our side! Jacob Lake was in the middle of winter.

Did I want a hypothetical pitch here? One trailer stood abandoned and snowed in on a large area. Now I could easily imagine why the road was closed to the northern edge of the Grand Canyon! At some point the road went slowly downhill. I tried to avoid using the brakes as much as possible and maneuvered with the engine brake so as not to slide. My God, I was so glad when the road became more grippy again! When we were down to 6,700 feet the haunting was over after about seventy kilometers and in the distance, I got a glimpse of the "promised green land".

286

I was ready for the **Zion NP**. Anticipating its altitude and its campsites without service, I filled my propane supply up to the brim, so at least the generator and the heater could run. I did not quite trust my information and wanted to be on the safe side.

From **Kanab** we came to a new red and white canyon world that went uphill again. But not as high as before! It was around lunchtime, so I wanted to try and find a home on the simpler campsite in the National Park. My entrance gate was the one on the east side with the tunnel. Going through it (twice within a week) was fifteen dollars. This tunnel was so low and narrow that it was totally forbidden for certain RV sizes and the rest of vehicles had to drive in the middle of the road so as not to get in the way. That's why rangers arranged a one-way street system here. The cars were so much smaller when this tunnel had been constructed.

The journey was breathtaking. I would document it when I go back. Today I had to hurry to find a place to stay. The south campsite operated on the basis of the "First Coming" (first come, first serve), Camping "Watchman" had electricity and was reservable, but for me there was no free spot. I had tried on the phone two days ago – I only wanted to stay in a commercial RV park here in an emergency anyway.

We were lucky and found a good location, right next to the river, a nice big pitch with lots of sun – if it was shining.

Now we'll stay here for the next few days and move away only for disposal. There is a free bus service throughout the park to protect nature from the environmental impact of vehicles. A measure that we in Europe should take as well!

We had "lost" an hour when transferring to Utah. That also meant that it would not be dark until half past eight and the day would not start as early. Therefore, there was lunch at three o'clock local time and a one-hour siesta. The need to concentrate while driving had made me tired. Later my dogs could spend an hour with me and drink from the ice-cold river water.

Then I turned my generator on for the permitted two hours. Twice a day, this noise pollution was allowed, and it was enough to survive in a simple camper if you do not install holiday party lighting. The bigger monsters did not get along with it, though. I had not decided how long we would stay yet. That would depend on the weather! I really wanted to see some stuff around here!

May 12ᵗʰ
Zion Canyon – for the first...

The night was cold but not icy: enough to start the heating in the morning. Until I took my dogs out on their walk, it was toasty warm in the "living room" for breakfast. The weather was variable: sometimes we had a blue sky; sometimes, peaceful clouds.

The shuttle buses to Canyon's end departed every few minutes from the visitor center. The bus stop was only a five-minute walk from the campsite. Before I left my dogs for their beauty sleep, I quickly paid for the next three nights. I wanted to hike some paths in peace and visit the museum. In addition, the pooches would be able to run around with me again.

Along the *Virgin River* there was a nice walk for the three of us and we could always go back to the fresh water for a break. Hopefully the weather and my toe would stay ok! Today I wanted to go by bus to the northernmost station and the Riverside Walk.

This simple trail leads one kilometer into the narrowest part of the canyon. From there it goes on, but

Zion NP
Shuttlebus System
„Angels Landing"
in the background

288

it is only convenient to take it when the water is low and wearing good waterproof shoes. Farther back, the walls almost collide.

Today, this route was closed due to flooding, but there were useful hints for branching hiking routes on the way. The enclosing walls bothered me because I had problems when measuring them proportionally; you couldn't really bring them into the picture, impressive though they were. Of course, a lot of people were hiking these easy ways, so I decided to walk down from the top station to the next one. I met only one person, several squirrels and three cyclists. Cars were banned anyway because of the bus system! A part of the path went along the torrent that has formed this mighty canyon since time immemorial. With the slightly crumbly Navajo sandstone, the river had an easy job. Time and again, I saw waterfalls and large moist areas, through which the invading water made its way into the open air. Just at these places they raised so-called hanging gardens because the moisture of the flora allowed its growth.

From the Big Bend stop, I took the bus straight to the last stop. It was already two o'clock in the afternoon, and my stomach was starting to growl. Actually, I wanted to take my siesta outside after lunch (snowstorm yesterday, today picnic under the awning – a crazy world!). But I got into conversation with some German neighbors and there was an interesting exchange of experiences. I had promised the dogs a longer walk, so we strolled around until half past three. I wanted to find out if my friends got a seat on the Watchman campground. We walked around for a while but no "Minnie" far and wide. Tough luck! They could not be found in the rangers' computer either. Unfortunately, we had no internet connection and I could only rely on chance. They would probably not think about calling my cellphone number either.

At six o'clock there was a small rainstorm and I turned on my power machine to load the equipment for tomorrow and write my reports. My mice were already hungry, but I had to use this time to work. No excuses! They certainly did not starve. Besides, they had to get used to the time shift.

personal notes

Zion National Park

 *personal notes*

May 13th
Smoking socks (Zion II)

It's six o'clock in the evening and I'm sitting at the PC to write about today's events with the door wide open and the generator rattling. My dogs had their last swim in the brass monkey cold Virgin River and they are patiently waiting for food. But unfortunately, first I must work! I did not want to do too much today. Go for a walk with the dogs, drive a bus, hike a light path, take it easy. I do not belong to the extreme hikers or mountaineers.

With the ladies I spent a comfortable hour along the river-walk, then I took the bus to the Canyon's limit. I would go again towards the valley end. At the *"Court of the Patriarchs"* I dropped off for the first time for a photo stop. A short steep path led to a small viewing platform with full view of the three biblical patriarchs: Abraham on the left, Isaac in the middle, Jacob on the right, a bit obscured by the Mormon Moroni – all had an approximate height of two thousand one hundred meters. I succeeded in capturing the power of these rock towers in my pictures.

I decided to visit the *Emerald Pools* because of the nice weather. There were three different trails: the lower (the most visited), the middle and the upper. Supposedly the road was made of concrete and could be easily walked. Just right for "older" ladies with an injured toe! It went up a bit and you got a better view over the whole valley. At the beginning I worried a little about how my pump would be affected by the altitude. But when it got used to the demands, it fulfilled its duty. Many, many busloads of Asians came to meet me. At present, Zion NP seemed to be crowded with Germans and Japanese. (I read it gets 2.5 million visitors a year! This must be appalling in late spring and summer! (Worse than Altötting – a more than famous place of pilgrimage in Bavaria!)

293

The first pool was picturesquely situated under a rocky out-crop and was fed by three smaller waterfalls. Presumably, they were more impressive after rainfall. It was enough to create a small oasis in this rocky desert. The way further behind the waterfall was a bit damp, but since I was here, I could at least look at the middle pool. My curiosity drove me on the way up. It started to get steeper and rockier. But with a little caution, I moved on without difficulty, taking a small photo break from time to time.

I was above the second waterfall now, the pools here were rivulets. Next up was the third pond. I gave up because it looked like I would need to do some climbing and I did not have the right footwear for this adventure.

Now I could decide between three return routes: the normal way out (boring), the one to Zion Lodge halfway up (sunny) or the shady way to the grotto, one stop north. I looked at all alternatives from where I was and opted for the last one. At first it was a bit bumpy and rocky down, but then the trail was pleasantly wide, with stunning views. At last I got an idea of the power of these sandstone cliffs (mind you – primeval sand dunes that are two hundred million years old!), the most impressive and highest in the world.

When I got to the bus, I decided to go home. Hunger and thirst were not so overwhelming that I could not survive until I got to the camper. Why spend unnecessary money in an expensive pub (Zion Lodge)? I could serve food on paper plates myself! At three o'clock I put together lunch and dinner, with a delicious mushroom steak and cauliflower – of course outside, with my girls expectantly sitting at my feet.

Siesta, a stroll for my four-legged friends and it was already evening. However, the world is "unfair": since I am not allowed to take my animals on any hiking trails, I am compelled to compensate them before or after. On two legs, I doubled the length of my walk compared to that of my four-legged friends: Wuschel and Knuffi each have four limbs!

May 14ᵗʰ
Let's take a break

We had a quiet day and I was thinking about staying until Sunday. This way, there was a greater chance of finding a campsite elsewhere, as the weekenders would have already left by the time I get to the next campground. For Saturday I did not expect the slightest chance, since I saw both places here absolutely packed!

After our morning walk, I went on an internet service search. There was no possibility for that in the visitor center, but there was one in the local information point at Zion Lodge. I took the bus and enjoyed the deep armchairs in the lobby of the luxury hotel. There were masses of wanderers today, many from abroad and traveling by public transport. A migration to the pools! I was so happy I had done the tour yesterday!

The Internet worked well, calls via Skype could be done and I was able to get cash too. Why drive to Springdale? Why not enjoy the peace and quiet at the campsite? Most guests were on their way. I made myself comfortable, studied maps and leafed through various camping guides for the next few days. From the beginning of the week it was supposed to be sunny again in Bryce National Park, but we would still have to wait for the weather to get warm. That's what happens when you're 2,800 meters above sea level! We could reach freezing point at night and I needed no more snow on the street!

The announced thunderstorm did not come in the evening. A few drops started to fall but there was no sign of thunder and lightning. These walls can endure a great deal of rain!

By the way, today I've bought a wickedly expensive hiking hat, a Canadian one that you can use while swimming, it is washable, supposedly crease resistant, keeps out rain, filters UV rays, it is breathable, holds a storage compartment in the "crown", it is windproof and looks good on my head! If lost within the first two years, it will be replaced by the manufacturer!

May 15th
No stress, please!

The crowds were probably streaming again through the gates of the park in the sunshine today. I didn't feel like mixing with them. Yesterday's forecast predicted thunderstorm took some time to come and the day started with clear air, intense colors and pleasant temperatures. I decided to stay at home. It was shady under the trees, we were not far from the river and we could enjoy the pleasant peace far and wide, because almost everyone was on the move. Why run around and sweat? The remaining trails were too exhausting for me. Here, in the 2,000 m high Watchman campground I had my majestic colored vis-à-vis in the strongest shades from dark red over to pink and then white. In addition, we had the blue contrast of the sky and the lush green of the vegetation and my camping chair in the shade. Simply comfortable!

After the first round of "toilets" I climbed back into bed and slumbered until half past nine! The next three hours I devoted myself to cleaning the sandstone in my camper and bed. Nice and slowly, so it was not too tiring in the thin air. Wuschel was sitting under the bench, and Knuffi watched her surroundings carefully from under the camper van.

Lunch at two o'clock, siesta and study of maps and literature, splashing and plunging in the water, sniffing mouse holes and before we realized it, it was six o'clock. Wuschel has developed a new special drinking technique in the torrent: why work when

 the water flows into her mouth by itself? She opened her mouth and let the water flow through as if she were a pelican. Shut up! There was so much water coming in that it came out again from the sides!

May 16th
Many, many rocks...

Today, as promised, I'll talk about the east side of Zion NP with its serpentine road and the narrow tunnel.

We started conveniently after nine o'clock, probably eagerly watched by a new contender for our cozy pitch. Disposal and fresh water were urgently needed after five nights. I was just too lazy to do it.

From the canyon's lookout tower, we headed up four miles of hairpin bends to the east. There were enough rest areas everywhere, so I could take pictures of the landscape in peace. Otherwise it was advisable to keep an eye on the road as much as possible!

I was so early that I had no waiting time in front of the narrow tunnel passage – a good mile long without illumination and with curves. Three air holes were drilled through the wall, but of course, to stop and peek was prohibited!

At the eastern end we found the trail to the "Overlook". Parking spaces were tight and rare. I had to wait until someone left. So, I stood in front of a car on the opposite side. A dangerous venture! How could I leave without heading back to the tunnel? I was lucky again with my big coach. A car of the same size as mine wanted to leave after five minutes of waiting time. If I managed to squeeze myself backwards into the gap, then I could later move without problems to the other side. There was not much going on, so for a moment I blocked the road when I was maneuvering. Damn tight! But with two corrections I was in my parking space and everyone could pass with no obstructions.

I quickly wiped off the cold sweat and then went up to the "Overlook"! Since many people were on the track, I thought that I'd walk there too! Not even close! The "walk" covers a distance of a mile for the round trip, but it goes up five hundred meters, and you have to climb stone steps and secure rock edges, along steep slopes, under a dry waterfall to get to the viewpoint. The path with its surrounding rock formations was terrific. The viewpoint overwhelming and worth the effort!

You saw the whole formation of the canyon in front of you, including the serpentine road to the tunnel. I did not just gasp because of breathlessness! The way back was easy, even if my osteoarthritis complained in my knees.

Now I had completed my compulsory program and left the Zion NP without the regret of having missed something. The road #9 had a "Scenic Byway" category and it had earned its name. Again and again, I had to stop to admire different rock formations. So many different colors and shapes in one heap! The clear morning sun helped make it even more impressive! At

a turnout, I heard something clatter behind me. Did three mountain goats just jump over the cliffs? They were not bothered by photographing tourists, ate with relish and they still had time to complain about the unnecessary disturbance! A nice sight, as they climb the smooth rock surface so cleverly! Now it was time to say goodbye to this sandstone mountain. We had something else to do!

The #89 continued going up north until we reached the top of the Zion Park. Its base is the Grand Canyon. Its highest peak is the base for the Zion NP and its summit heights are in turn the basis for Bryce Canyon. In other words, our night quarters today were at a height of about 2,400 meters. Cool! I did not want to stay anywhere else! As boring as the road was until the

#12 turnoff (alpine plateau on sandstone), the entrance to **Red Rock Canyon** (a taste of Bryce Canyon) was stunning. Great sandstone formations with a bright rock color!

Because of my early arrival I got a nice spot on the National Forest's campground for fifteen dollars a night. It had been modernized, because now (according to other descriptions) there were showers and acceptable sanitary facilities. However, you had to pay a fee to use the showers. You could use the generator until ten o'clock in the evening and dogs were accepted on the trails! The visitor center of the national park was twenty kilometers away.

Why should I deal with overcrowded campsites when I was comfortable, and I had plenty of space here? I can drive for a few meters! It's no big deal! The weather report for the coming days was not very convincing, according to the information office. We'll see! Tomorrow we will drive the circular route. The day before yesterday they had said there would also be a thunderstorm, and nothing had happened. Today, after a walk with the dogs, I was still on my chair laying lazily in the sun until about six o'clock.

Then there was food for everybody and now my generator is humming again for some time to allow me to work here. There are a variety of trails in this Red Rock Canyon, a bike path along the road and horseback riding possibilities, as well as a track for ATV (rural vehicles). But first you must get used to the altitude.

personal notes

Red Rock Canyon, Utah

 *personal notes*

May 17th
A canyon that is not a canyon!

Bryce Canyon! A big one like the Grand Canyon! 1.7 million visitors a year! That's what we wanted to look at! That had to be interesting! We were already out at nine o'clock in the morning. From our campsite it was not far to the gates of the park. The drive there was not particularly worth mentioning except for two unusual tunnels in the Red Rock Canyon. The name "Canyon", if we considered our last visits to several other canyons, was not correct.

It is the eastern edge of the *Paunsaugunt Plateau*, which rises several hundred meters above the *Tropical Valley* in the east. Between the edge of the boring plateau and the lower ground, there is an area of eroded sandstone that is about forty kilometers long. Over the course of millennia, pebbles, towers and sculptures were created in the rusty-brown rock. It was a land of fantasy – especially in the sunshine! The park administration had set up a shuttle bus system to relieve the traffic in the park, and you could use it whenever you wanted.

I parked my two ladies at the visitor complex "Ruby's" and promised them not too long a wait. I took the bus to the final stop, *Bryce Point* at 8,300 feet/2,667 m – the highest point of the plateau, which can be reached by shuttle bus! It  opened a fabulous panoramic view. No, I did not want to belong to the hop-on-hop-off audience. I wanted to walk! The trail along the edge to the next shuttle stop was two and a half kilometers. That was feasible for my breathing and my legs. I did not dare to go down the steep paths into the depths, although it would have been appealing to be allowed to move among the bizarre sculptures. The road was wide, dry and always going up and down, which slowed my speed enormously. In addition, I had to stop many times to take pictures. Don't judge my never-ending search for spectacular shots. It has one advantage: you look at the landscape much more intensely and attentively than a normal hiker. I needed twice as much time – I didn't want to miss a thing.

At "Inspiration Point" – another viewpoint – I decided to walk the next one and a half kilometers to "Sunset Point". If tomorrow's rain really arrives, at least I cannot blame myself for not having done enough! However, I was glad I could take the community bus back that drove straight to my ladies. A short stop at the park's own supermarket proved to be a failure. We would still have to get what we needed on the way. My mice almost had to spend four hours without me, so they greeted a weary and lame owner joyfully.

Thanks to the generator and yesterday's dinner, I had enough leftovers for my growling stomach and with the help of the microwave, the food was on the table within five minutes. It was my usual lunch time: three o'clock! I was drawn to my shady yew tree at the campsite. The few kilometers downhill were

done quickly and I spent the rest of the afternoon dozing, reading and going for a walk.

In the evening I sorted out over a hundred pictures I had taken today. Too bad that I couldn't keep them all! The selection was extremely difficult, because they were all very good quality.

Bryce Canyon

 *personal notes*

Bryce Canyon –
From one „Overlook" to the next

307

 *personal notes*

May 18th
Thousand-meter drop!

The bad weather front honored us overnight as previously announced. As a precaution, yesterday I had already cleared everything away, so it wouldn't be ruined with the rain. The clouds were broken, and the sun could be seen for a short time. Now it was cold but dry. I would drive the seventeen-mile-long spur road of Bryce Canyon Plateau. There were new viewpoints and before "Ruby's Inn", I quickly went online and my last reports from Zion and Bryce went halfway around the world. Then, I had to hurry up before the clouds changed their minds. I did not feel like getting into a hearty snowstorm again.

At the end of the road we had climbed up 9,115 feet (more than 3,000 m). We had a fantastic view, although not very clear due to the weather conditions. But the changing light conditions helped make the landscape colors extremely intense. At the end of the road, I got into conversation with a nice couple about the dogs. They were from Connecticut and on a break here in Utah.

Now I had visited all the individual stops and viewpoints from top to bottom. The most impressive one for me was the "Natural Bridge". Other deep views in isolated canyons were worth the stop as well. And again and again, I met the previously mentioned couple, each time with a friendly and interesting short conversation. The fourth time I got an invitation for lunch. They knew a good restaurant, not far from the Canyon. Why not? We went there together and had a nice conversation over a sandwich and a burger (good restaurant!). Once again, Wuschel and Knuffi have succeeded in organizing friendly people for me. Of course, also dog owners! I was invited to their place, if my return route would allow it. Let's see how far it takes me to get to the north! Maybe on my return from Canada?

By then it was half past four and a light snow had begun to fall. Fortunately, it was brighter in my direction than back to Zion NP. This was the goal of my new friends today – but by car. For me, it went downhill to the valley, to a height of 5,800 feet. It was milder, the vegetation lush, the villages poor. I was looking forward to the **Kodachrome Basin State Park**. This area was especially praised in my books. From **Cannonville** we left the #12, again in a rugged and mountainous area. I landed on the northern edge of the huge nature reserve of the **Grand Staircase-Escalante NM.**

This area is one of the most recent conservation projects, signed in 1996 by Bill Clinton. This vast landscape is character- ized not by anything in particular, but by a variety of natural wonders between high mountains and desert. The mentioned State Park is in this area. How the things had developed since the printing of my guide, I will find out at their visitor center in Escalante in the next few days.

Now I was standing in front of a full campsite! At least I wanted to look at it so I asked the rangers for permission. "We can still offer you one place today". It was, however, a group place and only accessible via a short gravel road. No problem! We arrived at a sandy pitch for us alone.

Tomorrow I will try to book two or three extra nights on the actual campsite. There are only twenty-two places available and they get booked quickly. According to a ranger I am quite likely to get one. I will be able to take pictures of the erected sand pillars tomorrow. The black clouds on the mountain side have almost disappeared. We all feel better again at this altitude: my water pump no longer rattles loudly, the Wuschelmobil doesn't spit its black diesel clouds when switching gears and I'm adjust- ing a little more easily the altitude. Now my toe would have to calm down – I survive all the hiking every day with only a pill!

May 19th
"Little Monument Valley"

Bright sunshine today: the threatening clouds of yesterday had completely disappeared. My ladies got me out of bed at half past six – mercilessly! Lousy 4°C outside, just 10°C in the apartment!

With these temperatures, the altitude of 5,800 feet cannot be denied, even if the area is classified as semi-desert.

While we were on our morning tour, I switched the heating on full blast. We came back and it was reasonably warm in the living room. Since we had breakfast very early, I laid down again until half past eight. I could not reach the rangers at nine-thirty in the morning that's why I got my doggies ready and made a pilgrimage to the office. Reservations were accepted except for three places (A, B and C) but only for one night. Well, then I would have to try my luck daily. There were only these three places available every day– on a "first come first serve basis". These can be occupied with luck for longer. And luck was on my side this time: one ranger recalled that place B would probably not be occupied today. He drove there quickly to ask. The place had been cleared! For the time being I was able to check in for three nights (I did not have any more dollars!) and could extend if I wanted. Yay! Weekend in sight! They would certainly be in the same situation in other places. Sixteen dollars a night, with shower and clean sanitary facilities...worth considering.

Since we could not move to the pitch right away – the predecessor was still cleaning it up – I did a little photo tour by car and we took a short hike to the natural arch of the park. From the hill we had a nice panoramic view of the area, up to Bryce Canyon. Unfortunately, we missed the well-known *Grosvenor Arch*, eleven miles from here, because the *Cottonwood Road* was a dirt road and only suitable for four-wheel drive vehicles. Never mind, we will see many other formations of this kind.

I think we got the ultimate pitch! The RV stands decoratively under a picturesque rock, the picnic bench is hidden around the corner and there's plenty of space to the nearest neighbor. I feel good and I already see myself getting an "extension" after the weather forecast for the next few days (they say it will be excellent). The power supply could be a bit problematic for so many days, as the generator can only run for a few hours in the afternoon and charging the battery takes some time. It also goes down faster than if it has been charged from a socket for a long time. But as long as we have enough propane and candles, that can be arranged! At some point I must go back to a serviced campground for a short time. But we are still here!

After lunch in the sunshine and a little siesta we walked off the nature trail. It was too warm for my ladies and I turned around quickly. Unbelievable, how the sun heated up during the day. In the summer I assumed the heat in the basin must be unbearable with the white stone reflecting the rays mercilessly. Right now, however, I'm enjoying my shorts. But in the evening long jeans and a sweater are in demand in the shade.

Today I'll try to light a campfire when it is not unbearably cold outside. The sun disappears after eight o'clock and I enjoy these longer evenings hugely and always go to bed later than usual. Days will be longer in the future as we drive towards the north and the summer.

May 20th
A hard desert life

… not only for us! Especially for all the vegetation here in this hot basin. You can see the trees fighting for survival. It's amazing how some plants can thrive in loose sand without even a square centimeter of fertile soil beneath them. Where is water? All creeks seem to have dried up and you can walk in the stream beds and still keep your feet dry. Wuschel and Knuffi search in vain for a small trickle of water. Dusty-dry! At midday we record thirty degrees, whereas at night it cools down to four degrees. It is understandable that these temperature differences can also erode the loose rock. We can only go for a walking treat in the morning or later in the evening. During the day we seek refuge in the shade. From time to time you can feel a little cool wind coming from the mountain edge. How can you hike here during the day? How do the other campers manage? They are exposed to the blazing sun most of the time on these trails. I would sweat myself to death!

312

This afternoon I'm sitting in the living room writing. By the way, the generator is humming, so my laptop and my batteries can recharge. My dogs are with me, because even in the shade it is too hot outside. We are waiting for the evening to come to go on another walk.

This morning we were already out at nine o'clock to hike the flat trail through the minarets and sandstone pipes (as the columns are called here). But any shade was already welcome at this early hour. The "Grand Parade Trail" led us along some rock formations and into two narrow canyons. With its two and a half kilometers, it had the right length for a morning walk. The light was inviting for photos, there was no wind and the sky was deep blue. Since the roads were narrow and I should stop my demons trampling the surrounding nature, we used our "troika" method: the power of my two arms was enormous when their nose got something to sniff, which happened often because lively rabbits dug their holes in the loose sand. We heard the buzzing of petite hummingbirds all around. Their quick wing fluttering produced a low humming noise. Some seashores would be happy with the fine sand quality they have here, produced by the slowly decaying sandstone. The dogs waited patiently when I asked them to stop every moment because a new opportunity kept coming up in front of the camera. Thirsty and tired, at eleven o'clock we returned and immediately disappeared into the shade.

I will make another round this evening (but this time alone) if the weather is cool enough. I want to go uphill. This is too strenuous with my two ladies on a leash. The wind is stronger and now the sky is covered with clouds of fog and this slightly reduces the quality of light. We'll see, otherwise I'll sit down again by the fire and enjoy our hard desert life!

 *personal notes*

Kodachrome Basin / State Park / Utah

 *personal notes*

May 21st
Desert storm

Despite the bright sunshine, we relaxed in our castle during the afternoon. There was an extremely strong wind in the basin that was unpredictably blowing from all directions. I couldn't look for a suitable shelter and it brought along carloads of fine sand. We literally bit on it or felt it while breathing – that's how I imagine the Sahara! My outdoor carpet, although weighted down with large stones, fluttered uncontrollably in the wind. The awning moved so jerkily that I was afraid it would bend or jump out of the brackets. The whole RV rocked with the force of the wind. Since my dogs hated it anyway, they were grateful when they could go into the car.

The day started today with a "heroic act"! I awakened my bike from its slumber. It had been sitting on the rack in the back all throughout Mexico. You can imagine how dirty it was. Although I had many covers, the road dust had come through all kinds of impossible cracks.

I dedicated the morning to my steel horse with cleaning and checking. Except for a broken handbrake and being in need of a coat of paint and some polishing, it had weathered the trip well. There was even enough air in the tires. I could live with the broken handbrake until I found a repair shop.

Why here and now? Because otherwise I would either have to walk all the way to the ranger's station or to dismantle my car and drive tomorrow. I was too lazy for both. I wanted to extend my stay for another two days. Besides, I would have to do that sometimes anyway. Now I can cycle to the office this evening – depending on the wind conditions. Most of the time, the gusts disappear when the evening falls and temperatures drop.

Last night I felt like staying home. That's why I could work diligently on my pictures and reports. When it was getting dark at around half past eight, I lit a fire and enjoyed the starry sky

317

with a cool non-alcoholic beer. Here in the wilderness, the night sky was not disturbed by any artificial light from a village or street. Sitting outside was comfortable until ten o'clock in the evening, as the rocks of the basin were still hot from the heat of the day. Nevertheless, the morning temperature outside was above 5°C and the inside temperature over 8°C this morning. The night cooled down enormously.

Today with the solar cell I tried to charge my battery for my daily needs. It seemed to work because the display was positive. I hoped it would raise the electricity level in general. But in the evening, I was down to half charge, just like without a cell, so back to just generator. Why is that?

With the dogs, I walked to the rangers to pay my extra time for the next two nights. Riding the bike would have been a fight against windmills. We all needed more exercise in the evening sun, even if it was windy. The atmosphere on the rock towers and columns was impressive. Now, in the evening sun, completely new stratification came to light. Sharp and edgy, the structures of the rock came alive. If it isn't stormy tomorrow, we will be able to take out the camera on the evening walk.

As night fell, the wind slowed down, and I enjoyed a campfire. I love this time when night approaches and I can watch the flickering flames: following various thoughts, finding new ways, coming to some solutions, seeing the stars glimmering, watching the moon and its shadow play with nature, feeling just fine, ...

A camping host in our latitudes would be horrified if someone started burning a fire in this drought or in the forest. Here in the States a fire ring is in most cases the basic offer in a State Park. Firewood is usually available for purchase or can be brought along. Unfortunately, in commercial camping places you don't usually get this luxury. Instead they set up an additional space, which increases the price!

In the meantime, it was already ten o'clock. I think I will go inside now. Therefore: good night!

318

May 22nd
Morning walk
Few words, great landscapes!

After a stormy night and flying tents, my neighbors invited me for an excellent breakfast. They parked their extra cars beside me yesterday, so that the park supervision could not grumble. It was a small walking group from Salt Lake City. My girls got some Bagels (delicious at first, but Wuschel spit them later!).

Despite gusty wind and dancing sand clouds, I made my way to "Angel's Palace Trail", a circular route of about two and a half kilometers, with views of the valley and basin. Beautiful! Although it was a weekend, I was almost alone on the slopes. The wind whistled around my ears, and as soon as I opened my mouth a little, I felt the sand inside. I was so happy with my new headgear from the Zion NP! The hat sat with its special wind holder on my head and braved every gust!

I was alone on my hike, as the trail was described as "moderate" and not "easy". In addition, the plateau of the angels rose forty-six meters above the valley ground, sometimes with steep slopes. Therefore, I was happy to know my girls were safe at home. The whole trip took a good hour and I did not force my knees or my stupid toe! By noon I was back in the camper because the sand devils outside were unbearable.

May 23rd
Fred Flintstone and Co

We made it! At night we reached freezing point! At seven o'clock in the morning the thermometer showed 5°C in the camper. The heating switched itself on! That was a sign! Emergency! This time I waited for a little bit before I took my first walk with the dogs, double layer of clothes and headband. My neighbors crawled out of the tent with blue noses and red ears. The women of the Air Force were tough!

319

After breakfast I hid myself in my cuddly corner. Why was I so tired? (Don't tell anyone! I continued sleeping until just after eleven o'clock! Guilty conscience? No, I am retired!).

I did not go for a walk before noon. It did not seem to be hot outside because the cold wind set limits to the heat of the sun. Let's see how far we can walk the "Panorama Trail" today.

First, we met "Fred Flintstone". If you looked closely, you could recognize his figure in the column. The road was wide and flat, not really a problem for dogs on a leash. Wuschel seemed to be in less of an athletic condition than me. She sought every imaginable place in the shadows and laid down making sure I saw it. Knuffi did the same. Her eyes seemed reproachful: "How can you walk around at lunchtime? Only our owner could come up with such a stupid idea!" Alright! I understood and after several pics of Fred Flintstone's companions, I turned around in sympathy. The wind got stronger and Knuffi's ears flapped vigorously with every gust. Close and careful, both ladies trotted behind me, back to the camper. Nooo, they didn't have to lay in the shade! Better to stay in the living room and wait, as it was almost lunchtime!

Now the generator is working until the notebook is recharged. Tomorrow I want to try to get back online. We will drive to Escalante, about seventy kilometers from here, and check in at a private park. Firstly, I need some electricity, secondly a washing machine, then I have to stock up on groceries and apart from that, the weather seems to be getting worse. They have announced snow above six thousand feet. The planned Highway #12 to Capitol Reef NP winds through a pass of nine thousand feet. The next camp opportunity is about one hundred kilometers to Escalante. I must check the weather forecast for the next days. I do not need another blizzard.

320

May 24th /25th
Two nights of luxury – one day of work

The past day was full of impressions, driving and activities. I was exhausted in the evening and just wanted to do some research on the internet.

I have enough time to write the report, because apart from work on the RV and a huge amount of laundry nothing else is going on today. Therefore, a short jump back to yesterday:

The weather forecast at the restroom stop predicted it! I didn't really want to believe it... The heating switched itself on again this morning! Then I looked out the window! Winter was back! Fresh snow! You cannot escape your fate! I wanted to avoid the winter and the cold found me in... Utah! Double layer of clothes, winter socks, headband from Alaska, dogs on a leash and a camera: fully equipped, I started our first tour at seven o'clock. The sun just came up over the ridge. How this little park has changed! It has a fantastic atmosphere and I completely forgot how cold it was.

The splendor did not last long, however, because as soon as the sun was up in the basin, it began to drip everywhere. When we left the campsite at ten o'clock, there was only some remaining snow on the northern slopes. I wanted to go to **Escalante,** seventy kilometers away, to check out the road condition of Hwy #12. The sun came through, the roads were clear, and no precipitation was expected.

I removed the State Park there from my list and drove north. The first section was already promising: between **Cannonville** and **Escalante** there were tremendous washouts and rock formations. This time the sandstone was yellow green. I stopped only for pictures and I passed some beautiful areas. It was just too much of a good thing!

321

Escalante (an almost seven thousand square kilometer area) despite its information center for the Grand Escalante Staircase region is still the cow village Bill Clinton declared a National Monument in 1996. Maybe there's a new corner shop or an extra restaurant. The hopes for a tourist boom walked past the village we're talking about.

The journey through the plateau was boring for a while. Then, suddenly in a curve we could admire a panoramic view! A fabulous world laid out at my feet. I was overwhelmed by the beauty of this spot. A mile-long view of the most absurd rock formations, bright and dark colors, intensified by the clouds in the sky, a daring road through the area: indescribable! The serpentine road down into the "valley" fascinated me. Again and again suitable reasons for stopping and astonishment. There was relatively little traffic, so it was an ideal place for motorcyclists!

I was interested in the campsite at **Calf Creek**. No chance for me to get there. Far too many hikers were on the way and I couldn't find a parking place anywhere. Four kilometers from there, a flat hiking trail led through a fantastic, picturesque canyon to a waterfall. We drove on. The hiking path could be taken in further stops.

From **Boulder** (an inconspicuous village in a fertile plateau) the landscape changed. The vegetation became high alpine: willows and many pines with black beef steaks grazing around them. We continued to climb up through the **Dixie National Forest**: 8000 feet, 8500 feet, 9000 feet, until we finally crossed the pass at 9600 feet (3200 m). My old girl (RV) had to work hard and spat black exhaust fumes (so-called diesel farts) as we were going up!

After the pass summit, a wide viewing point prepared a wonderful view of the **Capitol Reef NP**, which stretched along a red-brown earth crease: the "Water Pocket Fold". The strange name referred to (rain) water-filled erosion, popularly called "water pockets". This road was completed in 1985. In the past, the inhabitants had to accept a two-hundred-mile detour to overcome the sixty kilometers making a bee line between Boulder and Torrey.

From that point on, we quickly descended in several sections with a gradient of between eight and ten percent until we had reached seven thousand feet above sea level again – a total of 2,300 meters of altitude. I wanted to stay in **Torrey** for two nights, because my laundry bags cried out for some cleaning, I needed to do some internet work, my electricity had to be charged longer and the sand dust on my Kodachrome was waiting to be cleaned too. There was plenty to do and I settled in "Wonderland"-Park.

Shopping possibilities? Zero in this nest! So, I picked up all the stuff once more and drove to **Loa,** thirty kilometers away, further west, to stock up at the local supermarket. I hadn't done any shopping since Zion NP and I was quickly running out of food! We were tired and exhausted when we arrived at the RV Park at around seven o'clock. Today there were 225 kilometers between start and finish, which were accompanied by a constant hop-on-hop-off.

Until late in the evening, I was checking the Internet for information about free State Park sites for the upcoming weekend: an almost impossible job. Monday is Memorial Day, a "sacrosanct" holiday, so the weekend will find almost all Americans on tour. This holiday celebrates the beginning of summer. At the moment you can only guess this season. In Torrey the fruit trees are just beginning to bloom. Last night we had reached freezing again and my electric stove was set for continuous operation.

The weather forecast for the next days is excellent, so we will visit the Capitol Reef NP tomorrow, head for the Goblin Valley (got a place for one night), arrive at the Dead Horse Point State Park the day after tomorrow (unfortunately only for one night) and then look for a private camping at Moab for the weekend. I'm considering about whether I should drive the loop to the Natural Bridge NM or continue my way to Salt Lake City. I have time to modify my plans. My gas tank has been filled with (here expensive) propane. So, I am safe for at least two to three weeks in the wilderness, including the food in the fridge and freezer.

May 26th
Knocked out by rocks?

Tonight, poses the question "who's walking on a leash with whom?" I was so tired that I only stumbled after my dogs during the last walk. Have the many rocks of the day killed me? And I'm sitting again on a rocky campsite! All of Utah is a rock orgy for me today! But now, let me tell the story from the beginning.

Torrey was not far from **Capitol Reef National Park** and we could get going at half past nine. Slowly the rocks on #24 were getting closer and closer and became more powerful. They shone in a mix of deep dark red to brown. When we drove through the park entrance, I was disappointed by the scenery. Ok! I had been a little spoiled by the previous parks.

The sixteen-kilometer-long panorama road was narrow and curvy. This time it did not lead along a cliff edge, but rather the foot of the mountain crease. Thank God there were always dodges on the road where you could stop.

324

I discovered a junction. Gravel road! Maximum camper length twenty-seven feet! My camper was twenty-four feet. Let's go on to the "Grand Wash"! Bumpy and dusty, the road went on for about two miles into a canyon, which was cut deep into the dry rocks after rainfall water-bearing. At the trailhead I turned around, because the hikes from here were too long and too exhausting for me.

I wobbled at walking speed back onto the panoramic road and drove it to the asphalted end. Again, we found a gravel road and a height of twenty-seven feet! The curiosity and the thirst for adventure motivated me. My guide said something about a short hike to some "water pockets". The trip was exciting, slow, and even narrower – the mighty rocks came closer. Sometimes I thought I had arrived at the end but there were always new curves.

This time I parked at the trailhead. I wanted to see the ominous "water pockets". Here the guide was wrong! The trail was over a mile long, thus nearly two kilometers (twice as long as indicated) and the path to the water holes went a rocky way upward. Should I dare? Why was I here?

The canyon was brooding hot. The sun burned mercilessly at noon. It was warm between the white rocks. Only now and then you could feel a breeze, which was heated up on its long journey and therefore brought no refreshment. Shall I climb the height to the water pockets in the end? No question! We were only 0.2 miles away according to the board. But what 320 meters! They went over hill and dale, bare rock and high stone steps. Often you could only recognize the path thanks to the rock cairns that are found in the mountains all over the world. However, there were many hikers on the way – the orientation was easy for me. Alone it

would have been uncomfortable, so I let the hikers pass and continued climbing!

Then I stood in front of these puny water holes: one was dried out, in the second there was only some dirty broth, and the third hole in the rock was difficult to recognize, because the sun hindered the view. Have toiled all this way for this? Somewhat frustrated I started on my way back, partly dragging my ass over the rocks so as not to fall because it went steeply down. Whether age-appropriate or not, I didn't care! Without twisting my ankle or any other injury I arrived back at the bottom of the valley, in the stream bed. Today I had reached my limits and seriously thirsty, I trotted the shadowless way back. What a joy when I reached the car at the parking lot and opened my refrigerator. If I had been better informed about the path, I would of course have taken something to drink with me. I lamented a bit to the two ladies, pouring gallons of liquid down my throat, ate some bananas with biscuits and laid on my ear for half an hour. Maybe I was broken!

Soon it was half past three and we still had a hundred and twenty kilometers ahead of us. There were no more stops. The direction back to the road out of the canyon was as follows: the gravel road detour, the "scenic drive" back to the entrance and then, the #24 east to **Hanksville.** Despite all the tiredness I would like to mention that the road across the national park was beautiful, but a little curvy and bumpy. The rock colors changed from yellow to gray and jade green. And again and again you ran into the strangest erosion.

Around Hanksville I came across a moon landscape. The route led me through a strange area: Grey and black sand hills formed the most unusual arrangements. Their appearance probably changed after every downpour. I felt like I was in an area of huge coal mine dumps.

From now on, the #24 be-came flatter and so did its sur-roundings. Only here and there a rock formation defied the smooth landscape. The road to the **Goblin Valley** had been tarred since the printing of the travel guide: the description said there were thirteen kilometers of gravel road. Thank God, that was not the case! It was a nice campsite with only twenty-one

spots, at the foot of strangely eroded stones. Today everything was in the shade when we arrived.

We will be well-rested tomorrow when we discover the little "goblins". We have now landed at an altitude of 1,700 meters above sea level. It is noticeably warmer outside in the evening. Let's see what the heating says tonight! That's it! Now I am done and after adding the pictures to my report I will go as fast as possible to my cozy corner. See you tomorrow!

 *personal notes*

 *personal notes*

May 27th
Goblins and Gnomes

At around seven o'clock I woke up relatively recovered from the night. Relatively? Today I had some problems with breathing. Every activity was exhausting. Afterpains? Probably!

So, I took it easy and at ten o'clock we headed for the valley of the goblins (Goblin Valley). Last night we slept under the watchful eyes of these guys, but the center of the picturesque valley was a little further away. The campsite was beautifully situated on a slope of eroded rocks. The Goblin Valley got its name from the funny "goblins": strange stone sculptures created by erosion. You don't have to follow a fixed path in the valley, but you can walk between the elves. From the viewing point they looked quite reasonable, but when you went closer, they were an impressive size.

We strolled around this "museum" for a while and I tried to let my imagination work: there was a face with a medieval cap, here a chicken, a group of three friends, a proud noble lady with a headdress... The only disadvantage of the tour? It was hot! Short trousers would have been ideal and more shady places perfect for Wuschel. These temperature differences made me sick. This morning we had a pleasant temperature of 17°C when we woke up, but at that moment we were approaching the thirty degrees Celsius again!

At half past eleven I had taken enough pictures and we headed off for the next place to stay overnight – **Dead Horse Point State Park**, in the immediate (relative!) vicinity of Arches NP, about one hundred and eighty kilometers away.

We drove on #24 and turned north. The route led again through an inhospitable plain and later we passed yellowish sandstone *mesas* (table mountains). Where did the inhabitants of Utah live? I have never seen so many desolate and desert-like lands on one trip as here in this state – except in the Yukon.

There were no major towns in the area, just petrol stations, little villages, occasionally a house, that was it! Where did these people shop? Where were the nearest social services? What did they live from? Were there any jobs here at all? What prospects did the youth have? School education? Civilization was often miles away. The parks were beautiful, but to live here? Only nature could not fill one's stomach! These thoughts went through my mind, and before I knew it, I ended up on the I-70. How long had it been since I last drove a motorway? The last time was in the area around Phoenix. I enjoyed the next fifty kilometers going east, until it went off on the #191 to **Moab.**

The turn-off to **Dead Horse Point State Park** was twenty kilometers from Moab. Road #131 led west onto a huge rocky plateau with views of snow-covered peaks. I didn't think it would be that far to my final destination from here – thirty-five kilometers to the campsite! Slowly I was worried about the fuel gauge! Should have refilled before! Hopefully I'd have enough fuel going downhill to Moab. We will face the problem tomorrow. Today I enjoyed the magnificent view of the valley basin, which is two thousand feet above the ground from the visitor center. There was another point that was even more beautiful. I would check it out tomorrow at dawn.

Today I needed my rest, I was still not quite fit and needed my siesta. After all it was already half past three in the afternoon, when I shut off the engine on my parking lot. Short snack and an extensive mattress listening session, as we say in German! My God, it was hot here on the plateau! I could not use the air conditioning, because the power supply was too weak, so I opened all windows. Of course, that brought back the fine dust to my apartment. The day before yesterday, I had painstakingly removed it!

Two miles walk to the famous viewing point! In this heat? No, thanks! We will start very early tomorrow, and I can admire the valley from above in the morning light when it's cooler! Now it is nine o'clock in the evening and the sun is still shining mercilessly. It takes a lot of time to disappear, the horizon is miles away and there is nothing it could hide behind. My ladies will have to wait a little bit longer for their walk. I cannot extend the awning, because from time to time we are surprised by violent gusts of wind, which could lift the poles out of their hinges.

May 28ᵗʰ
(almost) homeless

The night was a bit restless, so I didn't get up as early as I had imagined. Consequently, at around nine o'clock we were still on our way to the viewing point. There it was already very lively. A movie was being shot in this unique environment, and everything they needed was brought in oversized containers. So, the street traffic was only one-way, because the directors, cast members, actors, technicians and script girls all needed to leave their coffee and their make-up suitcases somewhere!

The viewpoint, however, was almost empty and you had a fantastic view of the Colorado and its valley. This "Grand Canyon" of Utah is comprehensible to

me in its dimensions, whereas the real Grand Canyon is "incomprehensible" to me in the truest sense of the word.

I had ticked off this point in my program. Now it was time for program point two! Fuel, fuel and more fuel! The fuel gauge wasn't as low as it had seemed yesterday, probably because of the uphill movement. At the gas station in Moab I noticed that I had four gallons (scarcely sixteen liters) left. I would not have gone far with my thirsty box! Good that the tank was full again!

Now I started program point three: the search for nightly accommodation for the next three days. Since I was early, I indulged myself in the hope of getting one of the available open places along the Colorado River! Absolutely no chance! I then tried the numerous local campsite operators. Totally booked out! Even the sinfully expensive KOA had no place left for us. My last attempt was the "Sandflats" in the height, near the Slick Rocks. This was a real spot for mountain bikers on the smooth rocky peaks. It looked incredibly – and dangerous – when they drove over the rocks with their bikes or motocross machines. I didn't take the time to take pictures because I was looking for a place to stay somewhere in this wilderness. Absolutely hopeless! This "Memorial Day" on Monday seemed to be breaking my neck!

What to do? I would find the best possibility for a pitch far away from Moab. So, for now: goodbye Arches National Park – not seen! I turned south on #191. On the way there were two sights (Needles and Newspaper Rock). But I ignored them for the time being. The next place with an RV park was **Monticello**, close to the border with Colorado State -almost eighty miles (128 km) from Moab. The road climbed up; the wind got stronger. No dwelling far and wide, only nature! The air was filled with reddish sand: No environment for asthmatics. I coughed occasionally and felt the grains of sand in my nose.

Finally, Monticello appeared: an impossible village! The RV Park wasn't exactly the crème de la crème, but it had full hook-

334

up with showers, a weak internet signal and a free enclosure for the dogs for twenty-five dollars a night. I had to stay here – I had no other choice!

Now I'll have to rewrite my plans completely due to the situation. Until Monday there is no chance of staying anywhere else. If I go further south, I will reach the area of Lake Powell and there it should be as busy as in Moab. Now I will take day trips to the above-mentioned sights and the Natural Bridge. But then? I must think about it thoroughly and study the map!

My campsite is called "Mountain View", but there is almost none of that. The whirling dust prevents any view of the two snow-capped three and a half thousand peaks belonging to the **Manti-La Sal National Forest**. The wind blows so strongly that my dogs are afraid, and we prefer to stay inside the rocking "kennel" instead of being exposed to the strong gusts of wind outside. The temperature at this altitude (2,400 m) is still around thirty degrees. The air conditioning is running, because it is impossible to open a window or to extend the awning to get some shade. So, the three of us are a bit incarcerated in our small dwelling. But hopefully this will pass! In the meantime, some more guests have arrived. Probably the same unsuccessful seekers as us...

May 29th
...and rocks again!

I'm sorry! Utah has these in particular to offer on this trip! You'll see all kinds of rocks: with the highest degree of perfection and aesthetics, oversized, colorful, varied, breathtaking, terrific and often indescribable. How do the people who live here experience this environment? Do they care at all? Do they still see the beauty of what's around them every day? Is it possible to "bear" this constant greatness of nature? I noticed that this sublimity was slowly becoming too much for me. The power of

335

the rocks began to crush me. The barrenness of nature depressed me. I longed for some water, space and a green landscape. Seeing sand everywhere and nothing more than that was getting annoying.

Just negative thoughts? No, I admired this plateau with its protected zones. A smaller-sized landscape would perhaps be more human! One feels so small and abandoned in all this abundance of beauty.

After a comfortable beginning of the day we drove about thirty kilometers to the north. The terrible wind had died down and the air was clear and clean. Now you could see the landscape, which was wrapped in gray and brown yesterday. From the turn-off at **Church Rock**, which gives the impression of an Italian baptistery, we still had to cover twenty-two miles to the limit of **Canyonlands NP**. First, we went over a large plateau. The road was well developed. Nothing could have prepared us for the coming beauty. Later we descended steeply into Indian Creek. We came through a canyon, through which the brook with the same name flowed. Where there is water, there is life! Along the little river the landscape got greener, trees lined its course and meadows surrounded it on the valley extensions. Soothing for the eye!

The first stop was at **Newspaper Rock**. No one can tell today what news or stories have been written on the rock by the former inhabitants of this valley. Not even experts have found clear explanations of what they say, but they are the best-preserved petroglyphs I have seen so far.

We found a small rest stop that allowed us to jump into the creek. The water seemed to be cold! Just a short sip and some water treading and my ladies were back quickly!

The canyon opened and revealed a stunning view of countless sandstone rocks. It was exceptionally impressive. Of course, the weather contributed its part to the beauty. With several stops we approached "Needle District". I could only admire the "miniature"rocks with the same name in the distance. You could only get to them with 4x4 off-road vehicles or motocross wheels on dirt roads. What a pity!

We drove the "Scenic Drive" to its bitter end! Literally! The road ended at a gorge (Spring Canyon) and only offered hikers the opportunity to look behind the scenes. Nine miles to the confluence of the Colorado River and the Green River! Enough of this type of "reading", thanks! There were also remarkable rocks here. The comparison with an oversized cowpat forced its way into my mind. Pardon the expression – but look at the photos if you don't believe me!

Scenic Drive -
Needles
District

Spring Canyon

Another short tour led me to "Potholes" in the polished rocks, which fill up with water when it rains and create the basis for new life over many years. So, grasses, cacti, flowers and trees can survive in this harsh area. Natural art by life!

For our lunch break (at two o'clock – I rarely take it before) we looked for a shady picnic spot with a view of the canyons and the snow-covered peaks in the background. Beautiful and not too hot! Here my ladies were able to get some fresh air, because dogs are not allowed in the national parks on any hiking trail. A hard rule, but understandable for the many visitors: some dog owners don't pick up after their pets!

I was tired. Why not take a little nap in this grandiose environment? We have enough time to get home! The sun doesn't set before half past eight. So, all three of us snored for a while in the camper, with the door open and a refreshing air flow! Our "Wuschelmobil" had its advantages.

The return trip was as grandiose as the arrival. This time the late afternoon sun illuminated the rocks with a warm light. The venerable folds of our earth appeared sharp-edged; the colors shone more intensely than in the morning. I liked the strong contrast between the warm red tones of the rock and the intense blue of the sky, a little reduced by the surfaces of the white sandstone.

For the way home I decided to drive over the mountains. In recent years they had built a new paved road from Monticello over the local mountains (with a height of about 3,300 meters) to Newspaper Rock. Of course, I had to try that. Once again, we went up to the snow line. The view from the parking lot was indescribable. Unfortunately, it was very hazy in the distance and not even my telephoto lens could capture the real impression. Simply beautiful, when the whole Canyonland was at your feet. On the other side of the pass one could see far into the plateau up to Monticello. From the pass summit I went down steeply and almost dead straight into the valley. Again, I had to do the engine brake trick, in order to prevent my RV from smoke spitting. In this way I did not have to drive the #191 twice. During our round trip we covered two hundred kilometers. No kilometer was like the another.

May 30th
Nature as a bridge builder

I wasn't really concentrating today! Always tired and with constant pressure in the head! Nevertheless, I drove the hundred kilometers south to **Natural Bridges NM**. I didn't want to miss that. Since the road was excellently developed, we managed the distance in good time. As usual we went through endless

338

uninhabited land. The next bigger village on #191 was **Blanding** at a distance of forty kilometers, a nearly abandoned village with some tourist facilities that were quite sleepy. Behind the village we turned onto #95 which led to Lake Powell (northeast side). That was too far for me. I will probably have to do without the bridge over the Colorado for driving and accommodation reasons.

If the crow flew from Monticello to the natural bridges it wouldn't be that far, but it meant avoiding a mountain massif and several canyons up and down. The way was very steep. Poor motorcyclists, who had to stay behind me because of overtaking prohibitions! The sandstone changed its colors from red to yellow to white, and several off-road routes branched off several times! A paradise for passionate 4x4 drivers.

Today I was only a photo tourist, I didn't manage a trail! I gave up the first attempt as soon as I saw the freestanding ladder on a canyon wall! Please, no! Better from above! The physical conditions bothered me. What was going on? So better to go on slowly but surely! At some Anasazi ruins we took our lunch break. Since I had visited several of the same kind in other places, I ignored the old walls and preferred to take a nap in my corner for half an hour.

The following two bridges were quickly checked off and photographed in the Asian fashion! I wanted to go back and to stay at the small reservoir we saw on the way down, twenty kilometers from Monticello. The dogs also deserved a treat. The access roads to the recreation areas were a disaster, so I parked near the road and walked down to the lake with both ladies. That was a pleasure! They could not get out of the water, so I had done a good deed.

Although I still have a sightseeing point tomorrow, I'm now looking forward to two quiet days on the Colorado River. I'm trying to cram too much into very little time, and I must rest a bit again. I'm not thirty years old anymore! Then there is the Arches NP and "Island in the Sky". Meanwhile it is confirmed: On June 6th I leave Utah for Chicago!

 *personal notes*

Blanding – Natural Bridges – San Juan County/Utah –
Eastern edge of the Colorado-Plateaus
White und Armstrong Canyon

 *personal notes*

May 31ˢᵗ (Memorial Day)
A taste of Colorado

With a sightseeing detour of around seventy kilometers, I had three hundred kilometers ahead of me today. We were in no hurry because our overnight accommodation near Grand Junction in the state of Colorado had been reserved. This was the only and first option around Moab for tonight for a several-day stay. One hundred and sixty kilometers away! There was still a lot going on around Moab during this long weekend.

The "James M. Robb -Colorado River SP" (ouch, what a long name!) is (of course!) on the Colorado River, in a milder environment and at about 4,500 feet. I hoped to find water here for my dogs and a greener environment for my soul!

First of all, there were only wilderness and rocks. On our last but one excursion to Needles NP we hadn't managed the "Overlook" yet, because the way there was a long cul-de-sac. Today, our long trip back to Moab was a welcome part of our program. After the "church rock" we went a few kilometers further west, through the same plateau we had taken the first time. But this time we were on top and after about thirty-five kilometers we reached a viewpoint, which made me speechless at first. The whole basin, through which we drove to the national park the day before yesterday lay at my feet. The lookout was a small picnic place, directly at the edge of the cliff with a view to Dead Horse Point State Park and the Needles. The whole cliff edge was fenced so one could safely go to its margin.

It offered a breathtaking beautiful view into the depth. Sandstone rocks, which appeared huge while passing by, now shrank to miniature size. The face of our old earth was exposed with the furrows, warts, folds, wrinkles, fissures, scratches and pits of its long life. Incomparable! I was overcome with something like reverence for this natural harmony! I spent an hour in the overwhelming surroundings. There were hardly any tourists there.

343

You were alone with yourself, your feelings and the view! Then, however, we went quickly to Moab. It was around noon and there were still a lot of people on the streets. I met many dirty cars with trailers. All of them were driving the off-road area around Moab. On the one hand I imagined it was impressive to "ride" with a jeep or an off-road vehicle through many lonely canyons. Then I thought of the dust and the outfit I would be wearing later from the head to all body orifices! Better not!

A hundred kilometers to **Fruita.** We managed that in ninety minutes. It was exactly three o'clock when we landed in **Colorado SP**. It wasn't the cheapest type of campsite and they asked for a day pass of six dollars in addition to the place fee. Thus, the proud sum of thirty dollars came together, and on top of that amount they demanded additional fees for the showers! But the money was well spent. Each pitch had its own roofed cottage with a bench and a fire ring. The meadows were lush and green! The distance to the next neighbor was a dream! There was a path along the Colorado River. A bathing area and fishing possibilities in two small lakes were also part of it.

In the background you could find the Colorado National Monument, also a protected mountain region with a panoramic road. It was mild outside, and I could still work at 22°C with an open door. The dogs were several times up to their ears in the water. Which Bavarian dog could say that he had taken several baths in the Colorado River?

344

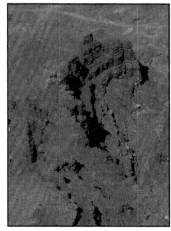

Dead Horse State Park – Overlook

 *personal notes*

Month June/July
2,800 km

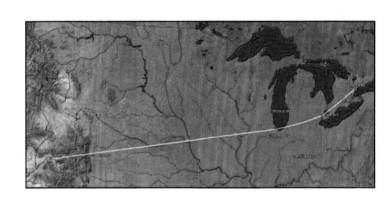

continent crossing

forced residence
Toronto
...and then?

 *personal notes*

June 1ˢᵗ
Fickle

Wasn't I planning on taking two days off? No sightseeing, just easy walks? Yesterday I already knew that I would not fulfill my promise. First of all, the State Park was directly on the way to the **Colorado National Monument**. Second, my fridge called for a visit to the Walmart in Grand Junction. Third, the weather seemed to get worse. And fourth, why not combine several activities today? If you have the National Park at your doorstep...

I arrived at the mountain (despite all my best intentions) at half past nine. The pass road with two narrow tunnels was interesting to drive. Various viewpoints on the fifty-kilometer *Rim Rock Drive* were impressive because of their location. I was curious about the small camping site at the visitor center. Nice location for ten dollars, and although it was not serviced it had a great view. On to remember!

All travelers should keep in mind that the direction of the road from Grand Junction will be even more interesting, as you will then drive directly along the slope and have the view stops in the direction of travel. It took me three hours with the photo breaks until I arrived at GJ – I only drove twenty interstate kilometers but it was worth it.

Driving around for a little I discovered one of the two Walmarts of the city. After one hour I crammed a full shopping cart into the motorhome. I was totally empty. No more dog food, hardly any breakfast food, not to mention my alcohol-free beer! Now nothing could happen to me for the next fourteen days! My last shopping tour was in Torrey or Loa. When? What, just a week ago? It can't be! Yes, it was! I checked it!

At three o'clock we arrived home. The desired siesta was impossible, because my whole bed was full of bags. This logistical problem had to be solved first: It took a while. But now hamster

349

Monika was satisfied again. All compartments were full to the brim – "winter" could come, so to speak! With a walk and some water splashing with the dogs this day was gone! And what will I do tomorrow?

June 2nd
That was good!

A top-class quiet day! No cleaning! No big laundry! No onboard cooking! No shopping! No obligations! Just reading, studying (preparing for Canada), planning the America crossing to Chicago, walk with the dogs, long siesta... pure relaxation, with a weather mix of rain, clouds, occasional gusts of wind, sun and temperatures around 30°C! Once again, a regular lunch at a decent hour. Actually, I would need another day like this! I'll probably get it at Green River State Park.

We will (hopefully) leave early tomorrow to have enough time for one of the last two National Parks. Our night accommodation is reserved and therefore we can take time in the evening and maybe enjoy the sunset with some natural arches! I calculate it'll take us two hours to the national park and another ninety minutes from there to the campsite. The sun doesn't set until half past nine. That gives us plenty of time.

June 3rd
Hot Island in the Sky

Not only in hell do sinners burn! It happens in heaven too. For technical reasons, today I decided to go to the part of Canyonland NP called **"Island in the Sky"**. There were fewer stops, and the region could be visited a little faster than the Arches NP. I'll save this last treat for tomorrow, because it'll take us less time to get there from the Green River State Park.

I drove the attractive route to the **Dead Horse Point SP** once again. I didn't stop but drove another six miles to the designated National Park. At the visitor center I had a hundred and eighty kilometers behind me from **Fruita**. It was already noon when we arrived there. The panorama road itself was sixty kilometers long. Until we got "home", I would drive another hundred kilometers. A full day's performance!

 It was humid and hot on the *mesa* but the different viewing points were fantastic. Unfortunately, the view into the distance was a little hazy and blurry. Basically, it was the same valley that laid at my feet here, like from Dead Horse Point SP or Needles Overlook, but from a completely different perspective. I got tired of the never-ending hop-on hop-off and although I had a quiet siesta in between, I was exhausted when I reached our destination for the day.

To my pleasant surprise, there was a well-known "Minnie" in the neighborhood! Karin and Klaus had been able to arrange it so that we could meet again before I left for Canada and they flew back home to Germany. We world travelers would not see each other for a while, because when I got home, they would already be on their way to Australia for a long time! That's how it was! Thus, I was happy to see them again. Our last meeting was just before the border crossing from Mexico to the USA. Some time ago!

First, I covered my fluid needs with more than one liter of water! Karin was in charge of the kitchen for the evening meal because she was already rested. I accepted the offer gratefully. Until eleven o'clock we sat around a cozy campfire and exchanged information. It was pleasantly mild outside, only the disgusting "black flies" in the twilight bothered our nice evening – they were everywhere on the plateau. They gathered under my hat rim, whirled around my eyes, looked for a way between eyes and glasses, hummed in my ear and tried to conquer my mouth! It was annoying! All the time I had to shoo them at least a little bit away from me! Nevertheless, I have survived!

The **Green River State Park** is a family park with lots of shade under cottonwood trees, clean sanitary facilities, with an access to the river and surrounded by a small golf course. There is no electricity, but we already had that! No problem for sixteen dollars. We had to make reservations for the weekend, because everything was fully booked. The mosquitoes seemed to get free accommodation everywhere! Thus, I closed the diary, in order to protect myself from further visitors with a lamp light outside!

Green River State Park

Colorado National Monument

 *personal notes*

June 4th
Goodbye arches and Co!

The departure to Moab could not take place as early as it was planned. I wanted to have a long farewell chat with the neighbors. At ten o'clock a last handshake and then we wouldn't see each other for a long time.

At eleven o'clock we stood at the gates of the **Arches National Park.** Since the weekend was approaching (Friday), a lot of tourists were on their way and we had to fight for a parking place at the different viewpoints. The temperatures rose again! How can one go jogging at an altitude of 2,000 meters, at thirty degrees in the shade along footpaths that were relentlessly exposed to the blazing heat? Why do they torture their bodies and circulation like that? This will remain a mystery to me forever! Even the shorter trails made me pant and sweat!

So, I heroically dragged myself to the viewpoint of "Park Avenue" and completed the Balanced Rock" circular route knowing it would take a while to get up there. I bravely hiked to "Turret Bow" and to the two window arches and boldly climbed around "Garden of Eden". At "Panorama Point" I needed a break. Since there was no tourist crowd here, I settled down for lunch. Later the sky got overcast and the warmth turned into humidity. Both dogs were having a hard time! Even a pee round outside was too hot for them and they quickly moved back into the RV. After a short, not very restful siesta we set off for the second part of the round trip.

At least I wanted to see the famous Delicate Arch from the distance. The way up there was almost 2.5 km long (one way), led over slickrock (polished rock), went up 146 meters and was exposed to the open sky. Despite all these strenuous conditions, the parking lot at the starting point of the hiking trail was full. I was able to resist this ambition with gratitude. Under the siege of black flies, the short route to the lower viewing point was enough for me. The upper one (1.6 km) was not even included in my intentions. Far, far away was this famous "window" of Utah, which you could also see on its license plates. Even my best zoom only created a blurred picture of the probably most famous sight of the park. But if you really want to see it masterly photographed, you can go online. There are excellent pictures from better photographers and more persevering hikers than me!

I would have been ready to take a breather and go back home. But I wanted to get to the bitter end and see the next campsite – one of the most beautiful in America and booked out for months. We drove the park road to the end, past the – cold – "fire furnace" (Fiery Furnace), the sand dune arch (didn't stop) and the Skyline Arch (photo stop) to the turning point at "Devil's Garden". When I saw the way through the shadowless gorge to six other arches (14 km) I got terrified and stepped on the gas brake! I had seen and suffered enough! There were two thousand catalogued "arches" in this National Park. It wouldn't matter if I hadn't seen more or less six of them! I was looking forward to my shady place, the green meadows around and the river for my animals!

A short fuel stop in Moab and at half past six we were home after a strenuous day! Despite all the effort and tiredness, I found this last day in Arches NP a highlight of the Utah visit! It was a worthy conclusion for this grandiose sightseeing tour. Tomorrow there will be another relaxing day before we start our continent crossing to Chicago.

Arches National Park

 *personal notes*

personal notes

Dear reader!

This is where the first part of our journey ends. But the round trip was not over yet.

We crossed the American continent from west to east, strolled through pretty and worth-visiting State Parks, saw friends in Chicago again and conquered Toronto in a hurry. The RV covered about three thousand kilometers in twenty days. Our next focus of the trip should be the eastern part of Canada with its maritime provinces and Newfoundland with Labrador.

But that wouldn't happen. Why? This is described in detail in the following epilogue.

personal notes

Epilogue

June 23rd / 24th
Fortune in misfortune

Now it's getting exciting! What happened? Where did we end up? Our route was planned and the next visit to friends in Kingston/Ontario was around the corner.

We left **Albion Hill (Toronto)** at about nine o'clock and hit some traffic. The city with its outskirts has five million inhabitants. Shortly after the last eastern suburbs I wanted to refuel. I drove #401 and took exit 401 to the next gas station. I picked up the nozzle and started refueling.

At 85 liters I stumbled over the tank hose and fell. Unfortunately, I could not answer the compassionate question of my neighbor ("Are you ok?") with a "YES". My forefoot was twisted. It was immediately clear that the foot in the ankle area was broken. I felt sick for a moment, but I recovered quickly. The gas station owner called the ambulance and the police. The dogs! A place to stay had to be found first for them when I was in the hospital. An officer called a public neighborhood assistance service. Knuffi and Wuschel were picked up while I was being treated with first aid. They trotted along calmly and without any problems. They had a feeling the situation was unusual. I was relieved that they were taken care of. So, I was transported to the next hospital. The RV was parked at the gas station and they tried to contact Richard and Karen from Kingston but unfortunately the callers only got the answering machine.

I was still on the outskirts of Toronto, in **Ajax**. They found a bed for me in the clinic and started the usual examinations and x-rays. But before that, I got a bill of $540. Without advance payment nothing would get started! The people from the ambulance were friendly and helpful. They stayed until I had disappeared behind a curtain – there were no private rooms for emergency cases. Despite the pain, I had the positive impression that the hospital was of a high standard.

Of course, the whole affair was associated with unpleasant torments and waiting times. Finally, I was given anesthesia, they put my twisted bones back into the right position and I got a provisional cast as I realized when it was all over.

My brain started to work. What could I do now? A friendly nurse at the reception got in contact with the animal help and then called a taxi. So, we (dogs and me) almost arrived at the same time at the gas station. On all fours I pulled myself backwards into the RV. I couldn't walk and the steps were too high to jump! Then my somewhat disturbed darlings followed me. No usual jumping, no bad behavior, no excesses – as if they understood we were in an emergency.

The taxi driver picked up the motorhome and drove me to a simple motel. No chance – no dogs! Thus, a campground would be the best solution. There I had electricity and water and all the essentials close around me. I could move with one foot from here to there, could get help in an emergency, was not alone, had everything around me within reach and a lot of seating in the car. Next Monday I would get the walking cast (as I thought). I would be able to survive until then.

We found the place we were looking for about fifteen kilometers west of Ajax, so back towards Toronto. It was a communal camping area of the city and it was located in a forty-two square kilometer large leisure area. I checked in for a week. Probably it would be a lot longer. It was a big pitch with lots of shade and green around – cheaper than Albion Hill.

The lady at the front desk was very friendly and helpful. I asked her if perhaps any member of the staff would be willing to help me out for a fee and walk the dogs a few times a day. She came back with a 2.10m tall gentleman in his fifties who seemed a little unusual to me. David came from the state of New York, was stationed on the campsite because life had placed his longtime love back in his path here in Canada. He was totally bankrupt and took any job to get some cash. Why not? So, one hand washed the other! It could not be better for us, because now I was helpless – which I wasn't used to and I absolutely hated it. The dogs loved the funny guy immediately. I appreciated his kindness and cordiality.

Now I have a "houseboy", who washes the dishes for me, prepares the food, thinks for me, always entertains me with his life stories, does the shopping and sometimes drives me to the internet place. He is content with fifty dollars a day and I can count on his help at any time, as he is only a few pitches away from me. "Press the horn in an emergency!" David is a likable character, a big child who never grew up, with a big portion of free spirit and a totally high self-esteem. Such a unique character!

I was convinced that my body was now using violence to bring back the peace that I had denied it in Mexico. My previous back pain was the first warning signal. I didn't want to admit it. Nothing happens in life without any sense or background! Now I had enough time to finish my projects! Think positive! I had the heavy suspicion that I would have to do without Newfoundland after this mishap. Losing six to eight weeks was not so easy to compensate – for the moment I could count on the healing process at least. I would devote all my time to New Brunswick, Nova Scotia and the Prince Edwards Islands and not sell my motorhome so soon!

June 24ᵗʰ
and following days

Angels

Guardian angels can be so different. If you can't recognize them by their wings, thanks to fate they will meet you at the right time when you really need them. Five years ago, after my total loss, the angel was a woman and her name was Dee; this time it is a man. His name is David and he is an absolute individualist with a somewhat peculiar philosophy of life. He loves to share his various life stories in different ways, to teach me new English vocabulary (which you won't find in the dictionary) and to involve me in the most impossible discussions. He loves my dogs, learns German dog commands with variations, rinses off, takes out the garbage and goes shopping. His helping hand is always there when I can't get up anymore. He cooks tasteful dishes for us imaginatively from the remainders of my food. He serves me every meal with a pretty presentation and the beer is given to me attentively. I could feel like "Countess of so and so ..." I hadn't been so spoiled in a long time.

Wuschel and Knuffi love him, even if it is hard for my two ladies to have to go for a walk alone with him. It is exhilarating to hear him pronounce the German commands. Hopefully, he will stay with me for a long time. I would be really lost without his help!

Today (June 25th) I was able to contact the ADAC (German travel insurance) in Munich and Orlando/Florida via Skype. There is a lot of paperwork to be done until the agency can decide if they will pay for my trip back home or support an extended stay here for recovering. For this reason, I need the operation on Monday and then they will give me the medical report and the expected recovery time. In any case, the process for this important matter has been started. I was able to cancel my ferries and camping reservations and saved a lot of money this way. However, this should not have been necessary!

In the meantime, David sits around patiently and had to be reminded to be quiet every now and then during my Skype conversations – like a lively child. There is a lot of fun in between and I feel comfortable in his presence, despite all the misfortunes. I do not know yet what tomorrow's going to be like, as his sweetheart has a job interview in New York City after the weekend so she's traveling back to the States with a "Greyhound". Selfishly I motivated him not to accompany her, but to let her go her own way.

July 1ˢᵗ (Canada Day) ….
Preparations for the journey home

I was given a cast and last Monday (July 28ᵗʰ) I was advised to go home, because of the seriousness of the injury. Damn! The last days were exhausting with the eternal hopping on one leg! David was tirelessly trying to relieve me of every move and cooked for us evening after evening. In fact, he was talented and conjured up good dishes from the available food. Meanwhile he has moved his little tent to my pitch. No 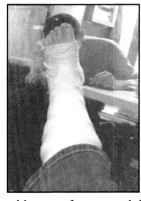 problem for me and if doing so he could save a few more dollars.

The last days we cleaned the RV together and emptied the cupboards. If I storage my camper now and send it into longer retirement, I don't need cheap T-shirts or outdated maps. I regretted a bit throwing away my good travel books. But sending them home would have been more expensive than buying new ones. Besides, I probably wouldn't need them for the next few years and by then there would probably be updated editions. Sack by sack, my "angel" transported the ballast outside. Fortunately, we had a large container available nearby.

Between the various clearance actions, I phoned the ADAC in Munich and Orlando again and again. Even the responsible

German doctor of the insurance company had contacted me. He had got all the necessary information from his opposite colleague in charge at the clinic here in Canada. I was lucky that I had bought a Canadian cell phone! The company and the staff did their job thoroughly and well. Yesterday I received my travel data, I am to be picked up from the campsite by a flown in doctor, cared for during the flight from Toronto to Germany and taken over in Frankfurt/Mainz by the Malteser emergency service. They will transfer me together with my dogs to Bavaria. I think the ADAC even reserved business class for me because there I had more space for my plastered foot.

Now we had to solve the problem with the dogs. The organization aspect then looked like this: the ADAC had taken over the reservation for the flight and ordered a bigger car for the transfer to my hometown. The fact that the payment had to be done by me personally was of course self-evident and peanuts, compared to the other costs. These were paid by my foreign health insurance. My third angel with "G" – Gabi from Mainz – would take care of my two four-legged ladies for the first few days until I could go back to my apartment from the hospital. Thus, one week after the stupid accident we were again in the green range and now prepared optimistically for the journey home.

David will take over my motorhome with the entire inventory. Thus, he has a roof over his head from now on. A meaningful use of the faithful companion, that has transported me on two big annual tours and covered about 75,000 kilometers through America, Mexico, the Baja California, West Canada and Alaska, with all the aches and pains of a used vehicle, but also all the reliability of an experienced lady! *Well done, old girl!* (... this should have been the title of our Newfoundland trip).

Yesterday there was a pleasant interruption of the waiting time. Karen and Richard from Kingston came to visit. I had met this couple together with Bob and Carolyne in Catemaco,

Mexico. They made a two-and-a-half-hour trip to see me before I left. They had received the address of a lovely 86-year-old lady who lived just around the corner and had invited us to visit her. Her son lived with his family in Munich. So, we went for tea to a senior woman's house who none of us knew! She was already sitting in the garden waiting for us. We spent a nice and fun afternoon with our hostess. Unfortunately, we couldn't stay for dinner as we had hoped, because Richard and Karen had to drive the long way home.

Today's holiday passed by more quietly. The English Queen visited Toronto to be celebrated by her former colonies. Yesterday a few thousand people cheered her in Ottawa! Thus, the security corps of the city was again in charge after the G20 summit.

It is pleasantly warm outside; angel David is cleaning his wings (his car) and I enjoy the silence on the bed for writing. Tomorrow we will do the rest of the cleaning together. The flying doctor is arriving in Toronto in the evening. Let's see how he contacts me. Then it will be high time for action: "MoWuKnuffels return" will mercilessly and inexorably start. But Canada should prepare itself for the fact that I will come back again sometime. Postponed doesn't mean canceled!

Looking back, all my trips home from the American continent have been a special experience. After the first trip I arrived in Germany without luggage, only with the dogs in tow. After the total loss of my German motorhome, although it was not my fault, all my belongings had to be shipped across the Ocean in a container.

After my second round-trip I missed the plane in New York due to wrong information and traffic chaos. One day before my visa expired, I was still on American soil. It was an expensive and stressful affair to find a hotel for the three of us in the middle of the night and then a flight for the next day.

This time the ADAC had to be involved as a rescue service. I probably went through all the (not life-threatening) possibilities of a return journey. Maybe should that be enough for me for a while...?

July 4th and 5th
transport back

Now I am sitting with my leg high and my joint screwed up in my – Augsburg (Bavaria) – hospital bed and feel motivated to describe our trip home as a positive conclusion to this travel book. It was a masterpiece of organization and logistics by the automobile association.

As already mentioned, the doctor arrived on Saturday, with all the necessary medication in his luggage. We discussed the procedure for the next few days. He was a real dog lover (again a stroke of luck) and my two ladies immediately took to him. However, they looked at the kennels with a skeptical eye.

For the departure day I ordered the taxi for two o'clock, because I had received no further information from the ADAC about the airport transfer. The flight left at 18.30, so we had enough time. The doctor was also there with his rental car.

During our last preparations we were astonished by a black stretch limousine with a styled chauffeur, which passed again and again, touring the campsite. Finally, the car stopped at our place. I couldn't believe it! Everyone's mouth fell open at first. It was reserved for us and already paid! Was the club aware of this? Probably the ADAC ordered a bigger car for all our stuff and the rental company only had this model available! So, I drove back to Toronto like the Queen with darkened windows on the Interstate #401, accompanied by many spectators and curious faces. When did a limousine arrive on an ordinary campsite? That was of course the sensation – not only for me! And my dogs could sit down on the worn-out leather seats.

370

The task now was to take all the cargo to the right place at the airport. A wheelchair with staff was already available for me. The check-in was done by my doctor. I had nothing to worry about. What a pleasure! From now on I could relax, and it felt like a weight had been lifted off of me!

Because of my stiff leg we traveled in the business class, therefore we could also use the VIP waiting room and shorten the time comfortably. Unfortunately, the dogs had to enter their "cabins" a little earlier than usual. Knuffi jumped into the kennel without any problems, but Wuschel resisted with all four paws. I could understand her feelings and had to secretly wipe off a tear. It was comforting that she wouldn't have to go through this torment again any time soon.

Well, at least now we had got rid of the heavy luggage. We both still had our hand luggage, the crutches and the doctor's case. Here, the airport staff of Lufthansa was friendly and help-ful as well. I was led through the strict security checks and we avoided all the queues. So, I was able to jump directly from my wheelchair to my comfortable travel seat.

So far, I had never flown business class for financial reasons, and I enjoyed the comfort of (relative) freedom of movement and proper crockery. Even non-alcoholic beer was available on board! The night was not a real night, because due to the time difference and my elephant foot I could not sleep, while my companion was sleeping soundly. He had already taken care of several other patient transports and was used to this kind of traveling. But how long could one endure such a life?

We arrived in Frankfurt/Main earlier than expected. A wheel-chair with an escort was also arranged here. Now my flight at-tendant had to handle the luggage with the dogs alone. This time no helping hand for my four-legged friends was available. So, we went to the exit and through customs on several stages. An ambulance was already waiting for us. It was indeed so spacious that we all found room to accommodate ourselves. I was strapped to a seat and the dog cages on the stretcher(!). Wuschel could sit at my feet. The two drivers confirmed that they had never done such a transport before. It shot through my head that we were just something special! Of course, several pairs of eyes turned towards us when they pushed Knuffi out of the car on the stretcher at a service area! We had to go for a pee tour. Too bad, I had no opportunity for a photo at this moment!

In about four hours we reached my home where my girlfriend Gabi was waiting for us. Suitcases, cages and dogs were delivered. Then we got to the Augsburg Central Clinic as quickly as possible. The ambulance staff stayed with me until I was personally handed over to the doctor in charge. As soon as they knew that I was under expert care, they started their way back to Frankfurt.

The foot was secured together with screws and now looks forward to healing. This will take some time and Newfoundland and the travelogues will have to wait. That interesting piece of earth has not been included in my program because of this unfortunate incident. Someday, in the near or far future, we will travel again to Eastern Canada, of course with a foreign health insurance plan!

The further fate of my RV? Since David is a mechanic – according to him the best in the world (!) -he will renew my beloved vehicle step by step. Music of the future: should there be a return for me to the American continent in a few years, he will make it available for me to use. What more do I want? With its high mileage (325,000 km) and its age (16 years) it is not worth selling it anyway. But I also have to say that it is still too good to be scrapped in the next few years. So, it will be maintained and meaningfully used by an expert. Who knows what will happen in three or four years? I don't want to speculate about that today. But maybe there will be a reunion and then I will tell her: "Well done, old girl!"

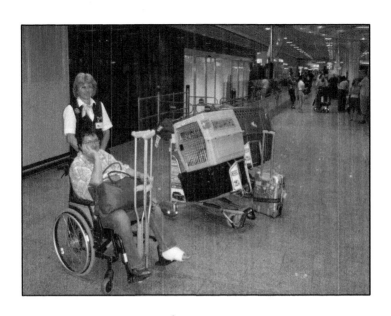

Back to Germany
Toronto - Frankfurt

 *personal notes*

Table of contents and itineraries

personal notes

Further travelogues of the enterprising trio Monika von Borthwick and dogs

Highways und Gravel Roads - Volume I
* With the MoWuKnuffels in a motor home right across the North American continent – from New York to Alaska
German and English Edition

Highways und Gravel Roads – Volume II
* A sequel story
* From the Arctic Circle/Alaska to the Tropic of Cancer/ Baja California
German and English Edition

Winter Wings
*Emigrate like storks in Portugal
German
English edition in progress

Chorizo & Co
* A Bavarian dog spends the winter in Spain – with a difference
German
English edition in progress

 *personal notes*

Carpe Diem! Use the time!
* By camper through Canada's eastern provinces
German
English edition in progress

La Cucaracha
* The colonial cities
* Central Mexico and the Yucatan   Peninsula
German
English edition in
Progress

All books are also available as e-books in relevant online stores.
Further information about the books, the purchase in the book trade or directly with the author can be found under:
www.mvborthwick.de
info@mvborthwick.de

380

Thank you

Normally at this point we should be reading a thank you to the helpers of the author such as lecturer, publisher, counseling, helpful wives, critical comments, …

Since the present book was created in absolute self-direction (images, layout, writing, language...), my thanks go to the following:

* My two dogs Wurschtel and Knuffi, who have faithfully gone through everything, helped me to never feel alone and to give me security as a guard and reliable alarm system.
* All the friendly and helpful people I met on my journey mentioned in the book and interested in our company.
* My reliable friend Patricia, who has translated this story into English with great love, competence and patience
* My English friend Jennifer in Saydo Park in Mollina/Spain finding the last spelling mistakes
* My open-minded email readers and good friends who gave me the idea to publish my notes as a book.
* The indulgent readers of the book, who overlooked one or the other error devil benevolently. If you discover one, you are welcome to keep it!
* Last, but not least, the helpful hands at home, which took care of the vacant apartment during my absence, monitored my mail and never let the connection to the home break. Without them such a tour would have been impossible.